"As always, he has listened before he has spoken. With a brilliant mind and a warm heart, Josh has spearheaded the work of a lifetime that could transform a generation."
—DR. RAVI ZACHARIAS, *Ravi Zacharias International Ministry*

"Josh McDowell's newest apologetic, *Right from Wrong*, bears the familiar stamp of authenticity which has made his published work famous. It is, like its predecessors, overwhelmingly research-based, uncompromisingly factual, passionately persuasive."
—DR. D. JAMES KENNEDY, *Coral Ridge Presbyterian Church*

"Once again Josh McDowell is on the cutting edge with a book that is destined to become a classic. Its need, relevance, and clarity make *Right from Wrong* one of those rare imperatives for every home and church."
—DR. BILL BRIGHT, *Founder and President, Campus Crusade for Christ International*

"Josh McDowell provides a much-needed analysis of and guide for overcoming the serious ethical and moral crisis that meets our young people on every corner of our culture."
—DR. R.C. SPROUL, *President, Ligonier Ministries*

"Josh McDowell has delivered us a classic. *Right From Wrong* will challenge you, convict you, inspire you, and give you practical answers for passing on biblical values to the next generation."
—DR. DANN SPADER, *Founder and Director, Sonlife Ministries*

"Josh McDowell dismisses all thoughts that responsibility for today's youth should fall anywhere but squarely onto our shoulders as parents, pastors, teachers, and youth leaders."
—BEVERLY LAHAYE, *President, Concerned Women for America*

"This is not about a book, it's about an issue! *Right from Wrong* is an underlying issue that must be addressed, and addressed now by the whole body of Christ."
—BILL ANDERSON, *President, Christian Booksellers Association*

"This is a most strategic book. Bible-believer McDowell demonstrates in a crystal-clear, vividly personalized way that while the tragic amorality of modern North American culture ruins young people, God's unchanging standards still make superb human sense."
—J.I. PACKER, *Professor of Theology, Regent College*

"People don't know how to think clearly about truth and error, right and wrong, or anything else that involves absolutes. This book will help those of us who lead see *why* this is so, and help us with the "how's" of practical, remedial ministry to families and individuals."
—JACK W. HAYFORD, *Pastor, The Church On The Way*

"Josh McDowell and Bob Hostetler have touched a raw nerve. They have addressed the problem of the lost morals and have proposed a Christian response. This book is going to make a difference."
—DR. TONY CAMPOLO, *Professor of Sociology, Eastern College*

"If you're concerned about the youth of our country, you need to read *Right from Wrong*."
—**RICH BUHLER,** *Speaker, Author, Host of "TableTalk"*

"Once again Josh McDowell has hit at the core of the problem with our society. If you care about our future and the hearts of our young people, please read this book."
—**STEPHEN ARTERBURN,** *Co-Founder, Minirth Meier New Life Clinics*

"Right from Wrong supplies a much needed analysis, provides the right answers, and offers concrete steps to influencing our declining western culture—one individual at a time."
—**DR. JAMES M. BOICE,** *Minister, Tenth Presbyterian Church, Philadelphia, Pennsylvania*

"This book, based on instilling strong biblical principles into our families, will serve as a beacon in the dark, messed-up world."
—**BARBARA JOHNSON,** *Best-selling author of* **Stick a Geranium in Your Hat and Be Happy!**

"A 'must read' for all of us who want to understand the context into which we carry the life-changing power of the gospel."
—**DR. JOSEPH M. STOWELL,** *President, Moody Bible Institute*

"Right from Wrong is a must for every family that wishes to develop a home with a solid biblical foundation."
—**DR. GARY SMALLEY,** *President, Today's Family*

"If you want insight into understanding the American teenager and how best to serve him or her, you must read this book."
—**DAWSON MCALLISTER**

"I pray God will use *Right from Wrong* to shock the Church and Christian parents out of complacency into obedience to His command to "love God . . . keep His commandments . . . and impress them on your children."
—**ANNE GRAHAM LOTZ,** *AnGel Ministries*

"Right from Wrong is required reading for those interested in preparing students to practically live the truth in a relativistic age."
—**RICH VAN PELT,** *President, Alongside Ministries, Adjunct Professor in Youth Ministry, Denver Seminary*

"America is in trouble. We need a 'Family Reformation.' I pray this book will be used by God to help bring about that reformation and rebuild our families and our national conscience."
—**DENNIS RAINEY,** *Executive Director, FamilyLife Today*

RIGHT
FROM
WRONG

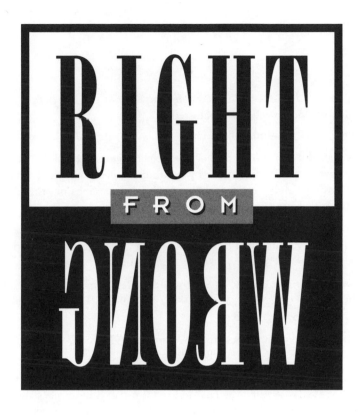

JOSH MCDOWELL
& BOB HOSTETLER

WORD PUBLISHING
Dallas·London·Vancouver·Melbourne

RIGHT FROM WRONG: What You Need to Know to Help Youth Make Right Choices by Josh McDowell & Bob Hostetler.

Copyright © 1994 by Word Publishing.

Unless otherwise indicated, Scripture quotations are from the New International Version of the Bible, published by the Zondervan Corporation, copyright © 1973 by the New York Bible Society. Used by permission.

Scripture quotations marked NASB are from the New American Standard Bible. Copyright © 1960, 1962, 1963, 1968, 1971, 1972, 1973, 1975, 1977, the Lockman Foundation. Used by permission.

Scriptures marked NKJV are from The New King James Version. Copyright © 1979, 1980, 1982, Thomas Nelson, Inc., Publishers.

Scriptures marked RSV are from The Revised Standard Version of the Bible. Copyright © 1946, 1952, 1971, 1973 by the Division of Christian Education of the National Council of the Churches of Christ in the U.S.A., and are used by permission.

Scriptures marked KJV are from The King James Version of the Bible.

Interior design by Toni Richard and Alyse Lounsberry.

Library of Congress Cataloging-in-Publication Data
McDowell, Josh.
   Right from wrong: what you need to know to help youth make right choices / by Josh McDowell & Bob Hostetler
       p.   cm.
     ISBN 0-8499-1079-X (hardcover); 0-8499-3604-7 (trade paper)
     1. Church work with youth—United States.   2. Youth—United States—Conduct of life.   3. Youth—United States—Religious life.   4. United States—Moral conditions.   5. Christian ethics.
I. Hostetler, Bob, 1958–   .   II. Title.
BV4447.M37   1994
259'.23—dc20

Printed in the United States of America
5 6 7 8 9 BVG 9 8 7 6 5

Table of Contents

PART 2
The Defense of Truth

PART 4
The Research Analysis

Dedication

To our wives
Dottie and Robin

Acknowledgments

A book of this magnitude could not have been written without the extraordinary contribution and collaboration of many people. We wish to thank the following people for their involvement in this project:

George Barna and The Barna Research Group, Ltd. for the expert service of directing the "1994 Churched Youth Survey" and for George's insightful analysis of the initial research;

Marcus Maranto of Josh McDowell Ministry Research Department for hours of compiling research related to numerous chapters;

Dr. Norman Geisler and Daryl McCarthy for reviewing the rough draft manuscript and providing valuable insight and counsel;

David N. Weiss for the benefit of his expertise and input on these pages;

Becky Bellis for laboring long and hard at the computer and for the insights she offered;

Bob Evans for technical expertise and selfless support that kept the project going at a crucial moment;

Alyse Lounsberry, editor at Word, Inc., for the expert editing and insight she brought to the manuscript completion;

Marsha Hamann, the Kotners, the Turners, the Shevelands, the Yerkes, the Kornweibels, the Wallaces, the Zunigas, and the Kuhns for participating in the focus group and providing such practical insight and guidance in the final shaping of the book's emphasis;

Laura Minchew, Word, Inc. Vice President of Children's Products, who believed in this book and shared in the vision of reaching children with the message of "Right from Wrong;"

Joey Paul, Word, Inc. Vice President of Trade Division, who provided immeasurable insight, wisdom, and support for this book and who championed the "Right from Wrong" Campaign throughout Word, Inc.;

Dave Bellis, my (Josh) co-worker for seventeen years, for designing and coordinating the development of the entire "Right from Wrong" Campaign from facilitating the denominational symposium, to coordinating the research, to proposing the campaign focus, to developing and producing the many products in the campaign, to overseeing the product marketing. Dave's involvement in this book, however, deserves special mention. We are grateful for his tireless work in hammering out the concepts of the book, in providing rough drafts, rewrites, and edits for many chapters, and overall in guiding and molding the book into its final form. In many respects, Dave could be considered a "third author" and we are deeply grateful for his contribution.

And, finally, to the many Christian brothers and sisters who reviewed the book and offered suggestions for its improvement and support for its mission, we thank you.

Josh McDowell
Bob Hostetler

PART 1

THE CRISIS OF TRUTH

A Generation in Crisis

SIXTEEN-YEAR-OLD Elizabeth Pena and fourteen-year-old Jennifer Ertman made the mistake of taking a shortcut.

It was 11:30 P.M. on a hot, steamy June night. The two had just left a party at a friend's house. They called home before they left, to tell their mothers they were on their way. They never made it.

Elizabeth and Jennifer cut through a wooded area near the White Oak Bayou in Houston, Texas, and stumbled into an initiation ritual of the "Black N White" gang. Gang members had descended on the isolated area to drink beer and engage in a macho induction that involved the gang's newcomers fistfighting other members. The gang gathering had just begun to break up when the girls appeared on the scene.

"Let's get 'em," cried one of the gang members.

Elizabeth's and Jennifer's naked bodies were found four days later. They had been raped repeatedly. Both girls had been strangled; one with a belt, the other with a shoelace. Apparently the girls did not die quickly enough. A police spokesman reported, "To ensure that both of them were dead, the suspects stood on the girls' necks."[1]

The six gang members charged with the murders (police reported that all six participated in the rapes and murders) ranged in age from fourteen to eighteen years old. One of the gang members had appeared on a local television show the day before the murders; he hoisted a beer and boasted into the camera, "Human life means nothing." Another of the boys, upon hearing that they might be charged with murder, is reported to have exclaimed, "Hey, great! We've hit the big time!"

■ KEEPING SCORE ■

Nineteen-year-old Billy Shehan claimed the lead in the game with sixty-six points. His closest competitor, twenty-year-old Dana Belman, had scored sixty-three times.

A basketball game? Card game? Archery?

No, the game these boys were playing was called sex.

Billy and Dana were members of the infamous Spur Posse, in Lakewood, California, a middle-class suburb of Los Angeles with cookie-cutter houses and neatly clipped lawns. The Spurs became famous when (after nine of them, ages fifteen to eighteen, had been arrested on charges of rape and molestation) the media learned that they had devised a scoring system to keep track of their sexual conquests. The Spurs, whose numbers ranged from twenty to thirty boys, scored one point for each different girl they "hooked up [had sex] with."

Mike Weber, one of the most feared Spurs, explained the code the boys used to communicate their latest score. "When somebody would be with a girl, he would say I'm [baseball player] Steve Sax [uniform number 7] or I'm [football player] Barry Sanders [uniform number 20]."

As the boys' tallies increased, so did accusations of intimidation and rape. One sixteen-year-old girl reported that a Spur removed her clothes during a sexual encounter in a park and refused to return them until she had sex with other Spurs; she believes she averted a gang rape by screaming until her clothes were returned. An eleven-year-old girl said that she was sleeping over at a girlfriend's house when a boy snuck into her bedroom window (apparently a common Spur practice) and told her he wanted to have sex with her. She complied, explaining later that she did so because she had heard that Spurs would hurt girls who didn't cooperate.

The boys admitted that the girls they slept with were mere statistics. "It's got nothing to do with love," said eighteen-year-old Matt Nielsen. "It's got nothing to do with liking them" (indeed, the boys referred to their conquests as "whores" and "sluts"). And none of the Spurs seemed embarrassed, much less remorseful, about their conduct. "It was not a big deal," Mike Weber said. "If you had sex, you got a point. It was like bragging rights for the person who thought he was the biggest stud."[2]

■ A GRIM YOUTH ■

What is causing mere children to be so coarse, so brutal? What has happened to our society that teenagers can be so violent, so callous, so unmindful of right and wrong? As journalist Rowland Nethaway wrote in an article for the Cox News Service:

> Adults have always complained about their youth, but this is differ-ent. There have always been wild and rebellious kids who would go off the track and do something wrong. But they knew where the track was and what was wrong. Many of today's youth don't seem to know right from wrong. Children are robbing, maiming and killing on whims, and with no pity and no remorse.[3]

The question is far more serious than when Janet Leigh and Dick Van Dyke sang "What's the Matter With Kids Today?" in the movie, *Bye Bye Birdie*. Today's youth are not only playing loud music and wearing radical hairstyles; they have graduated, it seems, to a level of adolescent aggression, promiscuity, cynicism, and violence that bristles the hair on parents' necks.

It is not just happening in isolated areas, either. Research tells a statistical horror story of what is happening *every day* in America:[4]

- 1,000 unwed teenage girls become mothers
- 1,106 teenage girls get abortions
- 4,219 teenagers contract sexually transmitted diseases
- 500 adolescents begin using drugs
- 1,000 adolescents begin drinking alcohol
- 135,000 kids bring guns or other weapons to school
- 3,610 teens are assaulted; 80 are raped
- 2,200 teens drop out of high school
- 6 teens commit suicide

Neither is such behavior limited to young people that are sometimes referred to as "problem kids." The 24th Annual Survey of High Achievers, a recent survey of high school honor roll students, reveals alarming facts about today's teens. One in five of these girls—honor students, remember—said they had been victims of a sexual assault. One in three knew someone who had brought a weapon to school. One in three had contemplated suicide, and four out of five of these high achievers admitted to cheating.

Such statistics *are* disturbing. You and I may shake our heads and cluck our tongues at the dismal state of the younger generation. At times it's hard to believe the things that are going on "out there," in the world—to other people's children.

We comfort ourselves that our youth aren't like that. We feel confident that our four-year-old and eight-year-old children are protected from all that. We console ourselves that the kids in our church youth groups aren't like that; they're not without their problems, but they're good kids. Yet even as we congratulate ourselves, a fear gnaws inside us like a rat chewing through a piece of shoe leather. You are afraid—I am afraid—that the craziness out there will somehow, someday claim your youth. I am a parent of four children; my co-author, Bob, is a parent of two preteens—and we are scared. You, too, probably worry that your children will become less like you and more like the world "out there," where promiscuity, dishonesty, irresponsibility, and violence are a way of life.

■ LIVING ON THE MORAL EDGE ■

You're not alone in your fears. In fact, if you are like most Christian parents (or pastors or youth leaders), your number one fear these days is that you will not be able to pass your values on to the next generation. You fear the influence of the public school system; you dread the potency of peer pressure; you worry about the effects of MTV and the media; you tremble at the potential impact of a culture that seems to be blowing up in your face. You wonder if the influence of home and church will be sufficient to counter the forces that threaten your children. As it turns out, there is ample cause for concern.

In March of 1993, forty-two Christian youth leaders joined me for a symposium in Dallas, Texas, on the state of the youth culture. For two-and-a-half days, we discussed the most pressing problems of today's youth and what we could do to address the state of this generation. Those leaders shared their burdens for youth involved in such things as drugs, premarital sex, and violent crime. Over the course of those meetings, the group wrestled to identify not only the symptoms of the diseases that afflict today's youth, but the root causes as well. Do you know what these men and women identified as the most dominant problem facing youth today? One hundred percent of them ranked this generation's loss of a biblically-based value system as their number one concern. Interestingly, that is the same concern you and I share as parents, pastors, teachers, and youth workers.

But could we all be overreacting? Sure, there's cause for concern, but our kids can't be as bad off as those "out there." We send our children to Sunday school. They're involved in youth groups and summer church camps. We love them, and they love us. How badly can this culture be affecting our young people?

None of us could answer that question with any certainty . . . until now. With the cooperation of thirteen evangelical denominations, we conducted the most extensive research ever of churched youth. Under the expert direction of The Barna Research Group, a scientifically-designed process randomly selected youth groups from thousands of churches throughout the U.S. and Canada. Over 3,700 youth were extensively and confidentially surveyed (see the "Introduction to the Research" later in this book for more details about the survey process and participating groups). It is from this 1994 survey that we will be extensively quoting and thoroughly examining throughout this book. (The last four chapters have been devoted to a complete analysis of the study.)

These are your kids—and mine—that we surveyed. The participants are youth who are intensely involved in church activity (Sunday school, worship, youth group, Bible study)—*and* who overwhelmingly identify their parents as loving and their family experience as positive. Yet, as you will see, the survey reveals that our youth are living on the moral edge, closer to disaster than we ever imagined. The survey results reflect not only where our teenagers are now, but also where our children—ten, eight, six years old or younger—will be in just a few years.

Large proportions of our youth—a majority of whom say they have made a personal commitment to Jesus Christ—are involved in inappropriate, immoral, even illegal behavior. The survey reveals that in the past three months alone:

- Two out of every three (66 percent) of our kids (ages eleven to eighteen) lied to a parent, teacher, or other adult
- Six in ten (59 percent) lied to their peers

- Nearly half (45 percent) watched MTV at least once a week
- One in three (36 percent) cheated on an exam
- Nearly one in four (23 percent) smoked a cigarette or used another tobacco product
- One in five (20 percent) tried to physically hurt someone
- One in nine (12 percent) had gotten drunk
- Nearly one in ten (8 percent) had used illegal, non-prescription drugs

The data show that young people from good Christian homes are succumbing to the pressures of our society. By the time they reach the age of eighteen, over half (55 percent) have engaged in fondling breasts, genitals, and/or sexual intercourse. Half (50 percent) of our youth say they're stressed out. Over half (55 percent) say they're confused. Three-fourths (74 percent) say they're looking for answers.

I cannot stress enough the importance of the fact that these data reflect the behavior of our own youth. Two-thirds (65 percent) of these kids say they pray daily. Eighty-four percent of them attend Sunday school *and* youth group at least once a week, more than double the national average for teens. The respondents to this survey are not the kids you think of when you hear about teen promiscuity, drug abuse, and violence; they're the kids in your church, the kids on your street, the kids in your home and mine . . . and they're in trouble.

Our youth fare better than non-churched youth in virtually every area we've cited. But far too many of our youth are involved sexually. Far too many are lying, cheating, and stealing. Far too many are hurting other people.

It is painfully apparent that many of our own youth have lost the ability to distinguish right from wrong. Many no longer pursue their parents' dreams and values but instead absorb the warped values of a sick society. But how do you address this sickness before it infects your own children or church? How can you pass on your values to your children even when they're four, five, or six years old? How do you prevent them from being sucked into the way of thinking and behaving that is ruining lives all around you? How do you correct the problem pointed out by a philosophy professor when she said, "We may be one of the few societies in the world that finds itself incapable of passing on its moral teachings to young people"[5]?

The government says the solution is better education; they say more prevention programs will make a better society. Educators say the solution is more money; if we pour more money into our schools, we'll produce better kids. Activists say the solution is justice; they contend that we must eradicate injustice and oppression. Others say we need more police, more corporal punishment, more prisons, more job opportunities, more social programs.

Don't get me wrong; many of those goals are worthy. But they will fall short every time, because they address the symptoms. Our problem goes far deeper than the easy availability of guns or drugs; it defies prevention programs and social solutions. I believe it is a problem that will never be solved until we identify its source and deal with the root causes.

2

Truth Matters

A FRIEND OF MINE once contemplated buying the home next to his as an investment property. He lived in an area of town that had seen better days; the house next door had been occasionally rented to drug dealers and users, and had regularly been the site of domestic squabbles that required police intervention. Several times gunfire had sounded in the house or the yard.

My friend hoped that buying the house, investing "sweat equity" into it, and then renting it to good tenants would allow him to improve his neighborhood—and protect his family.

He persuaded one of his in-laws, who had experience in construction and home improvement, to walk through the house with him and help spot any potential problems. The building was in deplorable condition, and while my friend was disappointed at the amount of work the house required, he remained hopeful—until they entered the basement. There, his companion pointed out gaping cracks in the foundation and a sagging support structure.

"This place is falling down," his companion told him. "Nothing you fix up there"—he pointed his index finger to the upper floors—"will be worth a dime because of what's wrong down

here." He pronounced his judgment that the house would probably have to be condemned—because the foundation was cracked
and crumbling.

■ WHEN THE FOUNDATIONS ARE BEING DESTROYED ■

That house provides an apt illustration of the problems that face
your family and mine. We all sense that something is happening to
the moral foundations of our culture. Has teen pregnancy increased
over 500 percent in the past thirty years due to a lack of sex education? Has suicide among young people increased 300 percent in
less than thirty years because we live in a more complex, stressful
society?[1] Are violence, drive-by shootings, and guns in schools the
results of ineffective gun-control laws? Or is there something more
fundamental, more foundational at work here? I believe such
problems stem from a much deeper root cause. I believe it goes
deep into the very foundation of what people in our society—
and in our homes—believe, and how they look at the world.

Our craving for instant gratification and easy solutions will not
help us here. We won't find an answer for adolescent violence at
drive-through windows; a stop at a convenience store won't keep
our children from lying and cheating; we cannot solve our teen
sexuality crisis in the space of a sixty-minute television program.
We must dig deep. We must look beyond the symptoms and deal
with the fundamental root causes.

■ AN ISSUE OF TRUTH ■

I believe that one of the prime reasons this generation is setting new records for dishonesty, disrespect, sexual promiscuity,
violence, suicide, and other pathologies, is because they have lost
their moral underpinnings; their foundational belief in morality
and truth has been eroded. As journalist Rowland Nethaway said,
they "don't seem to know right from wrong."

Once upon a time, children were raised in an atmosphere that
communicated absolute standards for behavior: certain things

were right and certain things were wrong. A child's parents, teachers, ministers, youth workers, and other adults collaborated in an effort to communicate that the former should be heeded and the latter should be avoided. At one time, our society, by and large, explained the universe, humanity, and the purpose of life from the Judeo–Christian tradition: a belief that truth existed, and everyone could know and understand it. A clear understanding of what was right and wrong gave society a moral standard by which to measure crime and punishment, business ethics, community values, character, and social conduct. It became the lens through which society viewed law, science, art, and politics—the whole of culture. It provided a cohesive model that promoted the healthy development of the family, united communities, and encouraged responsibility and moral behavior.

That has changed drastically, however. Our children are being raised in a society that has largely rejected the notions of truth and morality, a society that has somewhere lost the ability to decide what is true and what is right. Truth has become a matter of taste; morality has been replaced by individual preference.

Today's youth are being raised in a culture that reflects Hugh Hefner's "Playboy Philosophy," the creed that "if it feels good, do it." Our children seldom hear the words "right" and "wrong" from Hollywood, Nashville, and Madison Avenue; instead, they are bombarded with thousands of hours of sounds and images that glamorize immorality and mock biblical values.

Our youth are being educated in schools that profess to offer "value-free, morally neutral" education. "We cannot tell you," the teachers and textbooks say, "what is wrong and what is right. You must decide that for yourselves. We can only make you aware of all the options." William J. Bennett (former secretary of education), in his book, *The De-Valuing of America,* quotes a 1985 *New York Times* article:

> The article told of one counseling session involving fifteen high-school juniors and seniors. In the course of that session a student concluded that a fellow student had been foolish to return one

thousand dollars she found in a purse at school. According to the article, when the youngsters asked the counselor's opinion, "He told them he believed the girl had done the right thing, but that, of course, he would not try to force his values on them. 'If I come from the position of what is right and what is wrong,' he explained, 'then I'm not their counselor.'"[2]

It's not hard to see that such messages are not value neutral at all; they teach relativism—the belief that what is true for you may not be true for me. If a counselor tells teens that what is right or wrong is completely their decision, that counselor is conveying a philosophy that denies the existence of ultimate standards of truth and morality.

Count on it—if they have not already done so, your children will soon encounter an educational environment that rejects the notion of truth. The opening sentence of Allan Bloom's book, *The Closing of the American Mind,* states, "There is one thing a professor can be absolutely certain of: almost every student entering the university believes, or says he believes, that truth is relative."[3] A great many high schools and universities today not only reinforce and advance such thinking; they have evolved from institutions that aid in a search for knowledge to institutions that deny the possibility of knowing anything objectively!

In such a climate, it is not surprising that 70 percent of today's generation (both churched and non-churched youth) claim that absolute truth does not exist, that all truth is relative. Most of them say that everything in life is negotiable, and that "nothing can be known for certain except the things that you experience in your own life." In other words, they don't believe that anything can be definitely defined as right or wrong. This view has been expressed to me over and over, by parents and young people alike, who refer to a certain behavior, and say, "I feel it's wrong—for me—but people have to decide for themselves whether it's wrong for them; I can't push my beliefs on others." There is much to be said for respecting others' views, of course. But our society has so emphasized personal choice and tolerance that practically an entire generation of young people have rejected an absolute standard for right and wrong. And this thinking has greatly affected your children and mine.

■ OUR YOUTH ARE CONFUSED ABOUT TRUTH ■

What emerges from the data is a portrait—of our own churched youth—of ambivalence and confusion regarding truth. An intense emotional and intellectual (and, perhaps, spiritual) battle is raging within them. A significant portion of our youth—more than half—acknowledge the existence of truth in certain circumstances, but then deny that view when the question is phrased differently. For example, 72 percent say that the Bible provides a clear and indisputable description of moral truth; yet only 44 percent assert that humans are capable of grasping the meaning of truth. Apparently, they recognize there is a relationship between God's Word and moral truth, but their answers to other questions reveal a high level of confusion about that relationship.

Our survey included seven statements about objective standards of truth and morality. The reactions to the statements reveal that our young people are not at all sold on the biblical view of right and wrong. For example, 57 percent of our young people cannot even say that an objective standard of truth exists. Though that percentage is not as high as among unchurched youth, it reveals that even if your children are actively involved in church, they are likely to approve the view that "there is no such thing as absolute truth; people may define truth in contradictory ways and still be correct."

Only 15 percent of churched youth disagree with the statement: "What is right for one person in a given situation might not be right for another person who encounters the same situation." In other words, 85 percent of churched kids are liable to reason, "Just because it's wrong for you doesn't mean it's wrong for me." Their idea of the distinction between right and wrong is fluid, something that is subject to change, something that is relative and personal—not constant and universal.

A mere 29 percent disagreed with the statement: "When it comes to matters of morals and ethics, truth means different things to different people; no one can be absolutely positive they have the truth." This means that less than one in three of our youth believe that recognizable standards of right and wrong apply to everyone.

Just over one-third (38 percent) of our kids disagreed with the statement: "Nothing can be known for certain except the things that you experience in your life." Such matters as morality and ethics are up in the air for two-thirds of churched youth.

Forty-five percent of our churched youth could not disagree with the statement, "Everything in life is negotiable." The astounding implication of that statistic is that almost half of our young people are unable or unwilling to recognize some things in life as non-negotiable. It's unlikely, of course, that they realize the devastating effects of such a view, but that's part of the whole problem.

More worrisome than any single response, however, is the fact that, on a cumulative basis, only 9 percent of our churched youth provided a "pro-truth" reply to each of the seven statements. In other words, less than one in ten could articulate a cohesive, consistent view of objective morality!

As we examine our children's views about truth and morality, it is apparent that the foundations upon which many parents, pastors, and youth leaders attempt to build are crumbling. Traditional biblical concepts are eroding; a Judeo-Christian world view is being undermined. Most of our youth lack the most basic moral perspectives that previous generations took for granted. Many of our young people are struggling with the concept of truth and how they are to apply it to their own life and experience. Their inconsistent responses to the above statements reveal that, even when they express a "pro-truth" position, they do so with little conviction or assurance. Our kids are confused about what truth is and who defines it; they are uncertain about what truths are absolute and what makes them absolute. Consequently, they are making conditional decisions, choosing what seems to be the best alternative at the time, without reference to any fundamental set of precepts or underlying principles to guide their behavior.

<h2>■ WHAT IS ABSOLUTE TRUTH? ■</h2>

Many of our youth simply do not understand or accept absolute truth—that is, **that which is true for all people, for all times, for all places.** Absolute truth is truth that is objective, universal, and constant.

We all have established various family rules and guidelines. For example, I have established a curfew with my thirteen-year-old daughter, specifying what time she should be home after a football game. I have told her, "It is not good to stay out beyond 11:00 P.M." I have set a firm guideline to be followed. If she obeys the curfew, she is *right;* if she violates it, she is *wrong.* I want my daughter to consider curfew as a hard and fast rule. And, in most cases she does.

But should we consider that guideline—to be home by 11:00 P.M. after every football game—an absolute truth? No. It is not applicable to all people, at all times, in all places. Communities, states, and governments may create various ordinances, regulations, and laws that are to be obeyed, but they are not necessarily absolutes. Ordinances change, regulations expire, and some laws only apply in certain states. In fact, even the curfew rule for my daughter may change someday. An absolute truth, on the other hand, is objective, universal, and constant.

If our children are going to learn how to determine right from wrong, they must know what truths are absolute and why. They need to know what standards of behavior are **right for all people, for all times, for all places.** They need to know who determines truth—and why.

<h2>■ WHY TRUTH MATTERS ■</h2>

You may say, "Come on, Josh, all this talk about absolutes seems so abstract. Do you really think that my children's views about truth will really make a difference in their behavior?" That is one of the astounding insights of this research. The study indicates that when our youth do not accept an objective standard of truth they become:

- 36 percent more likely to lie to you as a parent!
- 48 percent more likely to cheat on an exam!
- 74 percent more likely to watch MTV!
- 2 times more likely to try to physically hurt someone!
- 2 times more likely to watch a pornographic film!
- 2 times more likely to get drunk!
- 2 and a quarter times more likely to steal!
- 3 times more likely to use illegal drugs!
- 6 times more likely to attempt suicide!

If your child fails to embrace truth as an objective standard that governs their lives, the study shows it will make them:

- 65 percent more likely to mistrust people!
- 2 times more likely to be disappointed!
- 2 times more likely to be angry with life!
- 2 times more likely to be lacking purpose!
- 2 times more likely to be resentful!

How our youth think about truth has a definite effect on their behavior—the choices they make, and the attitudes they adopt.

■ THE MAGIC LENSES ■

But what is it about truth that affects behavior? It works like this. When you believe there exists an objective standard for distinguishing right from wrong—that certain things are **right for all people, for all times, for all places**—you acknowledge that there are fundamental moral and ethical guidelines that exist independently of your personal opinion. You acknowledge that the distinction between right and wrong is objective (it is defined outside ourselves—it is not subjectively determined), universal (it is for all people in all places—it does not change from person to person or place to place), and constant (it is for all times—it does not change from day to day). When you accept an objective standard for truth, you adopt a moral and ethical viewpoint that guides your choices of what is right and what is wrong. Your "truth view" acts as a lens through which you see all of life and its many choices.

In the 60s and 70s, various cereal manufacturers attracted young customers with a "Hidden Picture" on the back of the cereal box. The hidden picture depicted an intricately drawn scene; but the instructions on the back of the box revealed that another picture lay hidden within that scene. The only way to discern the "Hidden Picture" was with a pair of colored spectacles that were buried inside the box (usually at the bottom). Once a young girl or boy dug those magic lenses out and slipped them on, the picture miraculously appeared in place of the old one. So it is, when a person views life through the *lens of truth,* they are better able to discern the "hidden" truth and distinguish what is right from what is wrong. When our youth are equipped with the proper "truth view," they will be better able to identify what truths are absolute and what makes them absolute . . . and they will have a fighting chance to make the right choices.

■ WHY THEY ARE ACCEPTING COUNTERFEITS ■

The reason, then, that youth who do not accept objective truth are more likely to lie, cheat, or get drunk, is that they are seeing their choices through faulty lenses; they have embraced a world view about truth that blinds them to the difference between right and wrong, the difference between the counterfeits and the real thing.

Many of our churched youth today believe lying to a parent can be justified, cheating can help them get ahead, or stealing can help even the score. But you say, "Can't they see how wrong they are or how much pain they cause?" No, most of them can't, because from their point of view everything is negotiable. If the circumstances warrant it, they think their actions *are* justified. They are thinking and living from a different perspective, a perspective that keeps right and wrong fluid and changing. But this way of thinking actually fools them into believing wrong choices are "right" ones. Consequently, they accept the counterfeits and think they are getting the real thing.

Most of the counterfeits our young people are accepting offer immediate "benefits," while right choices seem to offer more long-range benefits. Sin is packaged very appealingly in our culture, and it carries a promise of immediate satisfaction. That is why so many choose sin—it offers instant gratification. Right choices, on the other hand, often require postponing immediate satisfaction for better long-term benefits. Truth has a tough time competing with counterfeits for this reason. But a counterfeit is still a counterfeit—a substitute for the original. And far too many of our youth are suffering the consequences of choosing harmful substitutes.

I received a letter from a Christian father who had heard me speak. He said that he and his wife had always done their best to be good parents. They were members of a good church, and had always been proud of their children. But he told me that they had just discovered something about their oldest daughter, something that brought their world crashing down around them. He described his daughter as a pretty girl, but said that she'd never been really popular with boys. Until recently.

She started dating one of the boys on the football team, and—this father had just learned—very early in the relationship she had sex with him. She went from that football player to another. Before long, she had slept with the whole football team! This tortured parent wrote me, "Josh, they were passing my little girl around as some sort of 'team girl!'"

When these parents learned of their daughter's behavior, it had been going on for months. They sat down with their daughter and told her they knew what had been going on and cried with her. Then they asked her why—"Why did you do this?" The only explanation she offered was, "I just wanted to feel loved. It never lasted for very long, and I always felt bad about it afterward, but at least for a few fleeting moments I felt like someone loved me."

My heart goes out to that girl and to her parents. I can't tell you how many times I've heard similar stories—firsthand—that would melt even the hardest heart.

Sometime ago a teenage girl named Monica wrote me a poetic but heart wrenching, letter. She penned, "Sex gave me the loneliest thrills I had ever experienced. It handed me fear as a gift and shame to wear as a garment. It blinded my eyes with false love and gave me a jagged tear in my heart. . . ."

That letter might have been written by your daughter—or mine. Our kids don't want "a few fleeting moments" or the lonely thrills they get from a "false love." They want the real thing. Without solid convictions about truth, however, our children will buy the counterfeits almost every time. It's like a downward spiral. When they reject truth as an objective standard, their view of life becomes distorted. When their view becomes distorted, they easily accept the counterfeits. When they accept the counterfeits, they begin to make wrong choices. When they make wrong choices, they suffer the consequences. The choice is, quite literally, truth or consequences.

■ THERE IS HOPE ■

It's a frightening prospect to raise our children in the midst of a "perverse and crooked generation." King David's words are as relevant today as they were when he first asked, "If the foundations be destroyed, what can the righteous do?" (Ps. 11:3, KJV). There are no easy answers, but there is hope. It is not too late to reinforce the crumbling foundations. If you and I are willing to set aside the "quick fix" mentality and face the stark reality of what we as a Christian community have allowed (and perhaps unwittingly adopted ourselves), I believe there is hope. But it won't be easy.

I have no miracle cure for our corrupt culture. I cannot offer sure-fire methods with a "moneyback guarantee" for raising perfect children. We live in an imperfect world and none of us are perfect parents, pastors, teachers, or youth workers. Even youth from the best of families and the best of churches make tragic mistakes. Ultimately, each of our children will make their own decision regarding truth.

But while there are no easy answers, there are still *answers*. Throughout this book, we will explore a practical way to identify what truths are absolute. We will explain a basic method of answering why those truths are absolute. We will examine how to teach young people, even children, to identify what truths are absolute. We will apply the truth to eight crucial areas: chastity, honesty, marriage and family, love, justice, mercy, respect, and self-control. And, most importantly, perhaps, as you see the truth applied to those values, you will be equipped to apply it to many more in your own life and in the lives of your youth.

In the chapters to come, we will introduce three fictitious families, and show you how each has confronted the crisis of truth. But these families are more fact than fiction, because their situations and responses are based on reality. They are composites of the many letters and counseling sessions we have had with young people, their parents, pastors, and youth workers. Each story also reflects the research we have conducted among churched youth.

The pages that follow provide some tough medicine—but I believe it is medicine that will bring healing, renewal, and a rebirth of biblical values among us and our young people. You *can* equip your children to counter the culture. You *can* rebuild the crumbling foundations. You and I may not be able to turn this perverse culture around, but *we can* turn our Christian youth and families and churches around—one at a time.

3

A Seismic Shift

SEVENTEEN-YEAR-OLD Philip Milford entered his grandfather's nursing-home room behind his parents. The room was dark, with a medicinal, musty smell. What little light there was in the room entered with a struggle, filtering through a dirty window and past the loud flowered pattern of the curtains

Philip's mother strode directly to the window and yanked open the curtains. She whirled and spoke to the old man in the high-backed chair. "There, now, isn't that better, Daddy?" The man smiled weakly and nodded at his daughter, the pastor's wife. He noticed that his granddaughter, nine-year-old Sarah, stood with her father, James, at the door, but he said nothing.

"Sarah and I have to run some errands, Dad. We'll be back later," James said.

"Okay, Jimmy boy, you can go but don't lose that little girl there." The old man cracked a smile.

Philip stared at his grandfather. The eighty-year-old man was almost a stranger to him; Philip's grandmother Hughes had died before he was born, and his other grandparents—whom he knew much better—were much younger than Grandpa Hughes. But this visit was part of a school assignment, and he needed to bring his grades up.

After a few minutes of idle chatter had passed between his parents and his grandfather, Philip's mom asked Grandpa Hughes if Philip could ask him a few questions for a school project; she spoke to him as she would to a child. When the man nodded, Philip's mom patted his hand and said they'd be back in a little while.

Philip cleared his throat nervously and drew a pencil and pad out of his coat pocket; he hated this kind of stuff. His grandfather wasn't looking at him. "I guess I should ask you when you were born first."

The man's eyes shifted slightly in Philip's direction, but no answer came. Philip glanced at the clock. Finally the man spoke. "I was born first," he started, emphasizing the last word with a smirk, "in 1914. I was born a second time some years after."

Philip stared for a moment after the man finished speaking. Then he cleared his throat again and scribbled on his pad. After a moment, he raised his head and asked, "What was it like back then?"

"I don't remember much about 1914," the man answered. "I slept most of the year." The smirk creased his face again. "But I guess I know what you're asking."

Silence descended on the room again. Philip had expected his grandfather to keep speaking, but he only stared at the wall, as if he were waiting for a movie to start. Philip felt like tossing his pencil and pad in the trash and forgetting this whole thing. He'd taken a "zero" before. He could do it again. Finally the man spoke.

"My earliest memories are of my father cutting wood. We were kinda poor, even in those days—this was long before the Great Depression—and it seemed like my father spent most evenings chopping wood for the wood stove that heated our house. When I got older, I cut wood with him.

"Since I was the oldest, it became my job every morning to light the fire in the heater to warm the house for the rest of the

24

family, and as soon as I'd light it, I'd jump back in bed until the rest of the family got up."

"Did you have electricity?"

He smiled. "No, we used kerosene lamps for light, for homework, for reading, and for after-dark family games like dominoes, checkers, and Parchesi. That was before television, of course, long before Beavis and Butthead."

"You know who Beavis and Butthead are?"

"Sort of. Do you know who Plutarch and Virgil are?"

"Who?"

"Never mind. What else do you want to know?"

"What did you do for fun?"

"I already told you; we played games together, the whole family. I can remember when we got our first radio too. I must have been about ten or eleven. It was battery-powered, and we had to use a headset to hear it. It didn't have a speaker. Oh, and we would go on picnics during the summer, and we'd swim in the river and play in the sand pits. A carnival would come to town once or twice a year."

"Did you fight a lot with your parents?"

The man looked at Philip for the first time. "No," he answered. "I don't think so. There were things I didn't like. I didn't like having to chop wood, or start the fire every morning. But they were my parents, and I pretty much did what they said."

Philip had stopped writing. He was thinking that his grandfather probably just didn't remember what it was really like to be a kid.

"Of course," the old man continued, "it wasn't that way with everybody. I remember when Viola Kenton—she was two years older than me—Viola got her hair cut in a bob and started wearing short skirts and rolling her silk stockings down to her knees like the flappers. I remember my parents talking about poor Mrs. Kenton."

"Did she end up pregnant?"

"Mrs. Kenton? No, Viola was her youngest."

"No, Grandpa, I'm talking about the girl."

"Oh! No, she was just wild, that's all. She wasn't that kind of girl."

The door squeaked and Mrs. Milford poked her head into the room. "Are you almost done?" she asked, as if she were tickling a baby.

"Yeah," Philip said. "I think so." He stood up, and his parents entered the room. "Thanks, Grandpa."

The old man nodded. "Come back sometime," he said to the boy. "I'll tell you how I had to walk two miles to school every morning, and twice that to get home!"

"Sure, Grandpa," Philip said.

"And tell Jimmy good-bye for me."

"Dad doesn't like to be called Jimmy anymore, Grandpa," Philip said.

"I know." The man smiled. "I'm just tryin' to keep the preacher humble."

The man leaned his head back on his chair and closed his eyes.

■ A LESSON IN HISTORY ■

The worlds of Philip Milford and his grandfather are not only separated by most of a century; they're divided by a philosophical chasm as well. In Grandpa's world, a father and his son cut wood together, families read together and played games together; it was a world in which people depended on God and each other. In Philip's world, most children don't grow up to work in the "family trade," parents spend mere minutes a week with their children, and the overall culture reflects a dependence on man rather than God.

The gap between Grandpa's world and ours did not occur within the last few decades. And neither is our current crisis of truth a modern phenomenon. Our crisis has occurred because of a significant, long-term shift in the way human beings look at God and the world. So, before we discuss how to help our youth determine right from wrong, we must take a close look at this shift in light of history. This is very important because, unless we understand this "seismic" shift, we are likely to miscalculate—and underestimate—the problem.

The shift dates back to the Garden of Eden, when the serpent induced our first parents to trust their own reason instead of simply obeying God's command. But this shift also has its parallel in Israel's history.

During the days of Samuel, the last of the Old Testament judges, the leading citizens of Israel held a convocation. They came to Samuel at his home in Ramah and said, "Appoint a king to lead us, such as all the other nations have." The elderly Samuel had grown up in a society that acknowledged only God as king, a society that attributed the mighty acts and wise judgments of such men and women as Moses, Joshua, and Deborah as the result of their reliance on God. When these leaders approached him about appointing a human king, Samuel did what his people had done for generations—he consulted God.

God told Samuel, "They have rejected me as their king. . . . Now listen to them; but warn them solemnly and let them know what the king who will reign over them will do." Samuel obeyed, and told the leaders of Israel all that would result if they insisted upon usurping God's place on the throne and crowning a man king in His place:

> This is what the king who will reign over you will do: He will take your sons and make them serve with his chariots and horses, and they will run in front of his chariots. Some he will assign to be commanders of thousands and commanders of fifties, and others to plow his ground and reap his harvest, and still others to make weapons of war and equipment for his chariots. He will take your daughters to be perfumers and cooks and bakers. He will take the best of your fields and vineyards and olive groves and give them to his attendants. He will take a tenth of your grain and of your vintage and give it to his officials and attendants. Your menservants and maidservants and the best of your cattle and donkeys he will take for his own use. He will take a tenth of your flocks, and you yourselves will

become his slaves. When that day comes, you will cry out for relief from the king you have chosen, and the LORD will not answer you in that day (1 Sam. 8:11–18).

The people rejected Samuel's warning and persisted in their demands. Samuel (with God's permission) acquiesced; the people of Israel were ruled by a paranoiac (Saul), an adulterer (David), and a megalomaniac (Solomon), until finally—a mere three generations later—the nation was split by the foolishness of the nation's fourth king.

But what was the big deal? What was so bad about wanting a king? What was wrong with the people of Israel wanting a human ruler to lead them in battle? The problem wasn't so much that Israel wanted a king; it was that they wanted to look to a man, not God, for leadership and judgment. They made the mistake of thinking that human leadership would be more immediate and effective than God's methods. Like a sailor who foolishly takes his eyes off the stars and chooses to navigate according to the positions of his fellow crew members, the Israelites arrogantly supposed that they needed to look no higher than to one of their own number—a man—to steer their ship of state, according to their own ideas of what was best for them.

God wanted His people to look to Him for guidance and direction; He wanted them to depend upon Him for leadership and judgment; He wanted to provide for them and protect them better than any mortal king could do. He knew that even the greatest man among them lacked the omniscient, eternal perspective necessary to protect and provide for His people. He knew that that shift away from dependence upon Him, the Source of all good things, would deny Israel innumerable blessings and substitute poor counterfeits.

■ THE BIRTH OF MODERN CULTURE ■

A similar shift has occurred over the course of modern history; in fact, to a large extent, it is what separates modern history from antiquity. Israel's mistake (for which it paid dearly) was rejecting an infinite, immutable God as king and substituting a mere man. Our modern culture has similarly dethroned God as the ultimate source of truth and morality, and enthroned man in His place.

Stanley Newbigin has said, "Every kind of systematic thought has to begin from some starting point."[1] For centuries in western culture, that starting point was the nature and character of God. The purposes of science and philosophy were to discover God's design; art and music were intended to reflect His glory. The highest form of learning was theology. Life and death—and the meaning of human existence—were understood in the context of a universe created and governed by God, who was the Source of all good things. And, most importantly, concepts of truth and morality were inextricably linked to His nature and character. The acknowledgment of an infinite, immutable God made sense of the whole of human experience, and provided a valuable foundation for questions about right and wrong.

What David F. Wells writes about the prophets of the Old Testament and the apostles of the New Testament was also true about men and women in the "pre-modern" era of western history:

> They had a certainty about the existence, character, and purposes of God—a certainty about his truth—that seems to have faded in the bright light of the modern world. They were convinced that God's revelation, of which they were the vehicles and custodians, was true. True in an absolute sense. It was not merely true to them; it was not merely true in their time; it was not true approximately. What God had given was true universally, absolutely, and enduringly.[2]

That, to paraphrase Walter Cronkite, is "the way it was," the way men and women thought, and what western culture reflected. But that all began to change during a period of European history we now call *the Renaissance*.

The Renaissance began in Italy in the 1300s and, over the course of the next two centuries, spread throughout Europe, lasting through the sixteenth century. The Renaissance was characterized by great strides in literature, learning, art, and architecture. Writers and artists such as Petrarch, Boccaccio, Giotto, and Michelangelo sparked an era of extraordinary human accomplishment. The Renaissance also marked a significant shift in human thought. In contrast to the middle ages (in which the major theme of art, literature, and philosophy was glorifying and serving God), Renaissance artists and thinkers exalted man and his abilities. This shift gave birth to a doctrine called humanism, which stressed human dignity and ability and regarded man as the center of all things, the master of his fate, the captain of his soul—an emphasis that led eventually to an unbiblical view of man and his relationship to his Creator. As this way of thinking began to take hold, men and women's dependence upon God as the Source of truth and morality began to wane.

The Renaissance may have had minimal impact on man's thinking, had it not been followed promptly by a period of history known as *the Enlightenment,* or the Age of Reason. The Enlightenment began in the 1600s and lasted through the next century. While the Renaissance mind acknowledged God (but removed him from the throne, so to speak, replacing him with man), many leaders of the Enlightenment (such as Voltaire and Descartes) claimed that if there were a God who had created the world, He had no contact with it now—which meant that men and women were left to discover truth on their own; they could expect no help from God. Man had to depend upon his powers of reason if he hoped to discern the truth. Standards of right and wrong were not based on the nature and character of God; they were the products of human reasoning. In the Renaissance, man (not God) became central; in the Enlightenment, man's reason became transcendent. The error of the Enlightenment was not in recognizing human reason as a wonderful thing; it was the attempt to crown man's reason as king in God's place, refusing to acknowledge any standard or reality that reason could not fully comprehend or explain.

Two more historical influences have shaped how many modern people—including our own youth—think and act today. The first of these is *the Industrial Revolution.*

The Industrial Revolution overlapped much of the Enlightenment period, extending from the 1700s through the 1800s. It was an explosive period of human productivity and advancement. The inventions, innovations, and improvements of the Industrial Age fueled more than factory furnaces; it stoked the fires of human confidence. The progress that men and women saw all around them encouraged them to look to themselves for hope and guidance. Man no longer felt the need to look upward (to God); he need only look inward (to himself).

The furnaces of the Industrial Revolution still blazed hot when the theories of Charles Darwin, a former theology student, completed the seismic shift that the Renaissance had begun. "The publication of The Origin of the Species in 1859," says Ernst Mayr of Harvard University, "ushered in the greatest intellectual revolution since the proclamation of Christianity, two thousand years earlier." Darwin's theories presented an alternative to a theistic understanding of origins; God was no longer "needed" to explain or understand how the world—and man—came to be. These theories became known as *Darwinism*.

This shift in thinking had succeeded in convincing men and women that they were the arbiters of truth and morality, not God. Human reason had replaced God as the object of modern man's worship. Human accomplishments had made man arrogant and confident in his own abilities to create good and judge evil. Finally, with the publication and increasing acceptance of Darwin's theories, God became *persona non grata*—unnecessary and unwelcome—leaving man free (in his mind, at least) to judge truth, to reach his own conclusions about right and wrong independent of God and His decrees.

■ THE TWO MODELS OF TRUTH ■

The shift brought about by these four historical influences—the Renaissance, the Enlightenment, the Industrial Age, and Darwinism—has resulted in two distinct models of truth. They reflect two opposite ways of looking at God and the world:

31

Model #1: Truth is defined by God for everyone; it is objective and absolute.

Model #2: Truth is defined by the individual; it is subjective and situational.

The first model acknowledges that God—not man—is central, that He is the Source of all things, and that He rules over all. God is the repository of truth, the author and judge of right and wrong.

The second model, on the other hand, places the individual in control of moral matters; because the standard is within the individual, it is particular to that specific person (subjective) and circumstance (situational). In other words, each person considers himself or herself the judge of whatever is right or wrong in any given circumstance. It is an anthropocentric model; that is, it is man-centered, not God-centered.

Our culture, which was once guided by the first model, has fully embraced the second model. "Western culture," writes Chris Wright, "has been systematically and deliberately sucking out the transcendent from its public heart and core."[3] This shift from the first model to the second has affected every aspect of our society, from the arts to music to literature to politics.

Consequently, the second model—a relativistic model—is the model most of our youth use today. It has shaped and molded their world view. It is the lens through which they view life's choices, the basis on which they make life's decisions.

When the Bible says of Christ, "in him all things hold together" (Col. 1:17, NIV), it is in the context of the natural order, but it is also true of a person's world view, of a man or woman's philosophical base. God is the glue that holds everything together; He is the clue that solves the puzzle; He is the infinite that defines the finite; He is the absolute that makes sense of it all. As Francis Schaeffer said:

If there is no absolute moral standard, then one cannot say in a final sense that anything is right or wrong. By absolute we mean that which always applies, that which provides a final or ultimate standard.[4]

There must be an absolute if there are to be morals, and there must be an absolute if there are to be real values. If there is no absolute beyond man's ideas, then there is no final appeal to judge between individuals and groups whose moral judgments conflict. We are merely left with conflicting opinions.

■ AS TIME GOES BY ■

Even after the upheaval of the Renaissance, the Enlightenment, the Industrial Revolution, and Darwinism, most people in western culture lived far from Descartes and Darwin, and from those who declared God dead (in one way or another) and enshrined man as the new god, the cause of progress and judge of right and wrong. For the most part, all those lofty ideas about the greatness of the human spirit and adequacy of human effort just didn't enter the mind of the working man with an impossible boss or the mother of four children who fell exhausted into bed every evening.

As a result, the generation that was raised in the early part of the twentieth century (now called the "Seniors" by researchers and trend-watchers) came of age in a world that was vastly different from the one that exists at the dawn of the twenty-first century . . . though already a storm of monumental proportions loomed on the horizon.

"But," you may say, "all those things happened before this century, before my grandparents were even born. Why does it seem like things have come to a head now, in this generation?"

The explanation lies partly in the fact that cultural change does not occur suddenly; ideas and philosophies are not sold like hot dogs on a New York City street. It unfolds more like a tropical storm.

Before any major tropical storm, changes begin to occur in the climate. At first, these changes are nearly imperceptible—dark clouds gather, the barometric pressure drops, the wind increases. Each of these changes is gradual and insignificant by itself; but cumulatively, these conditions set the stage for a storm of cataclysmic proportions.

Similarly, the fundamental shift in the way people look at the world happens gradually, over centuries. As time goes by, each generation embraces more new ideas. Francis Schaeffer explained the slow dissemination of these ideas in his book, *How Should We Then Live?*

[The loss of traditional values] spread in three different ways to people of our own culture and to people across the world. Geographically, it spread from the European mainland to England, after a time jumping the Atlantic to the United States. Culturally, it spread in the various disciplines from philosophy to art, to music, to general culture (the novel, poetry, drama, films), and to theology. Socially, it spread from the intellectuals to the educated and then through the mass media to everyone.[5]

The ideas and observations of people like Descartes, Darwin, and others, which for years had been drifting among the intelligentsia like snowflakes in a gray sky, finally began to settle to the ground. From the turn of the twentieth century forward, the transmission of traditional values from one generation to the next began to diminish, like old cars disappearing from the road.

That loss of traditional values was facilitated by the vast societal changes that have occurred this century. These changes are not necessarily harmful themselves; they have had a calamitous effect, however, because of the ways they have contributed to the crisis of truth by allowing the shift from a God-centered world view to a man-centered view to take hold among us. Cumulatively, they have created the generational storm that is now raging all around us. Wittingly or unwittingly, you and I may be contributing to the very forces from which we so desperately want to protect our children.

■ THE ADVENT OF MASS MEDIA ■

One of the most influential societal changes of the twentieth century has been the advent of mass media. Seniors (those who

were born before 1927) can remember the first radios and talking movies. Builders (born 1927 to 1945) can remember the first
televisions. By contrast, most Baby Boomers (born 1946 to 1964)
cannot remember a time without television, and their children
cannot imagine life without MTV, HBO, VCRs, and CDs.

The development of radio, movies, television, and other
electronic media has changed the face of our society in three
critical ways.

First, mass media have shrunk the world and fostered the swift
dissemination of news and ideas. Because of today's media, the
world is smaller than ever before; its conflicts are closer, and its
problems are more immediate. The news of President Kennedy's
1963 assassination spread nationwide within minutes; the Vietnam
War became the first to expose Americans to the atrocities of war
in their own living rooms each night at eleven o'clock. The electronic media have brought us together, within our own nation and
with the people of other lands. But this "global village" created
by the electronic media has also sped the destruction of traditional
moral values. Phil Donahue, Bart Simpson, and Peter Jennings
have introduced ideas and perspectives into the home that present
a stark contrast to biblical views.

Secondly, the mass media have affected the way families inter-
act. "What's on TV tonight?" has replaced, "Dad, can you help me
with my homework?" in many families. Families used to linger
for conversation at the dinner table; now, instead of exchanging
news and views between parents and children, they consume the
evening meal in front of the television, watching reruns of
"family" shows in a room ironically called the "family room."
The average teen watches nearly three hours of television a day; the
average use per household is over six hours. Meanwhile, our
young people report that they spend under four minutes a day in
meaningful conversation with their mothers, and two-and-a-half
minutes a day talking things over with Dad.[6] It's not just television,
of course; music and movies also tend to frustrate effective family
communication. It's no wonder parents doubt that they're passing on their values to their children—teens spend 2,800 percent

more time with Beavis, Butthead, and Madonna than they do with their mothers and fathers!

Thirdly, movies and television present a totally unrealistic model of actions and consequences. Movie heroes can solve the most insurmountable problems in less than two hours (usually with a blow to the head or a burst from an Uzi submachine gun). The small-screen heroes can do it in under an hour. Such models may have an effect on your child's approach to problems. But more poisonous still is the impact of a daily diet of characters and shows that display little distinction between right and wrong and little relationship between a person's actions and the consequences that result from his or her behavior. For example, of all the television and movie characters who have engaged in illicit sex, can you name any who have contracted chlamydia or HPV (Human Papilloma Virus) or one of the other fifty-seven sexually transmitted diseases? Probably very few, because television and movie characters seldom clean up their own messes or suffer the consequences of their immorality.

■ THE URBANIZATION OF SOCIETY ■

Another factor in the disintegration of traditional views of truth and morality has been the effect of a major population shift in western society. This century has seen an unprecedented movement of families from rural environs to urban settings. Author Os Guiness points out,

> America in 1940 was still a rural, small-town nation. Incredible though it seems today, fewer than 50 percent of all Americans then lived in cities with more than ten thousand inhabitants. But vast social changes [took place] in the forties and fifties. By the beginning of 1950, two out of three Americans had moved into one of the great metropolitan regions.[7]

This population shift has—for the first time on such a scale— separated children from the supportive network of extended family. To previous generations, grandparents and other members of the extended family were an important source of moral instruction and guidance. Their presence not only supported parents, but often provided sage advice to children when Mom and Dad were absent (or when it would have been imprudent to consult one's parents). Grandparents (as well as uncles and aunts) often served as mentors and tutors to children; the entire family participated in raising children and communicating important values and morals to them. Those resources have been lost to recent generations: fifty years ago, 60 to 70 percent of all households included at least one live-in grandparent; today, less than 2 percent of households benefit from that resource.

Secondly, it denied children the benefits of apprenticeship. On the farm, children worked alongside their parents and grandparents. They pitched hay together, pulled stumps together, washed dishes together, and fixed meals together. These shared tasks not only taught important skills to children; they also presented ample opportunities for parents to share family history and communicate important values. When Mom and Dad started working in distant offices while their children stayed with baby-sitters or in child-care centers, an important benefit was denied those children.

Finally, the shift from rural to urban lifestyles resulted in the loss of a process by which children learned that their actions have consequences. With the switch to urban or suburban lifestyles came a shift in the role each child played in the home. On the farm, each child was given important responsibilities, and even the youngest learned that irresponsibility would have consequences. Philip Milford's grandfather, for example, knew that if he failed to start the fire on a cold winter morning, it wouldn't get done—and the entire family would be affected. If the cows didn't get milked, there would be no milk; if the eggs were not collected, there would be no cake; if the wood didn't get chopped, there would be no heat. Children grew up with a keen understanding of the relationship between actions and consequences, an awareness that has largely disappeared with the shift to an urban lifestyle.

■ THE RISE OF MATERIALISM ■

A third factor that has shaped our youth and the way they look at the world is the unprecedented economic prosperity that followed the Second World War. In 1940, for example, 43.6 percent of Americans owned their own homes; by 1960, that figure had increased 42 percent (by contrast, 1920 to 1940 had seen a 4 percent decline). "Of the nation's total housing stock in 1960," writes Os Guiness, "one-third was built in the 1950s."[8] The nation's automakers retooled to meet the rising demand for cars. Television sets began to be snatched up by consumers. In the space of ten years, America's GNP (gross national product) nearly doubled.

This economic boom affected more than people's pocketbooks, however; it affected how they lived, how they thought, and how they raised their children.

This new prosperity encouraged a new materialism. A new era of consumerism had dawned; families began to acquire homes, automobiles, conveniences, and extravagances like never before. More importantly, these material possessions—and the means to acquire them—began to assume greater importance to people. A mere 15 percent of the "Seniors" generation (born before 1927) esteemed "having a high paying job" as very desirable; that figure nearly doubled among their children—those who reached adulthood during the post-war economic boom. Baby Boomers, who were raised in the affluent post-war atmosphere, value a high-paying job even more (34 percent); still more "Baby Busters"—56 percent—consider a high-paying job to be very desirable. The same trend occurs when individuals are asked whether owning a large home is a priority to them; 16 percent of Seniors consider that goal "very desirable," a number that rises steadily among the generations until it reaches 43 percent among our youth today. The message that emerges from these and other statistics is that prosperity has created an attitude that increasingly values material benefits above other priorities (such as having a close relationship with God, for example, or living close to other family members—values that have steadily declined over the last four generations).

It influenced the rearing of an entire generation with a predominantly economic—not moral—aim. The rising tide of materialism among our youth should not be a surprise when we recall that the most oft-stated aim of many parents of the 50s and 60s was "to give my children the things I never had." Pulitzer Prize-winning author James A. Michener refers to this trend:

> Starting about 1960, the flood of children born after the end of World War II and properly labeled the Baby Boom began behaving in mysterious ways. Their parents, especially their fathers who had undergone both privation and psychic shocks, were excessively lenient and indulgent with their offspring on the theory: "I want my child to have it a lot better than I did when I was growing up in the Depression." [9]

Thus, children of the 50s and 60s were raised, not with a primarily moral aim, as were their parents and grandparents, but with a largely economic mind-set. Parents regarded their main responsibility to be providing materially for their children. In so doing, many of them neglected to provide their progeny with a moral frame of reference.

Finally, it introduced the irony of more leisure time, yet less "family" time. The prosperity of the post-war era introduced many "time-saving" conveniences, such as dishwashers, electric washers and dryers, and hair dryers. However, these time-savers have resulted, ironically, in families spending less time together. With no dishes to dry and no wash to be hung out on the line, parents and children have more time—for their separate pursuits.

■ THE WIDENING INFLUENCE OF PUBLIC SCHOOLS ■

The final major factor in the disappearance of traditional values is the widening role of public schools in American society. Public schools have been a crucial, positive part of American society for generations. However, recent generations have witnessed three important shifts in public education that have contributed immensely to our inability to pass on strong biblical values to our children.

First, with the entrance of the "Baby Boom" into our nation's schools came a shift from neighborhood schools to "education factories." Prior to the entrance of the first Baby Boomers into the halls of academia, the majority of American children had been educated in small, neighborhood schools. These schools were often staffed by relatives and neighbors. The curriculum reflected the community. When the Baby Boom's first wave hit first grade, however, the sudden demand for teachers and classroom space changed the complexion of public education. Authors H. Stephen Glenn and Jane Nelsen point out that,

> On or around September 1, 1951, a mass of 4.2 million urban/ suburban babies hit the schools looking for classrooms, teachers, and books. Taking everyone by surprise—for few people had heeded the warning embedded in the soaring 1946 birth rate—five times the number of children who had arrived the year before to start the first grade arrived at school and said, "Where's my seat?" [10]

Students were herded into what Glenn and Nelsen call "education factories"—huge regional schools of thirty-student classes taught by teachers who didn't know these kids or their parents. As a result, a structure that had previously reinforced parents' efforts to instill traditional values in their children could no longer identify those values, let alone support them.

Another factor has been the growing federal presence in the public schools. Over the past thirty years, more and more public education curriculum has been influenced nationally, rather than locally. The establishment of a federal Department of Education in 1979 escalated the trend toward federal involvement in public education. As a result, fewer decisions are made by parents and other adults who are intimately concerned with the values their children adopt.

Most importantly, parents have changed their thinking; these days, parents expect professionals to educate their children. If I were to ask a group of 100 parents, "Who is in charge of your child's education?" I would expect the majority of them to answer something like, "Mrs. Johnson," "Mr. Phillips," or "St. Ursula School." Few of them would answer, "Me." The most important change in education in the last fifty years has not occurred in schools; it has occurred in the minds of parents, who no longer take primary responsibility for their children's educations. Mom, Dad, we have let someone else take charge of our children! We have slipped into thinking that we must support those who are in charge of our children's education, when we ought to be taking charge ourselves! This is true not only of parents whose children attend public schools, but also of private school or Christian-school parents. As youth pastor James Strole says, "Christian parents are not sacrificing for their kids. They are assuming that the Christian church or school is doing the job."[11] The vast majority of teachers, principals, and church youth workers that I know are crying out for parents to become more involved in the academic and spiritual educations of their own children; that is a tragedy, one that has contributed immensely to the decline of biblical values among our youth.

■ A GENERATION OF FIRSTS ■

Generally speaking, the Baby Busters, that generation now approaching or embarking upon adulthood, is:

- ■ the first generation in history to be raised wholly under the influence of television in an electronic media-saturated society;
- ■ the first generation in history to be raised without the influence of a close extended family;
- ■ the first generation in history to be raised largely by parents who have never known deprivation or want;

- the first generation in history to be raised by parents who assign the primary responsibility for their children's educations to someone else.

But ultimately, none of those factors—not the influence of mass media, not the urbanization of society, not the rise of materialism, not the widening public school influence—have created the crisis of truth that plagues our youth today. They have contributed to the wider dissemination of a world view that has its roots in the Renaissance and other historical influences, but things like television and the public schools are not the issue here. They have certainly contributed to the storm that threatens to swallow our kids. But I believe that the single most important factor in the loss of moral and ethical values among our children is the way their parents—you and I—have responded to the storm!

I realize we cannot turn back the clock of time. We cannot recapture those days before television, when most families lived on farms—nor would I want to, to be honest. In spite of our culture's malaise, this is an exciting time to be alive. But what we can do is learn from history. If we can understand how our culture—like ancient Israel—fell prey to this seismic shift, we can begin to respond to the dangers. If we can see how our failure to adjust to the vast societal changes of the past century has hampered the transfer of biblical values to succeeding generations, we will be better enabled to counter our culture. If at every turn we resist the culture's shift away from dependence upon God, we will be in a better position to equip our youth with biblical values and standards.

■ PASSING THE BATON ■

Have you ever watched a relay race? As the lead sprinter on each team runs the first leg of the race, the next runner gets set. He anxiously times his teammate's arrival, and begins running before the lead man overtakes him. Then the crucial moment arrives, and the lead man passes the baton to the middle man. The process is repeated twice more in the race, as each man surrenders the baton to the next.

A good track coach will tell you that the relay is often won or lost in the transfer of the baton. A miscalculation or hesitation at that point can cost the race.

We *can* transfer our values to the next generation, but a miscalculation or hesitation in the passing of the baton of truth can cost the race. Oh, there may be hindrances; the crowd may be distracting, and the track may be rough. But as in a relay, we have a limited zone in which to make the transfer. If we as parents, pastors, teachers, and youth workers heed the lessons of history, counter the culture to the best of our ability, and clearly articulate the objective standard of truth behind our own morals and values, we will help ourselves—and our youth—to make the transfer.

From Generation
to Generation

JAMES MILFORD, the pastor of Westcastle Community Church, felt awkward in the pulpit for the first time in many years. His eyes scanned the congregation of faces looking expectantly up at him, waiting for him to begin the Sunday morning sermon.

Pastor Milford had led this church for over four years, and he had never cried in the pulpit. He was determined that this Sunday would not be the first exception.

"I come before you this morning a different man than I was last week. Several things happened this past week that have made me aware of my own faults and failures. I will not tell you about the events that made me search my own soul, and my own actions, but I will tell you that this morning's sermon has come out of that experience."

With a gesture familiar to every member of his church, Pastor Milford scooped his wide black Bible off the pulpit and balanced it in his left hand. He moved with assurance, his six-foot frame as straight as a flagpole. He adjusted his glasses with his right hand, inhaled deeply, and stepped to the side of the pulpit.

"The ancient book of Judges tells of the generations of Israelites that grew up after the great events of the exodus and the
conquest of Canaan. Joshua's generation—who had witnessed
the parting of the Red Sea, received the tablets of the law from
Mount Sinai, and fought the Battle of Jericho—remained faithful
to God and His Law. These were the generation who knew the
Lord, and had witnessed His mighty wonders.

"The next generation—the children of Joshua, the children of
the men who fought beside him, the sons and daughters of the
women who gathered manna in the wilderness—cut their teeth
on the firsthand stories their fathers and mothers told of God's
deliverance and provision. They had not seen the walls of Jericho
come tumbling down. They had not heard the rumblings on
Mount Sinai; but their parents taught them such things day and
night, when they tucked them into bed, when they walked together through their fields. And *that* generation remained faithful.

"The biblical account tells us, however, that something went
wrong. Something happened to the third generation after the
exodus."

Pastor Milford gazed at the Bible in his left hand, and spoke
in a booming voice, charged with emotion:

> The people served the Lord throughout the lifetime of Joshua and
> of the elders who outlived him and who had seen all the great things
> the Lord had done for Israel. . . . After that whole generation had
> been gathered to their fathers, another generation grew up, who
> knew neither the Lord nor what he had done for Israel. Then the
> Israelites did evil in the eyes of the Lord and served the Baals. They
> forsook the Lord, the God of their fathers, who had brought them
> out of Egypt. They followed and worshiped various gods of the
> people around them.[1]

He looked up from the page of his Bible, and his eyes were
ringed with tears.

"What happened?" he asked plaintively. "What went wrong
with that generation? Their grandparents had seen the mighty hand

of God. Their parents had heard eyewitness accounts of the wonders God performed. But—for some reason—the third generation after the exodus were influenced less by their parents—who knew the Lord and what He had done for Israel—than by the culture around them, a culture filled with idols and counterfeits. How did it happen? How did that generation grow up knowing neither the Lord nor what He had done for Israel?

"Oh, well, of course, there was the influence of the culture. You know, they were surrounded by Canaanites and Jebusites and Amorites—all kinds of bad influences. Pagan temples were springing up and seductive songs were being played in the marketplace.

"And, of course, their lifestyles had changed drastically between these generations. Joshua's generation had come out of Egypt while they were still young; they knew privation and war. The second generation did not know war during the time they raised their children; they settled down and began to build homes of their own and grow crops of their own . . . for the first time in centuries. They said, 'I want my kids to have all the things I never had.'

"But it wasn't the culture that led this third generation astray. It wasn't the momentous changes in lifestyle that occurred in their society. It wasn't even the fault of the pagans—Canaanites and Jebusites were just as plentiful in previous generations as they were then."

Pastor Milford looked at his wife, sitting in the first row; seventeen-year-old Philip and nine-year-old Sarah sat on either side of her. His gaze traveled from his own family to Gary and Penny Marsh, and their children, Brittney, Lauren, and Michael. He glanced at Geena Santoro, a single mother whose daughter was newly married. He met the eyes of several others in the congregation before straightening himself to his full height and striding to the edge of the platform. When he spoke, his voice was low, but earnest.

"The third generation of free Israelites grew up not knowing the Lord nor the things He had done for Israel because—" he paused, "while their parents gave them many material blessings, they did not do as their parents before them had done. They neglected to tell their children the stories of how God had led them out of Egypt and had given them victory after victory over their enemies. They failed to repeat, over and over again, how God had given them the Law, and why His commands were so important. The mothers taught their daughters how to beat soiled linen on the river rocks; the fathers emphasized the importance of bringing in the crop; but they never got around to teaching God's precepts to their children. They had camels to trade, barns to build, parties to plan, weddings to attend—a hundred things to do—but moral and spiritual instruction never made its way into their busy schedules."

The pastor shifted his Bible into his right hand, closed it, and used it to gesture to his congregation. His gaze again flitted among various members of the crowd.

"I am convinced that 'these things were our examples,' as the Bible says, because the same things are happening today. We see a whole generation of children who are being influenced less by their parents than they are by the culture around them, a culture filled with idols and counterfeits, a culture that can't tell the difference between right and wrong, a culture that can't distinguish between human and animal, male and female, reason and madness, art and pornography, knowledge and ignorance![2] We see a crooked and perverse generation that neither knows the Lord, nor what He has done for those who follow His commands.

"Our children are not adopting our values and morals. They do not share our priorities and perspectives. And we cannot blame the media, we cannot blame society, we cannot blame the government, we cannot blame the Supreme Court, we cannot blame the public schools—*they* are not entrusted with communicating biblical values to our children—*we* are! We must not expect to change our culture (if indeed we could); we must change the way we respond to it. It does no good to bemoan our society; we must control how much we allow it to influence us and our children.

"You see, we can't blame television and movies for what our kids believe or how they behave, because we've allowed the media to influence them. We've used the tube to baby-sit our toddlers and entertain our teens. We've been too lazy or disinterested to preview movies for our children, relying instead on a ratings system to tell us what movies we should expose our children to! I'm not saying that Christians should not own a television set or attend movies, but I am saying that Christian parents need to take responsibility for the influences we allow in our kids' lives. We need to help them filter advertising messages. We need to help them evaluate the subtle (and not-so-subtle) media messages in movies, television shows, newscasts, and songs. We need to use the media as a tool to teach or reinforce moral lessons. To the degree that we have failed to do these things, we have failed to meet our parental responsibility."

A few faces in the crowd exchanged meaningful looks. Pastor Milford thought he saw skepticism in some faces, outright defiance in others. He began to pace from one side of the pulpit to the other, something he could not ever recall doing before.

"The reason our children are not adopting our values is not because of the state of American society, but because of how we, as parents, have responded to it. We have contributed to the fracturing of the family. We have not placed a high priority on establishing strong family and community networks; we have not mentored our children and taught them good work skills and habits; we have not devised new ways to entrust our children with tasks that will teach them the relationship between actions and consequences. We have tried to express our love for our children with 'things' instead of spending time with them and teaching our children to work and save.

"We have not only failed to take charge of our children's education; we have too often failed to take part in it. How many of us have gotten to know our children's principals and teachers? How many school board meetings have we attended? When was the last time we volunteered to chaperon field trips? I'm afraid we have expected others to take primary responsibility for what our children know and what they value."

The pastor inhaled deeply. He was tired. He set his Bible down on the pulpit.

"Most importantly—hear me now, people of God—we cannot expect our children to value honesty if we receive cable television without paying for it because of a cable company oversight. We cannot expect our kids to respect the law as long as we have a radar detector installed on our dash. We cannot expect our youth to value sexual purity when we've committed 'sexual indiscretions' ourselves. We cannot expect our children to develop a wholesome view of marriage if we bail out when the going gets tough.

"Here and now, we need to acknowledge that it is *our* responsibility—not the culture's, not the schools, not the church—to equip our children with a bedrock of biblical values that will enable them to make moral choices in an immoral world. We must take time with our children—leave the briefcase at work, forget your favorite television show, let the garden go for a few days—and begin now to teach them when they rise up, when they are in the way, and when they lie down to rest."

Pastor James Milford placed a hand on the flat surface of the pulpit. He swallowed hard and closed his eyes. Then he began to pray.

"Father God, I come before You in sorrow and repentance. I confess that I have failed in my responsibility to my children. I have expected the church to evangelize my children. I have trusted the school to educate my children. I have allowed the media to entertain my children.

"I have forgotten that 'children are an heritage of the Lord,' that they are a gift, a trust, and that my daily, hourly responsibility is to raise them in 'nurture and admonition of the Lord.'

"Help me, Father, to begin now—this moment—to acknowledge that it is *my* responsibility, and no one else's, to teach strong moral values to my children, values based on biblical truth, that will enable them to make moral choices in an immoral world. Remind me to take time with my children—not a moment here and there, but when they rise up, when they are in the way, and when they lie down to rest—to make sure they know You, and the things You have done for me. Amen."

Following the prayer, Pastor Milford descended from the pulpit and strode to the back of the sanctuary in silence. The people hesitated, and many in the crowd exchanged bewildered looks. There had been no closing hymn, no benediction. Slowly, the hushed sanctuary began to empty, as the crowd of worshipers trickled toward the doors.

Pastor James Milford stood outside the large doors of the main entrance, shaking hands and nodding gravely in response to people's comments.

Geena Santoro gripped the pastor's hand and fixed him with a steely gaze. "I must say, I did not find much encouragement in the house of God this morning," she said. "Some of us have done the best we can for our children under difficult circumstances." She drew a breath quickly, as though she were about to cry. "You will never know how hard it is to be a single mother, Pastor. I love my daughter, and I'm proud of her, and I raised her with very little help. I think I did a good job, and I don't mind telling you I'm offended by your suggestion that I bailed out of my marriage when the going got tough. I did what I had to do, what I thought was best at the time. That's all any of us can do."

The pastor nodded solemnly and absorbed her criticism without a word.

As Geena scolded the pastor, the Marsh family pulled out of the church parking lot. Gary and Penny sat in the front seat of the Volvo, along with their seven-year-old son, Michael. Their daughter Lauren, eleven, and Brittney, fifteen, sat in the back.

As they usually did, Gary and Penny discussed the events of the morning. After a few moments, Penny tilted her head to one side and eyed her husband.

"What did you think of the sermon?" she asked.

Gary inhaled. "Well," he began. But before he could finish, Brittney interupted.

"Pastor sure nailed you on your Fuzzbuster, didn't he, Dad?"

Gary smiled, and stole a glance at the device on his dashboard. "I think you missed his point, Brittney" He looked at his daughters in the rear-view mirror; who had leaned forward, to hear their father's response. "He wasn't saying that it's wrong to have a Fuzzbuster."

"He wasn't?" seven-year-old Michael looked up from the seat beside his father.

"No," he said. "He was just using that as an example, an illustration."

He noticed his wife out of the corner of his eye; she was studying his face as he spoke.

"He was saying," he continued, mentally scrambling for words, "that we need to teach our kids right from wrong, and I think we've done that."

"I'm sure," Brittney uttered sarcastically under her breath as she and her sister sank back into their seats.

Michael said nothing and turned to look out the car window.

Penny Marsh smiled at her husband, but her face wore a thoughtful, unconvinced expression. The rest of the trip home passed in silence.

More Fact
Than Fiction

PENNY MARSH felt like someone had kicked her in the gut.

She had taken off work early to come home and pack for the family's ski weekend in the Poconos. The house was quiet when she entered—no sign of her fifteen-year-old daughter, Brittney. Penny consulted her watch. *Brittney should be home from school by now,* she figured. Penny had set her briefcase down by the door, hung her coat in the hall, and climbed the stairs to the second floor. She rapped smartly on Brittney's bedroom door and poked her head into the room. What she saw next knocked the wind out of her.

The form of a naked boy rolled off the bed; Penny saw her daughter's nakedness for a moment until Brittney snatched the sheet from around her feet and pulled it up under her chin.

Penny studied the room speechlessly, panic surging up from her belly in a wave of nausea. The boy's clothes lay in a heap at her feet; she kicked them in the direction of the creature who cowered beside the bed.

"Get out!" Penny cried. Her first words echoed shrilly in the room and startled even herself with their venom. "Get out!" she repeated.

The boy collected his clothes and clutched them in front of him as he stole past Penny, without a glance in Brittney's direction, and disappeared into the hall.

Penny stood trembling in the presence of her oldest child, her fifteen-year-old baby. She peered at Brittney through swelling eyes, but her daughter would not meet her gaze. An acrid taste filled her mouth and she fought for control. She quickly lost the battle, however, clamped a hand over her mouth, whirled, and ran to the bathroom across the hall to throw up.

Late that evening, Brittney sat opposite her mother and father in the family room. Brittney and Penny's faces streamed with tears; forty-two-year-old Gary Marsh fought to control his temper.

"How long has this been going on?" Penny asked her daughter.

"Matt and I just started going out," Brittney answered.

"I don't mean just him, I mean you—have you been with other boys?"

The trio sat in silence for a few long moments, until Brittney answered with a long, drawn out, "Yes."

"Oh, sweet Jesus," her mother said, sobbing.

"How many?" Gary interjected.

"What difference does it make?" Brittney answered, finally raising her glance. "What's the big deal? Look, I've never had unprotected sex, if that's what you're worried about. Okay? Never. And it's not like I've slept around, either. You act like it's something to be ashamed of. Well, it's not! It's a way of expressing love for somebody, OK? What's so wrong about that?"

"You lied to us!" Penny's face registered pain and astonishment.

"Like, what would you have done if I'd told you?" She mocked her mother's voice. "'How did your day go, dear?' 'Pretty good, I had sex with Andrew Witson.' Get real!"

Gary was standing now, his six-foot-two frame towering over Brittney. "How can you sit there and tell me you don't see anything wrong with what you've done? You've been brought up in the church, Brittney Marsh! Hasn't a Christian home done anything for you?"

Brittney stood, and returned her father's angry gaze. "Yeah," she said, her voice rising in a confident, defiant tone. "It's taught me about love—and that's what all this is about. I love Matt, and you can't tell me that's wrong!"

She stormed from the room. Her father watched her leave, wondering what he should do. Finally, unable to come up with a satisfactory answer, he sat down beside his wife. "She's so young," Penny said.

They sat in silence without looking at each other.

"She's so young," she repeated.

Gary nodded. "But she's old enough to know better," he said.

Penny buried her face into her husband's shoulder and cried. They remained there for a long time, wordlessly sharing their grief, until sleep delivered them from their nightmare.

■ HOW OUR YOUTH VIEW LOVE AND SEX ■

That tragic scene is more fact than fiction. It is repeated all too frequently, believe me—I get the calls and letters from heart-broken parents and confused teenagers.

According to George Barna of The Barna Research Group, only 23 percent of the entire Baby Buster generation (churched and unchurched) claim to be virgins. More than three-quarters admit to having sexual intercourse with another single person. Two out of ten single Busters say they have had sex with a married person. One in fourteen married Busters has had extramarital sex. Almost half (47 percent) of the babies born to Baby Buster females in 1992 were born to unmarried mothers.[1] And girls are having sex much earlier these days; the median age for a young woman's first act of premarital sex has fallen from nineteen in 1960 to seventeen in 1990.

Those figures are disturbing enough; but our new research reveals that your kids and my kids—kids from Christian homes and good churches—are also crumbling under the constant pressures of a sex-crazed society. By age eighteen, more than one in four (27 percent) of churched youth have experienced sexual intercourse, and over half (55 percent) have engaged in fondling breasts. Perhaps most disturbing is the implication of the research that there is a one-in-four chance that your son or daughter will engage in sexual intercourse by the age of eighteen.

The study reveals that sexual behavior like Brittney's is not uncommon among our kids. It also reveals that her attitude—"What's so wrong about that?"—is also widely accepted. More than half (51 percent) of our young people could not state that fondling of breasts was morally unacceptable. Nearly a third (29 percent) view the fondling of genitals as moral behavior. And one in five of our kids (20 percent) see sexual intercourse outside of marriage as moral. Don't miss the implication of those results. The study reveals the astounding news that many of our kids think that heavy petting—even sexual intercourse—between two unmarried individuals is perfectly moral.

However, in spite of the fact that one in five of our kids (20 percent) said they think sexual intercourse between unmarried persons is morally acceptable, more than twice that number (46 percent) said that they would be more likely to have sex with someone if they "were in love with the person." In other words, nearly half of our kids would tend to agree with Brittney's attitude that love—not marriage—makes it right.

The message that continues to surface in all these statistics, like the recurring theme in a Beethoven symphony, is the fact that our kids, our precious children, are floundering and flailing; they are being tempted and tossed because they do not have a sound moral and spiritual standard to anchor them when they are faced with difficult choices. As we will see, that single factor—the possession of a strong truth view—will make a world of difference in what they think and do.

■ TRUTH MAKES A DIFFERENCE ■

When my children were infants, they were entertained for hours by a plastic toy clown. The round base of the brightly colored clown was weighted; my kids would push him or pull him and watch him bob right back up to a sitting position. No matter how often they tried to upend him, he would quickly right himself. Even when they tried to stand him on his head or hold his face to the floor, he would inevitably return to an upright position. Why? Because that's how he was designed; the weight in his round base kept returning him to a right position.

I don't want to make too much of a child's toy, but that is precisely what strong convictions will do for our children. A strong conviction about the existence of truth and objective moral standards will return them repeatedly to a right position, even when they are pushed and pulled by a culture in crisis. Without the weight of truth, our kids won't know which way is up or which choice is right; they'll be knocked down by the culture and, more likely than not, they'll stay down. This is not just something I believe; the cold, hard facts of the study bear it out.

According to the study, your kids are much more likely to accept sexual petting and intercourse before marriage as moral if they lack a strong pro-truth view. Youth who *do not* affirm the existence of absolute truth are twice as likely to classify fondling of breasts (between unmarried persons) as moral. Our kids who are not equipped with a consistent view of truth and morality are three times as likely to regard fondling of genitals (between unmarried persons) as morally acceptable. And kids who do not accept truth as absolute are four times as likely to approve premarital sexual intercourse as a "moral" choice.

Keep in mind that the data indicate that nearly all of the kids who define a behavior as "morally acceptable" have engaged in it. Consequently, it is likely that those kids who define premarital petting or intercourse as "moral" have succumbed (or will soon) to the temptation to engage in that behavior. Therefore, while a strong foundation of biblical views about truth and morality is no guarantee that your kids will not become sexually involved before marriage, the *lack* of a strong foundation may nearly guarantee that they will!

Put simply, the likelihood of your kids being persuaded to engage in premarital sex based on emotional or practical circumstances (not moral considerations) increases significantly if they are not equipped with solid, foundational views about truth and morality.

This study shows that the most important thing we can do for our children—the investment that will do the most good—is to find a way to equip them with a bedrock of biblical values, to establish in them a conviction regarding objective standards of truth and morality. The research indicates that doing that will double, triple, even quadruple our children's chances of experiencing the real love and maximum sex that God plans for them.

□ □ □

Beth leaned over the coffee shop table and clutched her friend Geena's hand.

"I'm sorry," Geena sobbed, clamping a napkin to her red, puffy face. "This is so embarrassing."

Beth McConnell and Geena Santoro had been friends for a long time, and had been meeting for coffee every Tuesday morning for several years. Their weekly klatch began when Geena's daughter left home last summer to enroll as a freshman at a small Christian college, where she met a promising young art student and married at the age of twenty.

"What's wrong, Geena?" Beth asked softly. She waited patiently while Geena dabbed her eyes and blew her nose; she nearly launched into a new round of sobs, but she quickly choked her cries and suppressed her emotions.

"Melissa called last night," she said, her voice quivering. Beth nodded at the mention of Geena's youngest daughter. "She and Don are getting a divorce."

Beth's expression stiffened. She swallowed.

"Oh, don't look at me like that," Geena said passionately, responding to Beth's change of expression. "You don't know how many times I've wondered if I did the right thing, leaving Kenneth," she said, gripping her friend's hand, in both of hers, like a vise. "To this day I don't know, I really don't. But I hoped, Beth, I really did, that I could keep my daughters from making the same mistakes I did.

"And I begged Melissa to try to work things out with Don—'You've only been married seven or eight months,' I said. 'How bad can it be?' But she insists it's just not working. I told her to give it some time, Don had only been in his new job for a few months, and they've had to make a lot of adjustments."

Geena's distress fueled her speaking as she poured out her anguish in relating details of her late-night conversation with her daughter.

"Finally I said, 'Go and see a counselor,' and she said, 'It wouldn't do any good.' I just—I don't know what to do. I don't know what else to tell her." Emotion swelled in her throat again, strangling her words.

Beth's face appeared hard. Her lips were shut tight, and she said nothing. Geena begged for compassion and understanding with tearful eyes. The two friends sat in silence, until finally Beth spoke.

"I don't judge you, Geena," Beth answered finally. Her face wrinkled with pain. "I'm sorry I never told you. My Richard is separated from his wife; the twins are taking it really hard. They see a counselor every week," she said; her voice cracked and her shoulders began shaking with silent weeping.

They gripped each other's hands tightly, and sat without speaking, numbly sharing their grief for many moments. The waitress breezed by and filled their coffee cups.

Long after the tears had stopped flowing, Geena spoke. Staring wistfully out the window, she said, "What's the matter with us, Beth? Why can't we stay married? Why are so many families torn to pieces?"

Beth didn't answer; she sighed and studied the faint lines on her friend's weary face as the coffee grew cold.

■ HOW OUR YOUTH VIEW MARRIAGE AND FAMILY ■

Beth and Geena's experience is not uncommon, unfortunately. Over the past thirty years, a revolution has occurred in our society, a revolution that has changed the face of the family.

For years now, many voices in the popular culture have proclaimed the demise of traditional concepts of marriage and family. New terms, like "open marriages," "domestic unions," "palimony," and "blended families" have been coined as a response to societal changes.

But recent research indicates that marriage is not an endangered species, and the family and family values still appeal powerfully to the human spirit. Most adults in America (not just Christian adults, but the entire adult population) believe that marriage is an important and solid institution; that divorce is a cancer on society and a person's own life; and that the benefits of a happy marriage are to be desired. Most adults also believe that the traditional family is critical to the health of the nation.

Our kids, likewise, espouse many traditional views regarding marriage and family. Nine out of ten (90 percent) affirm that God's intention was for marriage to last a lifetime. Three in four (73 percent) agree with the statement, "I would like to be a virgin at marriage." Among those who have had sexual relations, three in five admit that if they could change their past, they would wait until after marriage to become sexually involved.

In spite of the fact that our kids overwhelmingly attest that their parents love them and each other, they are wrestling with a disturbing degree of confusion, fear, and anxiety about marriage. Less than half of our kids (48 percent) say that they want a marriage like that of their parents. More than one-third say that they definitely do *not* wish to duplicate their parents' relationship. One-sixth of our kids claim that they don't know if they want a marriage like Mom and Dad's, suggesting that they may not like what they see (in their parents' marriage), but don't know if they can hope for anything better.

Our kids favor divorce—by a two-to-one margin—for parents who do not love each other. In other words, nearly half (46 percent) of our kids disagree with the statement, "if there are children involved in the marriage, the parents should not get divorced, even if they do not love each other anymore." One-fifth (21 percent) favor staying together for the kids' sake.

Among the many implications of the data is the revelation that our kids, the products of loving marriages and intact families, are not convinced that marriage is an important and solid institution, nor that divorce is an improper response to marital strife.

It is unsettling enough to know that our children lack a biblical view of marriage and divorce; our discomfort is magnified, however, by the realization that they will certainly—one day—*act* on their views. Their ideas and concepts about marriage today will dictate how they will respond to marital opportunities and crises in the future.

■ HOW THEY DEFINE FAMILY ■

You've seen the full-page advertisements in major magazines: "No Risk. No Commitment. No Kidding."

The ads are touting a book club, I think, but they might as easily apply to contemporary concepts of the family.

Recent studies on adults by The Barna Research Group indicate a major shift in the ways American adults define "family." In days past, people defined a family as a group of individuals related to each other by marriage, birth, or adoption. Today, however, a majority of adults define a family as "all of those people whom I deeply care about, and all of those people who deeply care about me."

Such a definition, of course, means that one's family tomorrow may not encompass the same group that constitutes the family today. Family members may be added or subtracted according to feelings; I may care for a different set of people tomorrow, or next month, or next year. Family is no longer based upon legal or biblical foundations; it is based upon feeling. In other words, a "90s kind of family" has assumed a very fluid and temporary meaning: no risk, no commitment. No kidding.

Believe it or not, our youth have adopted this viewpoint. They have been exposed to it at school, in the media, and in their relationships with their friends. And it has taken hold.

A large majority of our youth—three out of every five (60 percent)—buy into the idea of this "nouveau family," defining family as "those who deeply care about you, or whom you deeply care about." Only one in three (32 percent) possesses a traditional perspective of what constitutes a family ("people related to each other by birth, adoption, or marriage"). Five percent of our kids say a family is "people living together," and 4 percent consider "people sharing the same goals and values" to be a family. To put it another way, two-thirds of our kids, when given a choice of four definitions of "family," select a definition that reflects a "no risk, no commitment" kind of arrangement. Moreover, most of our kids possess a concept of the family that would define cohabitating couples and homosexual unions as a legitimate family; the study indicates that they do not fully realize the implications of their view, but it is there, nonetheless, to shape their reasoning—and their behavior—in the future.

■ WHY TRUTH MATTERS ■

The study suggests that convictions about truth provide a network of roots for our children's concepts of marriage and family. A kid's truth views can make the difference between choosing happiness and choosing heartbreak; it can supply the moral lenses a kid needs to sort between what is right and what "seemeth right unto a man."

For example, those youth who have formed a strong pro-truth view are more likely to say that God intended marriage to last a lifetime, and to characterize their family experiences as positive.

Kids with strong convictions about what is absolutely right and wrong are more apt to value chastity before marriage; they are 23 percent more likely to say, "I would like to be a virgin at marriage," and 30 percent more likely to say, "If I wasn't a virgin now and I could change the past, I would wait to have sex until after marriage."

Youth who believe in objective truth are 65 percent more likely to say that "if there are children involved, the parents should not get divorced, even if they do not love each other anymore." In other words, kids who lack a pro-truth view are 65 percent more likely to accept divorce as an option, even when children are involved.

According to the study, your children are also more likely to view the alternative family as legitimate if they lack a strong conviction about the existence of absolute truth and objective moral standards. For example, young people who hold a pro-truth view are 75 percent more likely to consider the traditional family as a vital part of a healthy society.

Youth who *lack* a pro-truth view are much more accepting of cohabitation (unmarried couples living together); they are 46 percent more likely to say that "a man and a woman who are not married but are living together and have had children together" qualifies as a family, and two-and-a-half times (150 percent) more likely to say that an unmarried couple with no children make up a family.

The gap between the attitudes of youth who accept objective standards of truth and those who do not is most striking when they are asked to classify homosexual unions. Young people who lack a consistent pro-truth view are four-and-a-half times (350 percent) more likely to say that two homosexuals—male or female—living together are a legitimate family!

What does it all mean? Just this: if our children are not equipped to evaluate moral matters in an objective way, they are liable to see marriage as an unnecessary (and usually negative) institution. If our kids' morals are not based on fundamental, fixed principals, they will tend to view divorce as an appropriate solution to marital difficulties. If our youth do not have a sound spiritual and moral standard, they will be more likely to regard "alternative" arrangements (such as cohabitation or homosexual unions) as acceptable "family" settings.

More importantly, however, our young people will not hold these ideas and opinions in a vacuum; what they think about marriage and family will determine their behavior in these areas. A young person who does not value marriage highly will enter a relationship with an entirely different point of view than some-one who believes that "Marriage is honorable" (Heb. 13:4, KJV). A young adult who sees divorce as an option will be more likely to "cut and run" when a relationship hits a difficult period. A teen who does not object to "alternative families" will not be easily be persuaded to "shack up" with a boyfriend or girlfriend.

The implications of the study are clear: in order to equip youth to prepare for and build a lifelong marriage and healthy family, we must endeavor to equip them with strong, reliable convictions about truth *and* the tools to put those convictions into practice.

□ □ □

Pastor James Milford escorted his son into the ninth-grade counselor's office. He placed a hand on Philip's shoulder as they walked. Philip shrugged it off angrily.

"Good morning, Mr. Milford," said the woman in the office as she came out from behind the desk. She turned to seventeen-year-old Philip. "How are you, Philip?"

The boy shrugged noncommittally.

"Are you ready to go back to school?" she asked.

He shrugged again.

The counselor turned to Pastor Milford. "Thank you," she said. "We'll take it from here."

Pastor Milford hesitated for a moment. He looked from the woman to the boy, and finally turned and left.

Later that day, Pastor Milford sat in his office with Carl Strickland, an elder of the church. "I guess it went pretty smoothly," he said, relating the story of his son's return to school after a four-day suspension. "Philip's still not very happy with me."

"I know your boy was suspended, James," Strickland said. "But you haven't told me everything, have you?"

Pastor Milford inhaled deeply and removed his glasses from his face. He folded them carefully and dropped them into his shirt pocket. His expression reflected the weariness of a man twice his age.

"The school called last Friday," he began. "Philip got caught cheating in one of his classes."

Strickland nodded his head with sympathy. "We've all been there, James. Teenagers all go through it sooner or later."

"No," Pastor Milford answered firmly. "This is not a stage, Carl." Pastor Milford shifted his weight to the edge of his chair, and related to his friend the events of last Friday. . . .

Philip Milford glanced at the teacher, Mrs. Brewster. She was busily engaged in grading papers at her desk. He cast a glance to his left, and another to his right, finally reaching under his desk with his left hand. He extracted a piece of paper from his notebook, and carefully slid it under his math test. Debi White looked his way with wide eyes, but he scowled at her and she quickly turned her attention back to her test paper.

Philip quickly became absorbed in his work, sliding the test paper back and forth to reveal sample equations and basic operations; with this information, the biggest math test of the semester was almost as simple as filling in the blanks.

Suddenly, a hand appeared before his eyes as he penciled in the answer to a question. Mrs. Brewster slid the notebook page from under his test. She inspected it for a few moments, then announced, "Mr. Milford, come with me."

Philip blushed a bright shade of red, and followed Mrs. Brewster out into the hall. She scolded him for his cheating, and ended by telling him to come back into the room, where she would write a note that Philip would have to take to the principal.

"No way," Philip answered, his voice rising in anger. "I'll go to the principal, but I'm not going back in there where everybody will be staring at me.

"I don't care about your stupid math test," he continued. He began shouting, punctuating his words with profanities, and calling Mrs. Brewster obscene and cruel names.

Mrs. Brewster stepped forward and placed a firm hand on his shoulder. Philip jerked his shoulder from under her hand, threw both of his hands up in front of him, palms outward, and shoved her into the lockers that lined the wall behind her. Immediately, he felt someone grip him around his chest, pinning both his arms to his sides. He kicked his legs, which no longer touched the ground, and shouted obscenities until his captor, Mr. Detweiler, a teacher from across the hall, dropped him into a chair in the principal's office.

Pastor Milford leaned forward, with his elbows on his knees, and spoke earnestly. "But that's not what bothers me most, Carl," he said. "That afternoon, after the school counselor had called to inform me of the incident and the fact that Philip was suspended for four days, I picked him up and brought him home. In the car on the way home, we talked. I was upset. I said, 'Philip, what got into you? Cheating on a test is one thing, but to use that kind of language, and to attack your teacher!'

"Then he lied to me, Carl. On top of all that, he lied to me. He tried to tell me that the teacher just had it in for him, that he hadn't cheated at all. He started to make up some elaborate story about how it all happened, and that's when I lost it.

"I started yelling at him. I told him his counselor had given me his cheat sheet, and told me the things he'd said to his teacher, and the words he'd used; I told him I'd never been so embarrassed in my life."

Carl Strickland nodded sympathetically. Pastor Milford continued.

"I said, 'How do you think that makes me look? The pastor's son cheating on a test and attacking a teacher! Is that the kind of impression you want to give people of our family? I'm ashamed to be your father,' I said. Then, as I pulled into the driveway at home, I said to him, 'That's no way for a Christian to act.'

"He jumped out of the car, but leaned back in and said, 'I *never said* I was a Christian!' Then he stormed into the house."

The two men looked at each other in silence. Pastor Milford leaned back in his chair.

"You know what the worst part of all this is, Carl?" The pastor's shoulders sagged and his face wore a dejected look. "I realized that he was right—I'd never stopped to think about it before, but I searched my mind and realized that Philip never actually professed to be a Christian. He's gone to Sunday school and church with us his whole life, but like he said, he never said he was a Christian. And I'm ashamed to admit I've never made it a point to lead my son to Christ, or to teach him about the faith."

"Even our children have to make their own decisions," Carl offered.

"That's not what I'm talking about, Carl. I'm not talking about what I learned about my son anymore . . . I'm talking about what I learned about me."

He leaned forward in his chair again. "This past week, I've talked with Philip about things we've never talked about before. I mean, I've lectured him plenty, you know that—I suppose everyone in the church knows that—"

"You've always been firm with your children; that's not necessarily bad."

"But last Saturday we began to talk—I mean really talk, back and forth, with me listening sometimes, instead of always talking. And I couldn't believe the things that were coming out of my son's mouth! He said he believes the Bible, but he doesn't believe that the events of Creation happened like the Bible says. He said he thinks Christianity is 'OK,' but that Islam and other religions are probably just as good, just different. He said he thinks that Satan is just a symbol of all the evil in the world. He's even experimented with some occult stuff, Carl."

A sympathetic look again surfaced on Carl Strickland's face. He opened his mouth to speak, but Pastor Milford continued quickly.

"But my point—and the point of last Sunday's sermon—is that all this has made me realize that sending my son to Sunday school is not fulfilling my responsibility for him, just like sending him to the dentist twice a year doesn't mean I don't have to make him brush his teeth. And I guess what's hit me most, Carl, is the realization that, if I haven't provided my children a biblical foundation, a Christian way of looking at the world, then Sunday school and youth groups aren't likely to have the effect I want them to have."

Pastor Milford's experience points out a stark reality—being raised in Christian families and taught in Christian churches does not guarantee that our children will adopt Christian belief, much less become born again.

As in other areas, our children's ideas about God, the Bible, and Christianity are important, not only because we naturally want them to accept and adopt our values and beliefs, but because "as a man thinketh in his heart, so is he"—belief leads to action, and actions have consequences.

The survey data indicate that about three-quarters of the teens who attend Christian youth groups have made a personal commitment to Christ and trust Him for their salvation. But many of them are confused about biblical truth and Christian doctrine. Like Pastor Milford's son, Philip, our young people seem genuinely perplexed when they're asked to express an opinion on such subjects as God, the Bible, the devil, heaven, hell, and salvation. In the majority of cases, one in five of our kids had to admit that they could not express an opinion.

On the positive side, four out of five of our youth (84 percent) asserted that "a person can experience a relationship with God personally," and seven in ten (70 percent) asserted that "the Christian faith is relevant to the way I live today." Most echo traditional Christian concepts of God and the Bible, but they suffer the greatest confusion when they attempt to relate biblical belief to other religions and lifestyles. For example, an alarming number of our children do not believe that their faith can be objectively shown to be true; four in ten (40 percent) endorse the statement, "no one can prove which religion is absolutely true."

One in five of our youth (21 percent) believe that "Muslims, Buddhists, Christians, Jews, and all other people pray to the same god, even though they use different names for their god." An identical number (21 percent) aver that "it does not matter what religious faith you follow because all faiths teach similar lessons." Not only that, but one in five teens (22 percent) agree with the statement, "if a person is generally good, or does enough good things for others during their life, they will earn a place in heaven," and the one in eight (13 percent) who conclude that "all good people, whether or not they consider Jesus Christ to be their Savior, will live in heaven after they die."

Thus, in the mind of one out of every five of our young people—youth who are predominantly from good church-going families and highly involved in church activity—Christianity is nothing special; it is no more true, no more correct in its teachings, no more central to salvation than any other religion.

■ TRUTH AND BELIEVERS ■

My two older brothers and I used to enjoy playing a family game called "Dictionary." One of us would look up an obscure word in the dictionary, one he guessed the others would not know. That person would then announce the word; each player would then jot down a fictional definition, which would be added to the true meaning of the word to make a list of definitions. Each player scored a point for selecting the correct definition and for every person who selected that person's fictional definition.

I loved playing that game, but I always lost, mainly because my brothers knew more words than I did. Not only did they occasionally know the word that was announced from the dictionary, but they also knew root words, and other words with similar meanings or pronunciations. The words they did know enabled them to recognize or understand words they did not know. Their vocabularies helped them to accurately evaluate whether certain definitions had the ring of truth.

Something similar happens in our kids' faith and experience. Those youth who have formulated cohesive views about truth are immensely better equipped in spiritual matters.

For example, our youth are more likely to be committed to church attendance if they are equipped with a conviction that objective standards of truth and morality exist. Moreover, if your child accepts objective standards of truth, he or she will be more likely to attend Sunday school, church youth group, and a Bible study group on a weekly basis.

The study reflects a relationship between spiritual disciplines and truth convictions. Our children are 32 percent more likely to develop a daily habit of prayer if they see truth as absolute and eternal: 83 percent of youth with a pro-truth view pray every day, compared to 63 percent of those who lack a pro-truth view. Similarly, youth who accept the existence of moral absolutes are more than twice as likely (125 percent) to read their Bibles daily.

Our young people's perspectives about truth also affect whether or not they make a lasting personal commitment to Jesus Christ. Nearly every young person who affirms a belief in absolute truth (98 percent) testifies to having made a personal commitment to Christ, compared to eight in ten (84 percent) of those who lack such a view. Similarly, youth who have formed a pro-truth view are 48 percent more likely to say that they will go to heaven when they die because they have confessed their sins and accepted Jesus Christ as their Savior.

Those youth who accept truth are 38 percent more likely to regard the Bible as "totally accurate in all of its teachings," and half as likely to say that "Jesus made some mistakes."

A solid view of truth will make our children 30 percent more likely to recognize a connection between their faith and their behavior, saying that "the Christian faith is relevant to the way I live my life today," and 34 percent more likely to consider witnessing to non-Christians a priority.

If our young people are equipped with a pro-truth world view, they will be nearly 20 percent more likely to posit a belief in a literal hell and, amazingly, more than two times as likely (136 percent) to believe in a real devil.

The impact of strong truth convictions is most apparent in young people's views about the relative truth and distinctiveness of Christianity. Teens who *lack* a belief in absolute truth are 83 percent more likely to say "it doesn't matter what religious faith you follow because all faiths teach similar lessons." Those who do not accept that truth is objective are more than two times more likely (115 percent) to say that "no one can prove which religion is absolutely true," and nearly three times more likely (188 percent) to state that "Muslims, Buddhists, Christians, Jews, and all other people pray to the same god, even though they use different names for their god."

The greatest disparity between those youth who espouse truth and those who reject it occurs in their understanding of salvation and the way to heaven. Youth who do not accept objective standards of truth will be over two times more likely to think that "all good people, whether or not they consider Jesus Christ to be their Savior, will live in heaven after they die," and nearly three-and-a-half times more likely to say that "if a person is generally good, or does enough good things for others during their life, they will earn a place in heaven."

In short, the study suggests that, if we wish our youth to remain active in church throughout their teen years, if we desire for them the assurance of salvation in Jesus Christ, if we want them to espouse biblical Christian belief, then equipping them with solid convictions of truth and morality may be the single most influential gift we can give them.

What our young people believe in these areas (sex, family, and religion) will dictate many of the choices they make—whether they engage in premarital sex, whether they cohabit or divorce, and whether they trust Christ for salvation, among others. Helping youth develop strong convictions about truth and morality beginning as early as four or five years old can equip them not only to believe what is right, but to do what is right as well.

But how do we do that? How do pastors, parents, teachers, and youth workers lead our young children and teenagers to develop convictions about truth? It begins with the Test of Truth.

PART 2

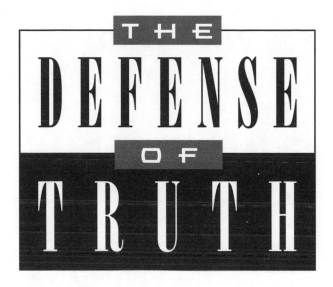

THE
DEFENSE
OF
TRUTH

The Test of Truth

IT TOOK SOME EFFORT, but Penny Marsh was succeeding. She was looking at her daughter, Brittney, without crying.

So much had transpired since last weekend when Penny came home early and discovered fifteen-year-old Brittney in bed with her boyfriend. Gary and Penny had spent hours crying together, and these days it seemed like a day was not complete without an angry confrontation between parent and child, with Gary issuing ultimatums, Brittney defying them, and Penny crying.

The three of them sat in the family room; the younger children, eleven-year-old Lauren and seven-year-old Michael, had been sent to play at a neighbor's house. Brittney slumped in the corner of the couch farthest from her father, who sat in the recliner. Penny took a seat next to her husband on the arm of the recliner.

"Brittney, I promised you that this wouldn't be like all those other 'talks' we've had," her father began. "I honestly don't want to yell at you anymore."

Silence descended quickly on the room, punctuated by a sniff from Penny. Gary looked at her; she wasn't crying—yet.

"I just want some answers," he said. He began to draw his daughter out, asking her many questions. It became a dialogue between father and daughter.

"How do you feel after you've slept with a boy?"

"I don't know."

"Do you feel guilty?"

"No."

"Because you don't think it's wrong?"

"No. Sometimes I feel sad."

"Why?"

"I don't know."

They continued, as Penny listened. At times, as she inspected Brittney's face and features, her daughter seemed like a stranger to her. At other times, she saw her baby, the finely featured dark-haired child who had nestled against her chest in a baby carrier slung over her shoulders.

The conversation turned, and Brittney was speaking.

"Why do *you* think it's wrong?" she asked, leaning forward, suddenly becoming interested in the conversation.

Gary flashed her a puzzled look. "What do you mean?"

"Why is it wrong? If I love Matt, why is it wrong for me to sleep with him? I mean, love makes it right for you and Mom to do it—at least I think you still do it—why do you think it's wrong for Matt and me?"

"I can't believe this," Gary said.

Brittney rolled her eyes. She slumped back against the couch and crossed her arms.

"Brittney," he answered abruptly, "your mother and I are married. That makes a big difference."

"Why?" she persisted.

"What do you mean, 'Why?'"

"What difference does that make?"

Gary fidgeted. He was beginning to lose his temper. "Because it's wrong, that's what difference it makes. You know good and well that sex before marriage is wrong. You've been taught that all your life, Brittney Marie!"

76

Penny, seated beside Gary on the arm of the chair, responded to the anger in his voice by pressing on his arm firmly.

"Look," he said, an edge still surfacing in his voice. "Some things are just wrong. They just are. Just like I know my name is Gary Marsh. Just like I know which way is up. Some things are just right, and some things are just wrong, and you and I both know that what you're doing is wrong."

Brittney's voice rose in reaction to his tone. "Well, you may think it's wrong, but I don't. You're entitled to your opinion, and I'm entitled to mine. Just because you believe something doesn't make it right, you know. This is the 90s. Things are different from when you were a kid." She rose from the couch and began walking out of the room.

"Brittney Marie, you get right back in here," Gary demanded.

"I've got to get ready for soccer," she answered from the top of the steps.

Penny pressed Gary on the arm again. His shoulders sagged and he looked at his wife; she returned his gaze, this time with unclouded eyes.

"You promised her this 'talk' would be different." Her voice was steady, but not loud. She looked at him unblinkingly.

Gary leaned back in his chair, closed his eyes, and wondered how the mundane things of life—like soccer practice—could possibly go on when his whole world was falling apart.

■ SHE BELIEVES SHE'S RIGHT ■

Gary and Penny want what you and I want—we want our young people to believe certain things are right and other things are wrong, so that they will make the right choices. The Marshes know Brittney is making the wrong choice, but they feel helpless to convince her otherwise.

Brittney, of course, believes she's right. In spite of her moral blindness, she still believes in truth; as Charles Sanders Pierce said, "Every man is fully satisfied that there is such a thing as truth, or he would not ask any question."[1]

What the Marshes (and all of us) want to know is this—how to get our children to determine the real right from the real wrong, so they can make the right choices. We know instinctively that some things are right and some things are wrong. Let Brittney discover, for example, that her soccer shoes were stolen from her school locker and she'll feel wronged. She would not argue that the thief is entitled to his opinion of right and wrong; she would appeal to an objective sense of justice because she would claim that she had suffered an injustice. In so doing, of course, she would appeal to a moral law that she believes every-one—not just herself—ought to follow.

C. S. Lewis wrote,

> Whenever you find a man who says he does not believe in a real Right and Wrong, you will find the same man going back on this a moment later. He may break his promise to you, but if you try breaking one to him he will be complaining "It's not fair" before you can say Jack Robinson. It seems, then, we are forced to believe in a real Right and Wrong. People may sometimes be mistaken about them, just as people sometimes get their sums wrong; but they are not a matter of mere taste and opinion any more than the multiplication table.[2]

In other words, while our young people may appeal philo-sophically to the second model of truth (truth is defined by the individual; it is subjective and situational), they expect others to treat them according to the first model of truth (truth is defined by God for everyone; it is objective and absolute). I have never en-countered a single exception to this rule; though I have met people who claimed to be relativists, I have never met a young person who did not expect or demand to be treated fairly. To the old maxim, "There are no atheists in foxholes," I would add a proverb of my own: "There are no relativists who expect to be treated relatively."

But for many people, accepting that "a real Right and Wrong" (to use Lewis's wording) exists is not the problem. The question for many people who struggle with questions of right and wrong is, "How do we know a thing is wrong?" What we need to answer is "What truths are right for all people, for all times, for all places?" Brittney certainly didn't agree with her dad on where the line between sexual morality and immorality ought to be drawn. *She* drew the line at "love;" her father drew it at the marriage altar.

Stephen L. Carter presents the problem this way in his book, *The Culture of Disbelief:*

> The hypothesis that dropped objects tend to fall to earth is a hypothesis about the natural world. If one wants to test it according to the rules of natural science, one would . . . set up an experiment that would yield one result if the hypothesis were false, another if the hypothesis were true—dropping lots of objects, say, and seeing whether they all fall to earth. . . . the trouble with claims about moral knowledge is that even today, more than two centuries after the Enlightenment, we have no settled rules by which to try to determine their truth.[3]

The majority of our youth would tend to agree with Stephen Carter. Fifty-six percent are not convinced that "humans are capable of grasping [moral] knowledge." Our children tend, like Brittney Marsh, to believe that "claims about moral knowledge" are simply a matter of opinion.

But that can't be right. If there is any validity at all to "claims about moral knowledge," then there must be a way to discover—and convey—what is right and what is wrong. What we need is a two-step process that will, first, test the truth to determine if it is absolute. This test compares a behavior or attitude to a standard of right and wrong that exists outside, above, and beyond ourselves. The next step (which we will discuss in the next chapter) is to evaluate the evidence of truth to show how it actually works in reality. If a truth is right for all people, for all times, for all places, we should expect it to work adequately in the real world.

■ TRUTH: COMPARED TO THE ORIGINAL ■

In the town of Sevres, a suburb of Paris, is the headquarters of the International Bureau of Weights and Measures, an organization that standardizes units of measure. The bureau establishes standards for metric measurements, and ensures a reliable standard for physical measurements around the world.

If I wanted to obtain the most precise measurement possible, I would refer to the standard they maintain. If I wanted to be absolutely certain that the millimeter divisions on my ruler were accurate, I would compare them against the bureau's standards. If I wanted to know whether the bottle of Diet Mountain Dew in my refrigerator contained exactly two liters of liquid, I could check it against the bureau's measurements.

Now, suppose you and I had a dispute about a length of wood I had cut for you. I measured it and told you it was one meter long; you measured it with your own meterstick and pronounced that it was less than one meter. How could we determine who was right? We could appeal to the standard; there exists an objective and universal standard in Sevres, France. To determine the validity of our individual measurements, we need only refer to the original.

That is just what our children need. They need to be convinced that a standard exists for settling claims about moral knowledge, a standard for right and wrong that exists outside, above, and beyond ourselves.

As we must do when measuring meters, we must also do in discerning right from wrong; to determine moral truth, we must first ask, *How does it compare to the original?* The first step in this process, then, is to test truth against the original. Webster defines truth, in part, as "fidelity to an original or standard."

The question is, of course, what—or who—is the original?

■ GOD ON THE STAGE ■

Back in the days of Julius Caesar, there was a Roman poet and playwright named Horace. Horace criticized the laziness of many playwrights of his day. He strongly criticized those writers who, every time a problem occurred in the plot of their play, brought in one of the many Roman gods to solve it. Horace instructed, "Do not bring a god on to the stage unless the problem is one that deserves a god to solve it."

The challenge of helping our young people determine right from wrong is one that deserves—in fact, demands—a God to solve it. It is impossible to arrive at an objective, universal, and constant standard of truth and morality without bringing God onto the stage. If an objective standard of truth and morality exists, it cannot be the product of the human mind (or it will not be objective); it must be the product of another Mind. If a constant and unchanging truth exists, it must reach beyond human timelines (or it would not be constant); it must be eternal. If a universal rule of right and wrong exists, it must transcend individual experience (or it will not be universal); it must be above us all. Yet, absolute truth must be something—or Someone—that is common to all humanity, to all Creation.

Those things—those requirements for a standard of truth and morality—are found only in one person—God. God is the Source of all truth. "He is the Rock, " Moses said, "his work is perfect . . . a God of truth and without iniquity, just and right is he" (Deut. 32:4, KJV). You see, it is God's nature and character that defines truth. He defines what is right for all people, for all times, for all places. But truth is not something He decides; it is something He is.

The basis of everything we call moral, the Source of every good thing, is the eternal God who is outside us, above us, and beyond us. The apostle James wrote, "Every good and perfect gift is from above, coming down from the Father of the heavenly lights, who does not change like shifting shadows" (James 1:17).

A lot of parents are like Gary Marsh. They think, "Some things are just right, and some things are just wrong." But trying to help our children develop firm convictions about right and wrong with such reasoning is like hanging our laundry on the wind; we must equip our youth with a sturdy framework of biblical reasoning. We must engrain within them the understanding that the reason we have this concept that some things are right and some things are wrong is because there exists a Creator, Jehovah God, and He is a righteous God. We must provide them with a truth apologetic—a ready defense of truth.

The reason we think that there are such things as "fair" and "unfair" is because our Maker is a just God.

The reason love is a virtue and hatred a vice is because the God who formed us is a God of love.

The reason honesty is right and deceit is wrong is because God is true.

The reason chastity is moral and promiscuity is immoral is because God is pure.

And the reason so many of our youth can't distinguish between the real and the counterfeit, between truth and error, between what's moral and what's immoral, is because many parents have stopped measuring against the original. We all have been influenced by the cultural shift away from God as the center of all things. Our culture has rejected the Source of Truth and has tried to come up with its own ideas about right and wrong. Gary Marsh's pitiful response to his daughter's "why" questions is typical of so many parents, youth workers, and teachers today, who measure right and wrong by their own ideas, rather than God's character. It's not enough to say, "You and I both know that what you're doing is wrong!" It's not what *I* know, nor what *you* know, that makes a thing wrong; it's *what God is* that makes it wrong.

Too often, parents and other adults communicate to young people that their actions violate *the adult's* standard of decency, or ethics, or morality. That would be perfectly appropriate if absolute truth were defined by the individual. But it's not. It is God and God alone who determines absolute truth. Truth is objective because God exists outside ourselves; it is universal because God is above all; it is constant because God is eternal. Absolute truth is absolute because it originates from the original.

Therefore, when Brittney—or anyone else—acts immorally or unethically, they are not just offending another person's "idea" of truth, they are transgressing *God's* standard of morality. We do well to adopt God's standards, of course, but we must be certain our young people understand that right and wrong are not measured by our own standards, but by the nature and character of God Himself—the original.

■ PRETZEL LOGIC ■

This point was driven home to me recently by a conversation I had with a superintendent of schools.

I took my daughter, Katie, to the county science fair soon after the news media had reported an incident in Oakland, in which students had laughed out loud during a showing of Stephen Spielberg's tragic holocaust epic, *Schindler's List.* I recognized the superintendent standing outside the school where the event was being held, so I joined him and engaged him in conversation.

"I've got a question for you," I said. I reminded him of the Oakland incident, and asked, "Would the educational system teach students that the holocaust was wrong?"

He indicated that it would, and I countered, "What would you say about *why* it was wrong?"

"We would say it was wrong," he answered, "because there are certain things that are true to all of us, and one is that you shouldn't kill."

"Are you saying that there is a universal moral absolute?"

He reacted quickly. "No," he said.

"What you're saying," I continued, "is that you—and certain other educators—have decided that it's wrong to kill. What would you say to an individual who disagrees with you?" I went on quickly to explain, "You see, Dottie, my wife, recently returned from a trip to China. She was assigned a loyal communist party member as a 'guide.' She, apart from the rest of her group, asked her 'guide' about the student protests in Tiananmen Square. The communist guide finally admitted, after much prodding, that many people had died in the 1989 uprising. Dottie asked, 'Don't you think that's wrong?' His answer was, 'No. So what if a few thousand people die? We have hundreds of millions of people. So what's the big deal?'"

Then I asked the superintendent, "How could you tell that man that killing is wrong?"

"Because it is," he answered.

"But wait a minute," I pressed. "Many Americans—not to mention the NEA (National Education Association) advocate cultural relativism. In other words, they think that each culture determines what is right and what is wrong."

He nodded.

"So how can we, as a nation, go to China and tell them that killing dissidents is wrong if their culture tells them it's right?"

"But all the people didn't agree with that."

"All Americans don't agree with the NEA. I don't."

"Well," he offered, still grappling to answer my initial question, "when two cultures come into conflict on morality, they go to war. We won the war with Germany, so that makes us right."

"What you're saying, then, is that might makes right?"

"I guess so," he admitted. "But you must understand—that's me speaking as an educator. My personal religious system and understanding of God would dictate a different answer."

You see, that man was struggling with the impossible challenge of trying to define truth and morality with no reference to the original. When we stray from the original—the nature and character of our Creator—and attempt to devise our own moral standards, the picture becomes indistinct, and muddy. That is why so many parents, the NEA, and our public school systems (as well as our government and media) are failing so miserably at communicating right thinking and moral behavior—because they are trying to do so without referring to the original.

■ THE BEGINNING OF WISDOM ■

But engaging in an intellectual or philosophical debate with our children will not necessarily motivate them to accept an objective standard of truth. And, ideally, this concept should be instilled in our children at a very young age. But how can a preschooler grasp such a concept? And how does a parent ever get through to a fifteen-year-old, like Brittney Marsh? How does one motivate a teenager to reevaluate his or her thinking once they have already formed a belief that truth is subjectively determined?

We must begin by instilling within our children—not just as teenagers, but even before they can talk—a healthy fear of God, an acknowledgment of His power and character. As Solomon said, "The fear of the Lord is the beginning of knowledge [wisdom]" (Prov. 1:7, KJV). It is the beginning of truth too.

I do not believe it is a coincidence that the fear of God disappeared from our culture—and our churches—at about the same time that our morals began to deteriorate. The same thing happened in Israel, in Jeremiah's day. God said to those people:

> Behold, I will gather [the Israelites] out of all the lands to which I have driven them in My anger, in My wrath, and in great indignation; and I will bring them back to this place and make them dwell in safety. And they shall be My people, and I will be their God; and I will give them one heart and one way, *that they may fear Me always, for their own good, and for the good of their children after them.* And I will make an everlasting covenant with them that I will not turn away from them, to do them good; and I will put the fear of Me in their hearts so that they will not turn away from Me" (Jer. 32:37–40, NASB).

What is the solution for a culture that has shifted from an objective (God-centered) morality to a relativistic (man-centered) morality? How do we help a family (or a person) that no longer looks to God for the definition of right and wrong? We must begin by restoring the fear of God: "I will put the fear of Me in their hearts so that they will not turn away from Me" (Jer. 32:40, NASB).

What this culture lacks, what our youth lack—and what I'm afraid many of us, as parents, grandparents, pastors, youth workers, and Christian educators lack—is a healthy, biblical *fear of God*, such as the prophets and apostles knew.

When Moses came near to the burning bush that symbolized God's presence, he was warned, "Take off your sandals, for the place where you are standing is holy ground." Moses obeyed, fell to the ground, and hid his face from God's greatness.

The prophet Isaiah's vision of God's greatness in the temple prompted him to cry out in fear and reverence, "Woe to me! I am ruined! For I am a man of unclean lips, and I live among a people of unclean lips, and my eyes have seen the King, the LORD Almighty."

When John the Apostle, who had known Jesus Christ and walked the dusty roads of earth with Him, saw the resurrected and ascended Lord in His heavenly glory, He "fell at His feet as though dead."

Those men of God knew the fear of the Lord. But when I talk about the fear of God, I don't mean fearing God the way we might fear Freddie Krueger or Frankenstein; God is not a monster from whom we must cower. Neither do I mean the kind of fear that churns the stomach and makes the hair stand on end, nor even the worry that keeps people awake at night, fearful of things that might come to be. The fear of God is none of those things. It is, instead, a profound awareness of God, and reverence for who He is and what He can do.

Some time ago, I was in South Africa, sharing evidence for the Christian faith to the Muslims. In one of my talks, I made a point about the consistency of the character of God: He always acts according to His righteous nature. What He *does* is always consistent with what He *is*.

After my talk, a young Muslim approached me. "Your concept of God," he said, "is not my concept of Allah. Allah is 'all-powerful.' Allah's 'powers' can allow him to do anything."

"Can Allah lie and cheat?" I asked.

"Sure," he responded. "Allah can do all things. He is not limited like your God. If he wants to love, he loves. If he wants to hate, he hates. Allah is 'all-powerful.'"

"Could Allah punish you for something you did," I asked, "even if it were good?"

"If Allah did not like it, he would punish me."

"Then you don't always know how Allah might respond, do you?"

He thought for a moment. "No," he said at last. "I don't always know what he would do." He stopped, but added quickly. "But I do know Allah is 'all-powerful.'"

I nodded. "You see, if I served Allah, I would be serving him out of fear. If he exercised the power to do wrong as well as right, simply because he desired to, he would be punishing me from his own selfish desires. That would be a dreadful motivation from which to serve God, because I would never know what angered him." He was listening intently, so I continued. "You see, I serve God out of love. God, being holy and perfect and almighty, is worthy of my fear, but because I know He is a loving God who always acts consistently with His nature, I can serve Him out of love too. I always know what angers God and I always know what pleases Him."

You see, because our God has revealed Himself as a God who loves us enough to die for us, we need not fear His caprice. Instead, because we always know what angers God and what pleases Him, we ought to fear Him enough to avoid the former and embrace the latter. Why? For many reasons.

We must fear God because He is God. It is natural for humans to respect and admire talents and abilities that are beyond their own. Albert Einstein's name is famous because his intellectual brilliance seemed so unattainable. Sandra Day O'Connor is admired by many as the first woman to serve on the highest court in the land. Michael Jordan became a sports icon because he performed athletic feats that seemed impossible. Yet the abilities of even the greatest among us are less than puny when compared to the might and majesty of God. He is so far removed from us in holiness, power, wisdom, and love, that we cannot compare to Him, we cannot fully comprehend Him, we cannot even approach Him without mercy.

Joshua and his generation had seen and heard "all the great works of the Lord." From birth, their children heard stories of the mighty power of Yawheh, the God of their fathers who saved Noah and his family from the flood, who destroyed Sodom and Gomorrah for their wickedness, who gave Abraham a son in old age, who delivered Joseph out of prison, who sent plagues on the Egyptians, who parted the Red Sea, who wrote the law on tablets of stone, who brought down the walls of Jericho. They instilled within their children a reverence for the Almighty, a God of love and mercy. With every story, every ceremony, every ordinance, every Passover dinner, they demonstrated their dependence on God. They acknowledged that God was infinite and they were finite. They acknowledged that God was all-powerful and they were weak. They acknowledged that God was all-knowing and they lacked wisdom. They were profoundly aware of God, and of their dependence upon him. *We must fear God because He is the Source of all good things.* God is the Source of all that we need. "He will fulfill the desire of those who fear him," sang the psalmist (Ps. 145:19, KJV). All that we are, He has made us. All that we have, He has given us. All that we lack, He can provide.

The Bible teaches that "Every good and perfect gift is from above, coming down from the Father" (James 1:17). Imagine how it would affect our children's attitudes and behaviors if they really believed that every breath they drew, every morsel they ate, every muscle they moved, every pleasure they experienced, was a gift from a powerful and loving God. Imagine the reverence, the dependence on God such an attitude would produce.

We must fear God because He is the judge of good and evil. As Solomon wrote, "The conclusion, when all has been heard, is: fear God and keep His commandments, because this applies to every person. For God will bring every act to judgment, everything which is hidden, whether it is good or evil" (Ecc. 12:13–14, NASB).

He will bring every act into judgment; He will measure it against himself. If it is consistent with His own character, then it is truth, it is good; if it is not consistent with His character, then it is error, it is evil.

We must fear God because He holds the power of life and death. "The Lord watches over all who love him," the Bible says, "but all the wicked he will destroy" (Ps. 145:20). Our lives are in His hands; "It is of the Lord's mercies that we are not consumed" (Lam. 3:22, KJV). When the children of Israel sang the song of Moses, they proclaimed the power of God over life and death. "See now that I, I am He, and there is no god beside Me; it is I who put to death and give life" (Deut. 32:39, NASB).

We must fear God because it is for our own good. God promises blessing for those who fear and honor Him: "And they shall be my people, and I will be their God; and I will give them one heart, and one way, *that they may fear me always for their own good, and for the good of their children after them*" (Jer. 32:39, KJV).

My wife has often described how, when she was a child, her father seemed, at the same time, the most loving and most awe-inspiring man in the world. She loved the smell of his after shave, she loved cuddling in his strong arms, she loved playing hide 'n' seek with him; but she also thought he was the smartest, tallest, and strongest creature on earth. That potent combination of love and respect delivered her from many dangers. She stayed away from the knife drawer in the kitchen. She played only where she was allowed. She ate her vegetables. You might say that her love for her father made her willing to obey him, and her fear made her unwilling to disobey him.

Similarly, God wants His children to love Him wholeheartedly, but He also wants them to fear Him, to respect Him, to reverence Him, because He knows that such a potent combination of emotions will be for our own good, and for the good of our children after us.

It is that fear of the Lord that we must reclaim and revive in our churches and families—and in ourselves. We must reverence Him; we must acknowledge Him. Not just in theory, but in practice. The fear of the Lord must pervade our lives; it must be in the stories we tell our children, in the way we live, in the way we think, in the way we talk. Then we will be able to better understand how to apply His truth to our lives.

■ MORALITY 101 ■

The fear of the Lord is the beginning of wisdom; it is not the end. We must convey to our children not only the fear of the Lord, but also an understanding of how His nature and character—the "original" from which all truth stems—are communicated in His precepts. This is apparent from the very first recorded words of God to man. God said to the man in the Garden of Eden:

> You are free to eat from any tree in the garden; but you must not eat from the tree of the knowledge of good and evil, for when you eat of it you will surely die (Gen. 2:16–17).

The man and woman in the garden already possessed the knowledge of good. They were surrounded by every imaginable blessing: a lush garden watered by a sparkling river and populated with birds and beasts, fruit trees and flowering shrubs. But God's first recorded words to man marked a moral choice, a choice between good and evil. With His first command to humanity, God identified Himself as a moral being, the definer of right and wrong, the Source of absolute truth. He drew a line around that tree that clearly marked the difference between right and wrong.

God spoke to Eve after she and her husband had eaten of the forbidden fruit, and inquired, "What is this you have done?" You see, God was revealing Himself to the man and woman as the arbiter of good and evil, as the righteous Judge, who would punish them by cursing them and expelling them from the garden.

When God spoke to Cain, who had murdered his brother Abel, He asked, "What have you done?" He revealed Himself as the God of life, who abhors murder. He cursed Cain and banished him to the land of Nod.

Throughout the pages of Scripture, God reveals Himself as the Source of absolute truth. He disclosed Himself to Noah as a righteous God who rewards righteousness and punishes wickedness. He proved Himself to Abraham as a trustworthy God who keeps promises. He showed Himself to David as a God of mercy. And through Jesus Christ, He proved supremely that He was a God of transcending love.

The revelation of God—in the Bible, in the Incarnation, and sometimes even through His body, the Church—reveals Himself as the fountain of truth, the origin of morality.

The Ten Commandments, which were given by God to Moses on Mount Sinai, represent the most famous codification of absolute truth in the history of humanity. But it's important to recognize that God didn't just invent the Decalogue because He was all alone on a secluded mountain with nothing else to do or just had a sudden urge to write. *The Ten Commandments were given to the newborn nation of Israel to reveal God's nature and help them enjoy the benefits of moral behavior.*

God commanded the Israelites to worship only Him because He knew the truth—that "all the gods of the nations are idols, but the LORD made the heavens" (Ps. 96:5). He instructed His people not to murder because He is the author, preserver, and governor of life (see Acts 3:15). He forbade lying because He is a God of truth, "who does not lie" (Titus 1:2).

The commandments of God are given to provide us practical knowledge of the character and nature of God and how to live in relationship to Him. His precepts point to His nature, and in turn point to truth that is true for all people, for all times, for all places. The laws He gives flow out of who He is.

■ GOD IS THE BASIS OF TRUTH ■

To develop a strong moral foundation within our young people we must teach them, first, to fear God and, secondly, to recognize Him as the basis—the original—of all truth.

For example, some people justify their rules with the explanation, "Because I said so!" Some will often explain a moral imperative by saying, "Because the Bible says it's wrong." Some, like Gary Marsh, will offer the unsatisfying argument that an act is wrong "because it's wrong." Such explanations may be inadequate for some people. The young person who rejects his parents' authority will not accept "Because I said so." The youth who questions biblical authority will not be persuaded to avoid immorality "because the Bible says it's wrong." For practical as well as theological reasons, we need to teach young people that the reason a particular action is right is "because God is like that."

For example, when I come home after a trip, I'll often take the kids out for breakfast. As I drive to the restaurant (or while we're all munching on our bacon and eggs), I'll suggest a situation in which we might be called upon to make a moral decision. The kids and I will discuss it, and try to decide what course of action to take, based on God's law.

First, we have to determine what law or commandment applies; but the important thing is to see how that law originates and grows out of God's character, and how it reflects His love and care for us. My purpose is to acquaint my children with the kind of God we serve, not just the kind of laws we follow, and to instill in them a foundation for evaluating—on an objective basis—what truths are right for all people, for all times, in all places.

Some time ago, I took my thirteen-year-old daughter, my seventeen-year-old son, and his girlfriend to see Stephen Spielberg's movie, *Schindler's List.*

As we left the theater, we were surrounded by a somber crowd, many of whom were commenting on the atrocities inflicted upon the Jews by the Nazis. I turned to my son.

"Sean," I said, "do you believe the holocaust was wrong—morally wrong?"

He answered quickly. "Yes."

Then, as we got into the car to travel to a nearby town for dinner, I pursued the matter. "Almost everyone walking out of that theater would say the holocaust was wrong," I said. "But what basis would they have for making that judgment? Could they answer *why* it was wrong?"

I could see the wheels in three teenage minds spinning as I continued. "Most people in America subscribe to a view of morality called 'cultural ethics.' In other words, they believe that whatever is acceptable in that culture is moral; if the majority of people say a thing is 'right,' then it is right."

At about that time, we arrived at the restaurant and continued the discussion over dinner. "That's why many Americans will say that abortion is OK, because the majority of Americans—and Congress and the Supreme Court—have accepted it. If the majority thinks it's OK, it must be OK, right?

"But there's a problem with that," I explained. If that is true, then how can we say the 'aborting' of six million Jews in the holocaust was wrong? In fact, the Nazis offered that very argument as a defense at the Nuremberg Trials. They argued, 'How can you come from another culture and condemn what we did when our culture said it was acceptable?' In condemning them, the world court said that there is something beyond culture, above culture, that determines right and wrong."

I also went on to explain that most of what people call morality today is simply pragmatism. "If we don't condemn what the Nazis did," people reason within themselves, "what's to stop someone from doing it to us?" And they're right, of course; they recognize the need for objective morality, but they cannot arrive at a true moral code—because they refuse to acknowledge the original.

Finally, after about two hours at the restaurant, I thought it was time to guide those three teens to a discovery. "Do you know *why* what you saw tonight was wrong?"

"I know it was wrong," Sean ventured, "but I don't know why."

"There is a truth," I said, "that is outside me, above our family and beyond any human—a truth about killing that originates in God. Killing is wrong because there is a God and that God is a living God, who created life and said, 'It is good,' and commanded us to preserve life and not to kill." That night I reinforced in my children and their friend that God is the original, the universal, the absolute standard for everything that is good and right. Without that standard, there can be no universal, absolute moral guidelines.

■ THE PATTERN FOR COMMUNICATING TRUTH ■

The reasoning I communicated to those three youth that evening applies to other ethical issues as well. Lying is wrong because God is true. Stealing is wrong because God is just. Hatred is wrong because God is love. These things are wrong, not because society or the church frowns on them, but because they are contrary to the nature and character of God.

But communicating such things to a generation that is losing its moral moorings can be a daunting task. How do we do that? How do we communicate the Test of Truth to our children, our grandchildren, our students?

We do it in much the same way we teach anything. Your mother didn't elaborate an overarching theory of linguistics before she taught you the alphabet. Your first grade teacher didn't expound the distinction between pure mathematics and applied math when he taught you that $1+1=2$. Your piano instructor mentioned nothing about chord progressions when she positioned your hands over the piano keyboard and instructed you to place your right thumb on middle C.

Communicating basic morality to our youth operates in much the same way. That is why God began His revelation of right and wrong with the Ten Commandments (actually, He began with *one* command—"you must not eat from the tree of the knowledge of good and evil"). God's commands—His *precepts*—point to universal moral *principles* which, in turn spring from the *Person* of God Himself. That is the divine pattern for communicating absolute rights and wrongs that have an objective basis in the nature and character of God.

☐ PRECEPT

Your first days in school may have been occupied with such mathematical concepts as $1+1=2$, $2+2=4$, and so on. Those were your "baby steps" in mathematics. Your five- or six-year-old mind may have been proud of your newfound ability to understand such quantities. Little did you know, of course, that you were not dealing in quantities; you were learning to express quantities through the use of numbers.

Similarly, few people realize that *precept*—the rules, regulations, codes, and requirements of Scripture—is but the first step in understanding basic morality. God said, "You shall not murder," "You shall not covet," and even, "Do not curse the deaf, or put a stumbling block in front of the blind."[4] He issued specific commands, like a parent telling a child not to touch the hot stove, in order to provide concrete boundaries for human conduct.

But the precepts of the Lord do not only serve as a long list of do's and don'ts that define right and wrong in explicit terms. They also point to larger moral principles. The Bible tells us that the law leads us by the hand, like a child going to school, to learn deeper lessons.

The apostle Paul wrote to the churches of Galatia, "Therefore, the law has become our tutor [literally, child conductor] to lead us to Christ, that we may be justified by faith" (Gal. 3:24, NASB). In the Greek-speaking world of Paul's day, there was a type of household servant called the *paidagogos* (the root of our word "pedagogue"). He was in charge of the child's moral welfare; it was his duty to oversee the child's character development. One of his responsibilities was also to take the child to school each day. He was not the child's teacher, but he was responsible to see that the child was, in fact, under the teacher's care.

Paul borrows this picture from the culture of his day, and says, in effect, that the law has the same function. The commandments and precepts of Scripture are designed not only to say, "Do this," and "Don't do that," but to lead us beyond the precept to a universal principle (one that applies to everyone) and, ultimately, to the God who expresses Himself through precept.

☐ PRINCIPLE

If all of God's commands are the first step toward knowing Him and distinguishing right from wrong, principles are the intermediate step on the stairway leading us from precepts to the person of God. Behind each specific command (precept) is a principle.

A principle is a norm or standard that may be applied to more than one type of situation. To understand the difference between a principle and a precept, think of a principle as expressing the fundamental truth on which a precept is based.

That's what Brittney Marsh was looking for in her conversation with her father. They communicated the precept to her; she knew they didn't want her having sex. But she did not understand the principle behind the precept, and when she asked her dad to explain why her behavior was wrong, he was unable to communicate it.

Principles help explain the "why" behind a command. A concern for safety is one of the principles behind a mother's command to look both ways before crossing the street. As I explained to my children after we saw *Schindler's List* together, reverence for life is the principle behind the command, "Thou shalt not kill." A principle behind the command, "You shall not give false testimony," is honesty.

By revealing to our young people the principles behind God's precepts, we will begin to equip them to apply the Test of Truth to moral matters. But there lies a greater moral truth beyond even the principles to which the law points, and that is the very person of God.

☐ PERSON

To know what we believe about God's precepts (and even the principles of truth that lie behind those precepts), and not know the Person from whom they derive, is worthless. Too many times we focus on God's *law*, and never see its extensions— what it teaches us about the character of God. The ultimate purpose of God in every precept is to bring people to the knowledge of Himself.

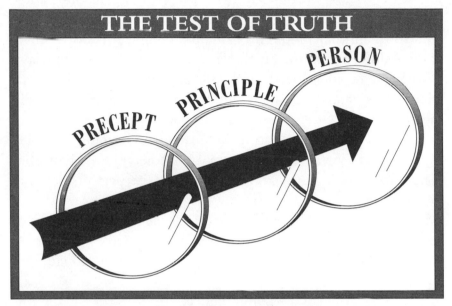

God's Word is filled with PRECEPTS—commands put there for our good. PRINCIPLES are the "whys" behind the precepts, and the PERSON behind the principles is God Himself. As we move from PRECEPT to PRINCIPLE, it leads to the very PERSON of God. It is through the Test of Truth that we compare our attitudes and actions to God's character and nature.

Moses, who received the law on Mount Sinai, apparently understood this progression of *precept-principle-person*. The Bible says that, after God spoke to Moses "face to face, as a man speaks with his friend" (Ex. 33:11), Moses prayed, "If you are pleased with me, teach me your ways *so I may know you . . .*" (Ex. 33:13, my emphasis). Moses recognized that learning God's ways—understanding His precepts and the principles behind them—would acquaint him with the person of God Himself.

Many Bible readers are tempted to skip over the chapters in Exodus and Leviticus that detail thousands of regulations concerning dress, food preparation and consumption, construction of the tabernacle, the forms of worship, and so on. Altars and acacia wood and cubits and blended fabrics seem totally irrelevant to us. But such prescriptions, instructions, and codes reveal the character of God. The purpose of those laws was to give Israel a lesson in purity, separating good from bad, clean from unclean, one kind from another kind. The principle behind the law—purity of life—flowed from the character of God Himself. Specific laws prohibiting mixing threads in the same garment or hitching different types of animals to the same yoke were tangible lessons in the character of God. His commands were intended not only to benefit His people, but also to help them understand what He was like, that He was a God who did not tolerate sin. Their obedience to those laws was to point them to the perfect model of God's holiness.

God's law is not an end in itself. Some of His commands were illustrative, others were practical, but all were   and are— an expression of His character. King David acknowledged,

> The law of the Lord is perfect,
>   reviving the soul.
> The statutes of the Lord are trustworthy,
>   making wise the simple.
> The precepts of the Lord are right,
>   giving joy to the heart.
> The commands of the Lord are radiant,
>   giving light to the eyes.
> The fear of the Lord is pure,
>   enduring forever.
> The ordinances of the Lord are sure
>   and altogether righteous.
>   —Psalm 19:7–9

Note carefully the words David used to describe God's law: *perfect, sure, right, radiant, pure, and righteous.* Why do you think the law possesses those qualities? Because they are qualities that belong to the Lawgiver—God Himself. You see, ultimately, the truth does not reside in the commands; it resides in God. The truth would not cease being true if the Law were to disappear from the face of the earth, nor would it cease to be true if there were no humans to discern the principle—because the truth resides in the person of God Himself, who is eternal.

We help our youth determine right from wrong when we teach them to fear God and to look to Him—His nature and character—as the measure of truth and morality. We help them take the first step in this process of distinguishing right from wrong through the Test of Truth, which asks, *How does it compare to the original?* An attitude or behavior is not wrong just because adults frown, stamp their feet, and say it's wrong. The truth, which flows out of the nature of God into His laws, is right for all people, for all times, for all places.

But, of course, today's generation may be slow to accept such a standard for determining truth; they want what is "real, relevant, and right now." For that reason, parents, pastors, educators, and youth leaders must be prepared to take the next step and have them evaluate the evidence of Truth by asking, "Does it really work?"

7

The Evidence of Truth

GEENA SANTORO hailed Pastor Milford from across the grocery store parking lot as he and his wife were preparing to unload their shopping cart into the minivan. He extracted his key from the car door and strode to meet the woman in the middle of the lane. He shook her hand and drew her over to the narrow space between cars.

"I wanted to apologize for the way I reacted to your sermon last Sunday," she said, blushing with embarrassment.

He smiled agreeably. She continued.

"I was talking with my heart, not my head. I do that a lot, you know." A pained smile twitched at the corners of her mouth. She went on to share the news of her daughter's impending divorce. Pastor Milford's expression quickly changed to reflect his grief; he had performed Don and Melissa's wedding ceremony.

"Anyway," she said when she finished the story of Don and Melissa's breakup, "I wanted to say I'm sorry for reacting the way I did."

He smiled indulgently. "You're not the only one who took me to the woodshed after that sermon," he admitted. "I came on very strong, I know, but I intended to. And those words were intended as much for me as for anyone. I've been taking a long, serious look at the kind of father I've been."

"I guess I didn't do such a great job with Melissa, either," Geena said.

"Oh, that's not the point at all, Geena. None of us have done as well as we'd like to, and none of us can guarantee that our children will share our values or live the way we'd like. But what I've really been convicted about lately is, am I doing everything I can to give them a fighting chance against our culture? Could I be doing anything differently, anything better, to equip them with a biblical way of looking at moral decisions?" He shrugged. "And I've come to realize that I've neglected some key things I should have been teaching my children."

Geena perked up. "What things?" she asked.

The pastor shared with her how he had begun trying to help his son relate morality to an objective—and eternal—standard. "I've been trying to help him see that what makes a thing right or wrong is how it corresponds to the character of God. I've been trying to help him see that certain things are right, not because I say so, but ultimately because that's the way God is."

"Has it had any effect?" she asked.

He wrinkled his brow and sighed. "Well, I think Philip understands what I'm saying, but I'm not sure he's convinced. Of course, these things take time."

The pastor glanced toward his wife, who waited patiently at the front of the car. "Why don't we get together in the next few days?" he suggested. "That way my wife and I will have more time to tell you what the Lord has been teaching us, and maybe we can learn a few things from you."

"I would like that," Geena said. She started to say goodbye and walk away, but she turned back after just a few steps. "What if—" she began. "Could I maybe invite a couple other people? I've discussed your sermon with several other parents who I think are interested in the kind of thing you're talking about."

"Well, yes," he answered with slight hesitation. "I don't see why not. I'll check my calendar and maybe we can agree on a time tomorrow after the service. How's that sound?"

"Super," Geena said excitedly. "I'll talk to the others."

Pastor Milford slipped behind the wheel of the minivan and smiled at his wife. She looked at him doubtfully.

"Where is all this headed?" she asked.

"I have no idea," he answered seriously.

■ THE REFLECTION OF TRUTH ■

Pastor Milford has discovered that the Test of Truth—that is, how does it compare to the original?—presents a struggle for some youth. If a teen doesn't know whether the Bible can be trusted, for example, he will be unable to look to it for moral direction. If a young person isn't convinced of the holy, loving nature of Jehovah God, you risk losing him or her completely if you talk about God's character as a basis for determining truth.

While the Test of Truth is an ideal place to start with a three- or four-year-old child, the Evidence of Truth may be the place to start with a teenager. It helps a young person see specific, substantive evidences that can help him or her recognize truth from error. It is evidence that will help the 58 percent of our youth, who say they don't believe in absolute truth, to reconsider their positions. For the 91 percent of our young people who lack a cohesive pro-truth view, the Evidence of Truth will help them "put all the pieces together" in their efforts to make moral judgments. Eventually, it is hoped, the Evidence of Truth will lead your child to embrace the objective standard of God's Word as a reliable model for making right choices.

■ TRUTH: CORRESPONDING TO REALITY ■

You'll recall Webster first defines truth as "fidelity to an original or standard." The dictionary goes on to define truth as "the body of real things, events, or facts; the property of being in accordance with fact or reality."

Most of us—unless we're college philosophy professors—have a pretty firm grasp of what is "real." If you've ever tried rollerblades, for example, you probably know that pavement is hard—*really* hard. That is a fact. It's part of "the body of real things."

We know—some of us better than others—that a steady diet of Hostess cupcakes and Twinkies will tend to make us "fluffy in the middle." That's a fact, unfortunately. You can't get much more real than that.

How do we know such things are true? We have witnessed them, we have experienced them; we have skinned our knees on the pavement, and we have seen our reflections in the mirror.

Our survey of nearly four thousand youth reveals that a primary issue for churched youth is the relevance and practicality of truth. In other words, our young people want to see *evidence* that moral standards apply to them in a practical way. They want to know if there are benefits to a moral lifestyle. To paraphrase Janet Jackson's hit song, they want to know, "what has truth done for me lately?"

The Evidence of Truth explores the relevance and practicality of truth. It seeks to evaluate morality in the light of the evidence. It shows how the Test of Truth—fidelity to the original standard— works in the real world, by asking, *How does it correspond to reality?* Brittney Marsh stumped her parents when she said, "You're entitled to your opinion and I'm entitled to mine. You know, just because *you* believe something is wrong doesn't make it so." She claimed that there were no objective means to determine which opinion was right and which was wrong. Gary and Penny Marsh needed to present clear evidence that God's view on premarital sex was the correct opinion; Brittney needed to see the Evidence of Truth.

■ SEATBELTS AND OTHER CRUELTIES ■

Seatbelts are a habit in my family. When our children were small, they were secured in carseats; when they outgrew the carseat, they learned to fasten their own seatbelts. I don't recall any argument or protest from them. It was just something everyone in the family did.

When my children's young friends ride in the car with us, however, they have occasionally responded indignantly when I required them to fasten their seatbelts. I have had young people from the ages of three to twenty-three sigh loudly, roll their eyes at me, and offer heartfelt protests.

Their responses communicate that they think I'm the meanest, most demanding, most unreasonable parent they've ever met. Their attitudes reflect a belief that I'm only making them wear safety belts in order to make them miserable.

That's not true, of course. I would much prefer to give in and save myself the grief their mournful cries cause. But I don't. Why? Because I know that the seatbelts could save their lives. My "safety regulations" are for their own good.

Many people—our youth included—react to God's laws the way young people react to my rules about seatbelts. They see His commands as constricting. They think that biblical morality is confining. They don't see the benefits to a moral lifestyle. They need help recognizing that God's commands, like those of a loving parent—"don't touch the stove," "look both ways before you cross the street," "eat your vegetables"—are not meant to spoil our fun and make us miserable.

God gave commands, such as "Flee sexual immorality," and "Husbands, love your wives," and "You shall not commit adultery," and all other commands because He wanted to protect us and provide for us. He didn't throw those precepts into the Bible just because He liked the way they sounded; He didn't concoct those rules to be a killjoy or to throw His weight around; He gave those commands because He knew some things we didn't. He knew, for example, that sexual immorality is a path, not to pleasure and fulfillment, but to emptiness and frustration.

Moses acknowledged this truth when he challenged the nation of Israel:

And now, Israel, what does the LORD your God require from you, but to fear the LORD your God, to walk in all His ways and love Him, and to serve the LORD your God with all your heart and with all your soul, and to keep the LORD's commandments and his statutes *which I am commanding you today for your good?*

—Deuteronomy 10:12–13, NASB, my emphasis

God issued His commands *for our good!* Looking down from an eternal, omniscient perspective, He can see things that we cannot, and He issues precepts to protect us and provide for us. We need to reinforce over and over again to our youth that all truth coming from the absolute character of God is for their good.

■ THE MORAL MAZE ■

When my children were very young, I watched them navigate a maze at a small amusement park. The maze was sunk into a pit, so that from my vantage point above the pit, I was able to watch the children thread through it. Their confused meanderings seemed so pointless as they pursued one dead end after another. *Of course,* I reflected, *anyone can see the way to go from up here.*

From His vantage point, God can see the way through the moral maze so much better than we; and His commands are given to keep us from heading down dead ends.

As Bill Hybels writes:

The Lord tells us specifically that His commands are never burdensome (1 John 5:3). By this, He doesn't necessarily mean they're easy to keep. Rather, He's telling us that they're never foolish. They are never unnecessary or purely arbitrary. He doesn't force us to observe meaningless formalities, nor does He impose rules that have no value.

On the contrary, every guideline, every law, every imperative in the Bible was crafted in infinite wisdom. They were given not only to honor God, but to benefit us as well. The entire book of Deuteronomy, for example, is a testament to this truth. In that book Moses repeatedly states that God gave the commandments for our good and promises to bless us if we obey them.[1]

106

"For I know the plans I have for you," God says in His Word, "plans to prosper you and not to harm you, plans to give you hope and a future" (Jer. 29:11). His desire is that people "will always fear me *for their own good and for the good of their children after them. . . . I will rejoice in doing them good*" (Jer. 32:39, 41a). Choosing right instead of wrong does not sap all the fun and excitement out of life; on the contrary, it accomplishes our good, because God's definition of absolute truth is based on His perspective, on His knowledge of what will protect us and provide for us.

While the majority of our youth (57 percent) acknowledge that "God established the limits for humankind," and that "acting in conflict with His laws has negative consequences for those people," they do not appear to apply that belief to their own behavior. The Evidence of Truth helps youth to do that; it explores the consequences of an action, and whether those consequences "give you hope and a future," or whether they bring frustration and disappointment. It looks at real things—at actions and consequences—and evaluates behavior in light of the short-term and long-term results.

■ WORDS OF WARNING ■

We must be careful, however, in discussing the protection and provision that result from knowing and following the truth, not to give the impression that bad things do not happen to moral people, nor that people who engage in immorality are never happy. That is not true, of course. Indeed, the prophet Jeremiah asked, "Why does the way of the wicked prosper?" (Jer. 12:1), and King David confessed, "I have seen a wicked and ruthless man flourishing like a green tree in native soil" (Ps. 37:35).

The Evidence of Truth does not pretend that morality is always rewarded and immorality is always punished. It simply views God's moral imperatives as furnishing an umbrella of protection and provision under which the wise will seek shelter. As we have said earlier, sin promises immediate satisfaction and does often deliver pleasure for a season. Some of the consequences of sin or rewards for righteousness may not be measured out until after this life.

A second word of warning is in order. We must be careful not to communicate the impression that God's commands are true because they are beneficial. Let me explain what I mean.

I learned the multiplication tables back in third or fourth grade. That knowledge has paid off many times over for me. It helps me complete my tax return and compare prices in the grocery store. You might say that I get something out of the right relationship of various factors and sums.

But $5 \times 6 = 30$ is not true *because* I get something out of it. It is right because it is right, because it reflects certain laws; it reflects reality. The benefit I derive from having learned most of my multiplication tables (I still have trouble with 7×8 and 7×9, for some reason) is not what makes those facts true; they are true whether I benefit from them or not.

Similarly, those things that are true and right are not so *because* of any benefit I may derive from them; they are true because they are true. As Os Guiness writes,

> Ultimately, the real "usefulness" of the Christian faith . . . depends on the conviction that the faith is not so much useful as true.[2]

The point of offering evidence for truth to your young people is not that the benefits or consequences of a belief or behavior make that thing right or wrong, but that it can help them learn to distinguish right from wrong—and, of course, choose that which is right. That is, ultimately, the purpose of evaluating actions according to the test, "How does it correspond to reality?"

■ IT CUTS BOTH WAYS ■

"The word of God," the Bible says, "is living and active. Sharper than any double-edged sword, it penetrates even to dividing soul and spirit, joints and marrow; it judges the thoughts and attitudes of the heart" (Heb. 4:12). Like a two-edged sword, God's words—His commands and judgments—cut both ways. They accomplish our good by a "two-edged" process: they protect and provide. In the words of the Lord to Jeremiah, His commands are intended to "prosper" us (provide) and "not to harm" us (protect).

■ SEEING GOD'S PROTECTION ■

I once knew a young man whom I'll call Greg. He lived down the block from a family who had an in-ground swimming pool in their back yard. He had never gone swimming in their pool, however; he barely knew the people, and a high wooden fence enclosed the pool. One dark evening, when Greg knew his neighbors were away, he and his girlfriend snuck behind the house, scaled the fence, and entered the pool area to go for a swim.

Greg threw off his shoes, climbed the ladder and, while his girlfriend was still taking her shoes and socks off, leaped off the end of the diving board.

He heard his girlfriend scream just before he lost consciousness. The pool held only a few feet of water; Greg's dive ended with a shallow splat of water and a sickening crunch of bones. Greg's late-night dive paralyzed him from the neck down for the rest of his life.

Greg ignored the fence that his neighbors had erected around the pool. He probably assumed it was there only to keep him and his girlfriend from having fun. In reality, it was meant for his own protection, and his disregard of that boundary cost him dearly. Similarly, when we disregard the moral boundaries that God has erected for our benefit—to protect us from harm—the cost can be devastating.

Dr. S. I. McMillen wrote a brilliant book nearly thirty years ago, called *None of These Diseases*, that shows how over two dozen divine commands or standards served to prevent such disorders as heart disease, cervical cancer, and arthritis—long before the advent of modern medicine! McMillen wrote in the preface:

When God led the Israelites out of afflicted Egypt, he promised them that if they would obey his statutes, he would put "none of these diseases" upon them. God guaranteed a freedom from disease that modern medicine cannot duplicate.[3]

I have often been asked, "Is AIDS the curse of God on homosexuals?" I answer, no, I don't believe it is; for one thing, the overwhelming majority of people around the world who have AIDS are not homosexual. But I do believe that God's commandments are like an umbrella. When you put up an umbrella, it shields you from the rain. But if you choose to move out from under that umbrella during a storm, you're bound to get wet.

As long as you stay under the umbrella of God's commands, you'll be shielded from many consequences. However, if you step out from under that protective cover, you should not be surprised if you suffer the consequences. Therefore, though I can't say that AIDS is a curse from God, I do believe it's among the many consequences of immoral behavior God wishes us to avoid.

■ SEEING GOD'S PROVISION ■

I went hiking in the Great Smoky Mountains National Park some time ago with my children. We set out in the morning to hike to the top of Clingmans Dome, the highest point in the park, a towering 6,643 feet.

It was a long hike from our campsite, much longer than we had expected. We grew tired, of course, but plodded on. My children's groans and complaints seemed to increase in volume and intensity with the altitude, and I began to wonder if I was being cruel, if I was expecting too much, perhaps pushing them too hard.

We finally reached the "dome," the bald spot at what seemed to be the top of the earth, and gazed in wonder at the breathtaking vista. The magnificent view made us forget our aching legs and throbbing lungs. My son wrapped an arm around me and whispered, "Thanks, Dad. This is great." His sister joined us in an embrace.

That view—and the sense of accomplishment at having completed a taxing hike—turned my children's complaints into appreciation. They realized, I think, that my insistence on completing our hike had provided a memorable experience, one that we will all probably treasure for many years.

That sort of thing may be what the psalmist had in mind when he wrote, "He [God] makes my feet like the feet of a deer; he enables me to stand on the heights" (Ps. 18:33). Obedience to God's commands not only protects us from harm; it also allows God to provide for us, sometimes in breathtaking ways.

You see, when Jesus said, "You will know the truth, and the truth will set you free" (John 8:32), He spoke not only of freedom *from* (freedom from things like disease, disillusionment, and disappointment), but also of freedom *to* (freedom to love and be loved, to trust, and to laugh). Being obedient to God's truths does not mean giving up the pleasures of sex and leisure, of satisfaction and liberty; it means being free to enjoy *maximum* sex, *maximum* leisure, *maximum* satisfaction, and *maximum* liberty, in the way that God intended.

Thirty years ago, I made a decision that I was going to wait until a loving commitment of marriage before I expressed myself sexually. Because I entered my relationship with my wife as a virgin, in twenty-three years of marriage, I have never had the slightest shadow of fear over what I was bringing into the marriage bed. I feel protected from the risk of sexually transmitted diseases, or the strain of comparisons with past lovers, for example. But the benefits of moral behavior do not stop there. I have also experienced a real peace, a genuine intimacy that I could never have achieved if I had not made right choices. The transparent, intimate relationship I now experience with my wife is an example of the provision that results from moral choices.

Our study of churched youth also illustrates the clear benefits of a moral lifestyle. The youth who were most discontented with their lives, by their own admission, were those who had already had sexual intercourse, those from broken homes, and those who rejected the existence of absolute truth and objective standards of morality.

The study clearly supports the notion that immoral behavior produces negative results. It indicates that moral behavior makes your children more likely to say they are satisfied with their lives, that they have high hopes, that they are respected by others. The study intimates that morality breeds a healthy self-esteem, making your youth more likely to characterize themselves as "achievers," "encouraged," and "reliable."

Immoral behavior, on the other hand, fosters negative attitudes, making your children more likely to say that they are "resentful," "lonely," "angry with life," "unmotivated," "disappointed," "confused," "skeptical," mistrustful of others, and lacking in purpose.

Expounding the Evidence of Truth to a young person can serve to reinforce the Test of Truth; it may even prompt a skeptic to grant the Test of Truth a fair hearing.

"But," you may say, "the Test of Truth relies on the precepts of God's Word. What if my young person questions the authority of Scripture? Is the Test of Truth and the Evidence of Truth going to work?"

Not likely. The Evidence of Truth and the Test of Truth rest on biblical principles and, therefore, on the authority of Scripture. If a person questions the Bible's reliability, they will find it difficult to grasp and use the Test of Truth and the Evidence of Truth.

And—count on it—at some point, your young person will have questions and doubts about the Scriptures. I have heard from hundreds of parents, pastors, and youth workers who lament how their "strong" Christian youth went off to universities and came back skeptics.

As a young university student, I was a skeptic myself. I thought Christianity was a joke, and I set out to disprove it. After two years of research, I came to the conclusion that Scripture was reliable and God was who He said He was—and I trusted Christ as my Savior and Lord. I have spent the last thirty years of my life speaking and writing on the evidences for the Christian faith. I have attempted to document the overwhelming evidence for our faith, including the reliability of Scripture in such books as *Evidence That Demands a Verdict, More Evidence That Demands a Verdict, A Ready Defense, More Than a Carpenter,* and one directed specifically to high schoolers, *Don't Check Your Brains at the Door.* I have written volumes on a defense for the faith; many other authors have done the same.

■ THE NEED FOR MORE EVIDENCE ■

I encourage you to obtain evidential books—such as those mentioned above—to use as references when you and your young person need them. But I would also like to provide you with a "quick defense" to use whenever you sense any young person doubting the reliability of Scripture. With this "quick defense," you can challenge them to examine the accuracy and veracity of the Bible. You can then use a book like *Evidence That Demands a Verdict* to provide the needed documentation.

I urge you not to disagree with youth when they suggest the Bible may not be accurate. Instead, challenge them to examine the evidence; say, "If the Bible is in fact an accurate historical document, it should be able to withstand the test by which all historical documents are tested." With that, you can explain that there are three tests for the historical reliability of any ancient literature: the bibliographical test, the internal evidence test, and the external evidence test (the following material is covered in greater depth in some of the books mentioned above).

The Bibliographical Test is an examination of the textual transmission by which documents reach us. In other words, since we do not have the original documents, we ask: "how reliable are the copies we have in regard to the number of manuscripts and the time interval between the original and the existent copy?"

The bibliographical test determines whether the text we now have is what was originally recorded. But it does not address whether that written record is credible.

The Internal Evidence Test establishes two criteria to determine a piece of literature's credibility. First, in the event of an apparent inaccuracy or discrepancy, the benefit of the doubt must be given to the document itself. In other words, the textual critic must not prejudge, but must consider the author innocent until proven guilty of a discrepancy. Secondly, the writer's credibility is judged by the nearness of the witness (both geographically and chronologically) to the events being recorded.

The External Evidence Test determines whether other historical material confirms or denies the internal testimony of the documents themselves. In other words, we look at what sources, apart from the Bible, for example, substantiate its accuracy, reliability, and authenticity.

Once you have exposed your young person to these three tests (which are used to examine any piece of literature), you are ready to put Scripture to the test. They will not only find that the Bible we have is reliable; they will discover that it is the most accurate and reliable piece of literature in all of antiquity!

The evidence is overwhelming: the Hebrew and Christian Scriptures are historically accurate and reliable. And once we confirm their accuracy, we establish them as a reliable source of authority. And that brings us back to the overwhelming evidence of truth: adherence to biblical truth protects us from harm and provides benefits—just as the Bible promises. It is that evidence—the evidence of God's protection and provision—that we can share with our youth in confidence. But the way we share it—the way we impart the Test of Truth and the Evidence of Truth (and even the evidence for the reliability of Scripture) to our children—is critical. It can mean the difference between our youth accepting or rejecting the truth.

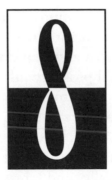

Teaching the Truth

"I DON'T WANT TO DO THIS!" Gary Marsh stood in the church parking lot, whispering vehemently to his wife. "You know I don't like this kind of thing."

Penny smiled at Geena Santoro and Beth McConnell as they walked by on their way into the church. When the door had closed behind them, she turned to her husband.

"We've got to do something, Gary, you know that as well as I do. And what we've tried so far with Brittney hasn't been working." She stepped close to him and looked up into his face. "Look, I'll tell the pastor you have laryngitis; you won't have to say a word." She touched his cheek. "Please?"

He nodded sullenly and they stepped into the church and made their way into the pastor's study. A desk with a computer on one corner took up most of one wall; the other walls were covered with books, neatly shelved in alphabetical order. A tight ring of folding chairs occupied the center of the room. Pastor Milford and his wife, Diane, Beth McConnell, and Geena Santoro smiled as they entered. Another couple, whose names Gary and Penny did not know, stood and introduced themselves as Dave and Tammy and their two-month-old, Renee Nicole. The pastor indicated the empty chairs in the circle.

Penny touched her throat as she sat down. "Gary's got a touch of laryngitis today, so he'll probably just listen."

Pastor Milford began, then, to explain the events that had led to this meeting: his experience with Philip, the reactions to his sermon a couple Sundays ago, his conversation with Geena. He went on to relate in great detail the results of his efforts to address his son's ideas about morality and Christianity. He distributed a photocopied handout he had created on the computer to share how he had begun to give his son an objective basis for judging right and wrong, based on the nature and character of God; he told how he was trying to help Philip see how moral precepts are based on universal principles, which spring from the very person of God himself. Finally, he said that he had only recently—in the last several days—realized that he needed also to point out to his son that the truth is not only true, but relevant as well, by pointing out how God protects and provides for us when we obey His commands.

When he finished, a thoughtful silence descended on the group. Diane Milford, the pastor's wife, finally broke the silence, and the group began to discuss the concepts the pastor had shared and to exchange their own stories of sons and daughters struggling to navigate without a moral compass.

"It seems so simple," Beth McConnell finally said, referring to the ideas Pastor Milford had shared, "that I can't believe I never thought to communicate it to my boys."

"It is simple," Pastor Milford admitted, "but it is not easy. I can't begin to tell you how much this process has made me aware of things in my own life, things that have been inconsistent with God's standards . . . things that have prevented me from passing on my values to my children. I have sinned—there's no other way to say it—in various ways, and my children have seen that inconsistency, and it has affected their ideas of morality. I've also wronged my children by not fulfilling the Scriptural command that says to teach God's commands to your children, 'when you sit at home and when you walk along the road, when you lie down and when you get up.' I have been very humbled these last few weeks, and I confess to you—" he looked around the circle—"that I have sinned, as a man and as a father."

A sober mood descended on the group. Geena Santoro began to cry quietly, and Beth rummaged in her purse and pulled out a tissue, which she extended to her friend.

Geena began to speak emotionally about her divorce, and its effect on her children—especially on her youngest, Melissa, who (Geena said) appeared to be repeating some of her mother's mistakes. "But I still can't believe it was wrong to divorce Kenneth." The group listened quietly, attentively, as she struggled to speak through a flood of emotion. "There was just no other way," she said. "It was like our marriage went down a certain path, and after a while, there was no turning back. There was just no other way."

Beth stretched an arm around her friend and began weeping with her.

Geena turned her face, splotched with tears, to the pastor. "Maybe if I'd known these things ten years ago," she said, "it might have made a difference in my marriage, I don't know. But I can't save my marriage *now*, can I? I can't help Melissa save hers either." She lifted the tissue to her nose.

DeVonne Davis, another single mother, whose daughter Darcelle was among the leaders of the church youth group, rose from her chair and knelt in front of Geena. She gripped Geena's left hand in hers and looked up seriously into the weeping woman's face.

"You're right, Geena," DeVonne said. "None of what Pastor said will change the past. Even if it could, though, there's no way to guarantee that our children will always choose God's best; we don't even do that ourselves. But it's never too late to help our children—even our grown children—see that choosing to live by God's standards of right and wrong, no matter how difficult it may be, is not only the right decision, but the most beneficial too."

Geena nodded. Beth produced another tissue from her purse, and Geena wiped her eyes, sighed deeply, and smiled at DeVonne.

The entire group was soon on their knees; most were praying and crying. The meeting adjourned with hugs and hearty back-slapping, and an agreement to meet regularly to report on their efforts and progress in communicating consistent, objective standards of morality to their children.

Gary Marsh did not speak until he and Penny were alone in the car, about a block from the church. "Don't *ever* make me do that again," he said sternly to his wife. "You know I don't like that kind of stuff."

Penny waited a few moments. After they had crossed the train tracks by Eisenhower High School, she braved a comment. "I'm glad we went, though," she said. "I think the pastor hit the nail on the head. If we start doing some of those things with Brittney—"

"What, like telling her it's all my fault she's been sleeping around? Like telling her I've been setting a bad example for her?" He held the steering wheel in a vise-like grip. "Look, I may not be the best father, but Brittney's problem is not that she hasn't been taught right from wrong; she knows, all right. She just doesn't want to do what we tell her."

Penny's soft voice contrasted with her husband's sharp tones. "I just think . . . "

"I just think the pastor needs to put his foot down with his own kid before he tries to tell me what I've been doing wrong with mine."

■ WHAT COLOR IS TIME? ■

The concept of the Test of Truth and the Evidence of Truth may be simple, but coming to terms with it, and then communicating it to a young person, may not be easy—not at first, at least. Every parent and youth worker knows that communicating with children—particularly, it seems, with teenage children—holds more perils than a melodrama. And trying to teach abstract concepts like absolute truth, even in a practical form presents a daunting challenge.

Peter Bocchino, executive director of leadership training for Ravi Zacharias International Ministries, delightfully depicts the dangers of matching wits with a child:

I truly enjoy spending time with my [seven-year-old] son Andrew. . . . However, it is our periodic philosophical conversations that I am learning to treasure.

One day Andrew engaged me in a dialogue that went something like this: "Dad, how do they get those big fire engines out of the desert when they get stuck?"

"What do you mean?" I said. "What are fire engines doing in the desert?"

"That is not my question!" Andrew replied. "I want to know how they get the big fire engines that got stuck in the desert out of the desert."

"Well," I said, "they get very large tow trucks and tow them out."

Of course, this was even more of a problem in Andrew's mind. "Wait a minute," he retorted. "The fire engines got stuck because they were so big. Why wouldn't the large tow trucks get stuck?"

At this point I knew I was in trouble. "Look Andrew," I said, "you are asking a question that really has no meaning."

He looked at me and asked, "What do you mean?"

Now it was time to really stump him by asking him to answer an unanswerable question: "Andrew, tell me, what color is time?"

Without hesitation, he bounced back, answering, "Oh, time! Time is red!" (Then I remembered that he was thinking of the clock in his room that has a red LCD).

I said, "Okay, tell me, how does green taste?"

Again, as if he had answered this question a million times, he quickly replied, "Oh, green—yuck!" I thought of all the green vegetables that he hates to eat—especially peas.

I had to think fast, so I tried one more question. "Andrew, what does the invisible man look like?"

He stared at me. I thought I had him until he said, "Hey, how should I know? I never saw him!"

Well, this was it. . . . I had finally met my match. I meekly replied, "Andrew, Daddy doesn't know how they get those big fire engines out of the desert. When you grow up, will you explain it to me?"

"Sure, Dad," he gleefully replied.[1]

Communicating a cohesive model of truth and objective morality to your children may seem nearly impossible. Not only do we have to bring abstract concepts into the "real, relevant, right now" world of young people, but it seems like a never-ending process. That's because it *is* never-ending. The responsibility of parents seems so daunting partly because it is so constant. But it is the constant, consistent element of our teaching that will instill truth within our youth.

God gave Israel the model for teaching our children when He said:

> "Hear, O Israel! The LORD is our God, the LORD is one! And you shall love the LORD your God with all your heart and with all your soul and with all your might. And these words, which I am commanding you today, shall be on your heart; and you shall teach them diligently to your sons (and daughters) and shall talk of them when you sit in your house and when you walk by the way and when you lie down and when you rise up. And you shall bind them as a sign on your hand and they shall be as frontals on your forehead. And you shall write them on the doorposts of your house and on your gates" (Deut. 6:4–9, NASB)

God's model for teaching truth to young people called not only for a constant process; He also prescribed a relational method. We are to teach diligently when we sit, walk, lie down, and rise up. In other words, God wants parents to teach His truths in every relational interaction with their children—even the most mundane. And His plan of parenting His own children—leading us from precepts to principles to an understanding of His person—is the same relational model we can use effectively with our children.

The word "no" was probably one of the earliest communications you exchanged with your children. Your infant son grabbed your glasses; you removed his hand and said, "No." Your one-year-old extended a hand toward a hot stove; you pulled their hand back and said, "No." Your toddling daughter broke free from your grasp at a busy intersection and dashed off the curb; you grabbed her and yanked her out of harm's way with a stern "No!"

What you were doing, in a very elementary way, in each of those cases, was teaching your child by precept. You were communicating the boundaries of safe and acceptable behavior by issuing clear commands. As your children grew, of course, you stated boundaries in more than a single word: "Don't play with your food," "Brush your teeth after meals," "Don't go near the street."

Many parents, however, fail to progress beyond precept in communicating with their children. They fail to communicate the principles behind their own precepts.

■ TO MTV OR NOT TO MTV ■

Some time ago, my daughter began pressing my wife and me for permission to watch MTV, the cable channel that plays rock videos. My wife and I refused. Several weeks later, she asked again. We refused again. Finally, after her question had been repeated several times—each time several weeks apart—we became exasperated.

"You've already asked us and we've already told you 'no,'" we said. "Why do you keep asking?"

"Because I keep thinking, 'Maybe I'm old enough now.'"

We explained to her that we weren't waiting for her to reach a certain age.

"Well then, why won't you let me watch it?" she asked.

Only then did we realize that in this matter we had never explained the principle behind the precept. We had never explained that the command issued from our concern over the messages that particular channel communicated and the long-term influence it could have on her. We had given her a command: "Thou shalt not watch MTV." But we had never revealed the principles—such as purity of thought—that lay behind our persistent refusal.

We were quick to correct our oversight, and not only explain the principle behind the precept, but shared how our rule to her related back to us as her parents. We said, "The reason we would rather you didn't watch MTV is because those singers and their songs convey messages that can be harmful to you;" we went on to explain, "because your mother and I are completely committed to Christ, we want our home—even the television shows we watch—to honor Him." Such a message not only revealed the principle behind the precept, it also showed our daughter something about her parents' character and personality.

Imitating the pattern of precept-principle-person in our relationships with our own children is crucial if we wish to equip them with the means of discerning right from wrong. But to do that effectively we must be sure three critical elements are present.

■ THE THREE PILLARS ■

Picture a structure in the classical Greek style, a foundation ringed by several steps that lead to a columned building. Now imagine that the steps represent precept, principle, and person. Those steps lead an individual into the structure itself, which is supported by three pillars. Each of the pillars is necessary, of course; the strength of each contributes to the effectiveness of them all. These three pillars symbolize relationship, example, and truth.

Keep that picture in mind as we discuss the three pillars that will help you to communicate biblical truth to your children, grandchildren, students, or friends.

■ BUILD A RELATIONSHIP ■

The first pillar of effective communication is relationship. That's what biblical morality is all about: our relationships with

God and with others. We cannot impart truth, therefore, apart from honest, meaningful relationships.

Simply occupying a position of authority, such as pastor, youth worker—even mother or father—by no means guarantees that you can effectively teach a young person right from wrong. Anyone who wishes to pass on biblical values to someone else must begin by developing a strong, positive relationship with that person.

I held a one-week conference at one of the largest evangelical churches in our country. I had counseling appointments with forty-two junior and senior high school students. Their number one question was, "Josh, what can I do about my dad?" When I asked what they meant, they made statements like:

"He never has time for me"

"He never takes me anywhere"

"He never talks to me"

"He never does anything with me"

I asked all forty-two of them, "Can you talk with your father?" Only one said yes.

I also asked the girls, "If you got pregnant, could you go right to your father and share this with him?" Most of them said they didn't think they could.

In the survey we've been citing throughout this book, 54 percent—over half—of teens in evangelical church families responded that they seldom or never talk with their fathers about their personal concerns, and over a quarter (26 percent) said they seldom or never talk with their mothers about such things. At the same time, the study reveals that youth who are "very close" to their parents are more likely to feel "very satisfied" with their lives, to have abstained from sexual intercourse, to espouse biblical standards of truth and morality, to attend church, to read their Bible consistently, and to pray daily. Those youth who lack a strong relationship with Mom or Dad are more likely to regard premarital sex as moral, view the purpose of life as personal fulfillment and enjoyment, lack a positive role model or hero, and reject the existence of absolute truth and objective morality.

No wonder so many young men and women are struggling—and failing—to develop sensible ideas of right and wrong; many of them lack relationships with people who are in positions to communicate those ideas.

These things illustrate the fact that truth is best understood in the context of a relationship. For example, if I need to correct my children, I begin by asking a question that appeals to my relationship. If the answer to that question is positive, then I can be confident that they will respond to my correction. I ask, "Do you know that I love you?" By asking that question before I offer correction, I appeal to them, not on the basis of my authority, but on the basis of our relationship.

A few years ago, I co-authored a book with my dear friend, Dick Day, entitled *How to Be a Hero to Your Kids*. In it we thoroughly examined the concept that "rules without a relationship lead to rebellion." Allow me to quote a page from that book, because it is so very applicable to this issue. In fact, I would recommend the entire book to you because it is devoted to how you can build a deeper and more meaningful relationship with your children.

> Dick and I have spoken to parents throughout the nation and around the world for the past fifteen years. Everywhere we go we find families who have rebels on their hands, parents at their wits' end, not knowing what they can do. It's easy enough to blame the culture in which we live. There are many likely scapegoats. If only those kids didn't watch so much television, see so many movies, or listen to that rock music.
>
> We're not denying that all of those pressures can do families serious harm. Our children are growing up in a culture that is not dedicated to helping a family; in fact, many of the values of our present-day culture are deadly enemies of family life. . . . But Mom and Dad, please realize that the real problem is not with the culture. We can try to excuse our weaknesses by blaming the culture, but the real cause of the problem lies deeper—right on our doorsteps and in our family rooms.

When parents try to lay down rules without first establishing a real relationship with their children, the natural result will be rebellion. Sometimes it will be outward rebellion that is easy to spot in the child's actions, but just as often it can be an inward rebellion, where the child appears to be obedient but is nursing all kinds of grudges and hangups, along with an unhealthy self-image and poor self-esteem.

We see the "rules without relationships lead to rebellion" principle being violated in every culture around the globe. Recently I spoke in the Philippines to over six hundred pastors and Christian workers. Afterward, over two hundred of these men lined up to talk to me. One of the major problems I dealt with that night is illustrated in the father—a pastor—who told me his family had turned against him. His three children—seventeen, thirteen, and ten years of age—were considered to be "the worst kids in the church" and were all rebelling in one way or another. He wanted to know what he could do.

"Forget the rules," I told him.

"What?" he said in disbelief. "That's what's wrong—they're not obeying any rules. They don't even think they need to."

"I know what you're saying," I told him, "but I repeat, forget emphasizing the rules. Take some of the ideas I talked about tonight and start building a relationship. You don't have anything to lose."[2]

Regardless of the ages of your children, it is not too late to build relationships. I recall a Portland woman whose four adult children had completely rebelled against her and caused her untold agonies and heartaches. Dick Day and I shared the relationship-building principles from *How to Be a Hero to Your Kids*, and she went home committed to the long, hard task of rebuilding those relationships. Five years later, we met that woman again. She said that her relationship with two of her children had turned around 180 degrees! She shared tearfully how attention to relationship—even with adult children—had paid rich dividends.

How do you determine the depth and breadth of your relationship with a child or teenager? Try asking:

When's the last time you laughed together?

When's the last time you cried together?

Do you know what his favorite (current) song is?

Do you know who she sits with in the school cafeteria?

When did she last seek your advice?

When did you last forget or cancel a commitment to him?

Do you more often ask questions of or make statements to her?

Have you recently admitted a mistake or fault to him?

What do you know—really know—about her spiritual life?

The answers to such questions may reveal the depth of your relationships—and may suggest places to start deepening them right now.

■ BE AN EXAMPLE ■

I received a note from a man about four or five years ago. He explained that he had come to Julian, the little California town where I live, and had waited around town until he saw me.

He watched me as I took my kids to eat at the Rong Branch Cafe, and followed me around town for a while, into the drug store, into the ice cream shop, and so on—all without me knowing he was there.

"I wanted to see," he wrote, "whether you live what you teach."

Whether you know it or not, you're being watched too. And the things you model—by design or by accident—powerfully communicate your convictions about right and wrong, about morality and immorality.

Thirty-five percent of our youth cannot identify any adults as their heroes or models for successful living. No wonder so few teenagers today can't sort through their ideas about right and wrong; they have no one to model their lives after, no one to imitate, no one to illustrate strong convictions and high standards of moral behavior.

I have a friend named Frank; his son is called Frankie. Frank is a man of few words; so is his son. Frank appears the most comfortable when his hands are thrust into his pants pockets; Frankie is no different. Frank is a skilled mechanic; Frankie is fascinated by cars. Not once has his father ever explained or taught these behaviors to Frankie; but he has modeled them continually, without even thinking.

If you want to pass on biblical values to your children you must model those values in your own life. If you wish your teenage son or student or friend to accept the idea that there are absolute standards of right and wrong—that some things are right for all people, for all times, for all places—you must let them see that you believe it yourself.

I can think of nothing that is more detestable to a teenager than a hypocrite. And they believe there are a lot of them. In fact, only 29 percent of the youth participating in our survey could disagree with the statement, "There are a lot of hypocrites in my church."

Only 27 percent of our youth say their parents frequently "admit when they're wrong or mistaken." The study indicates that our children see our mistakes pretty clearly; what they seldom see are parents who are open and honest enough to admit their failures, seek forgiveness, and keep trying.

I am not saying that you must live a perfect life before your child—merely a consistent life, a life that models biblical standards.

Parents who complain about neighborhood kids treading across their lawn and through the flower beds should not neglect to leave their name and phone number in the windshield of the car they scrape with the shopping cart in the grocery store parking lot.

The youth worker who instructs students to be honest must not "forget" to report every cent of income to the IRS.

The pastor who preaches against sexual immorality ought to evaluate his television viewing in light of those convictions.

For a number of years, I would speak regularly (about once every three years) at a large church near Denver. Not long before one of my engagements there, the church had hired a new pastor. When one of the church leaders picked me up at the airport to drive me to the hotel, I asked, "How's the new pastor working out?"

He sighed. "Josh," he said, "it's so wonderful to have a pastor who loves his wife." For most of an hour, the elder talked about his pastor. He never mentioned a sermon, never referred to the pastor's fund-raising abilities; he told me about the man's obvious love for his wife. He said it had transformed his church—and his own life. He said, "I'm more in love with my own wife now than I've ever been." That pastor was modeling biblical truth to his people.

How do you determine whether you are modeling the idea that there are absolute standards of right and wrong? Try asking yourself:

> What is there in my life that I don't want known to others?
> How has my behavior this week displayed my belief in absolute standards of morality?
> How has my behavior failed to display that belief?
> Do I forbid behavior in my children that I allow in myself?
> Am I open to criticism from others?
> Can I ask a teenager to help identify and correct inconsistent behavior in my life?
> What divine precepts or principles do I resist or disobey?

Ralph Waldo Emerson's famous words challenge us: "What you are stands over you the while, and thunders so that I cannot hear what you say to the contrary."

■ SHARE THE TRUTH ■

The man or woman who is modeling truth will be far more effective, in communicating biblical standards to the next generation, than those who attempt to teach without modeling. The sequence is important.

God said to Moses, "These [commandments] shall be on your heart; and you shall teach them diligently. . . ." (Deut. 6:6–7, NASB). The commandments must be upon *your* heart; then, you can teach them to your children.

And, as we have said, instilling biblical values in our youth requires a continual commitment. You cannot expect to explain it once to a child and be done with it. We must talk about it when we sit at home and when we walk along the road, when we lie down, and when we get up.

Early in my daughter's school experience, I remember asking her at the dinner table, "What did you learn today?"

She answered, "Nothing."

"You had to learn *something* new," I insisted.

"No," she maintained. "We just learned the same things we already knew."

I've since learned that's pretty much the answer I can expect to that question, because so much of education is involved in repetition and review.

Think about your own experience. Once you were taught the rule,

> "I before E except after C
> or when sounded like 'A'
> as in neighbor and weigh,"

the teacher did not abandon the rule and assume the lesson was taught. For days and weeks afterward, he or she assigned spelling words for you to study, and had you use those words in sentences for homework, and had you write them on the blackboard in class.

Teaching the truth requires a similar commitment. The Test of Truth and the Evidence of Truth must be taught to your children consistently, repeatedly, at every opportunity.

I like to take advantage of television shows, movies, even news broadcasts to teach truth—and consequences—to my children. From time to time the media does show negative consequences. For example, my son and I were watching a detective show in which two men sat at a bar; one purposefully lied to the other. That single lie got him wounded, jailed, and eventually cost him his family. When the show was over, I asked my son, "What can we learn from this? What were the consequences of lying?" We began a fruitful conversation about the Evidence of Truth.

I've used congressional hearings to discuss ethical matters with my children. I've used graffiti on walls to initiate a conversation that taught my children the Test of Truth. I read through Magic Johnson's biography with my two oldest children, and drew lessons from that; I pointed out how a lack of character can have devastating results.

If we are going to instill biblical standards of right and wrong in our youth, we must be alert to every opportunity to communicate that morality can be understood by tracing it through:

precept
principle
Person

and that moral choices can be evaluated by investigating which choice will:

protect
and provide.

The following chapters will detail ways to apply the Test of Truth and the Evidence of Truth to specific areas, particular values that are most lacking among our youth.

Before we examine those together, however, there is one more key to effective communication of truth and morality that cannot be overlooked. It is unquestionably the most important.

■ THE PERSON OF TRUTH ■

Nearly twenty centuries ago, a high government official, trained in politics and the law, asked a question that has echoed all the way into the latter years of the twentieth century. He stood in his elaborate palace, bedecked in regal clothes, and asked, "What is truth?"

Ironically, at that very moment, a prisoner stood before him who was and still is the embodiment of that word, "Truth." The official's name was Pontius Pilate; the prisoner's name was Jesus, who said of Himself, "I am the way and the truth and the life."

You see, we generally think of truth as an abstraction. It exists in our minds as a principle, or a quality. But truth is not merely an abstract idea. It is a Person, and that Person has a name.

We cannot separate the principle of truth from the Person who embodies it: Jesus Christ. A relationship with Jesus Christ is the integrating factor that makes it possible not only to understand truth, but to apply it to your life and relationships, to issues of morality and ethics and politics and all sorts of things. To return to the illustration of the columned building, this integrating relationship is like a roof on that structure; it completes the design and makes the place "liveable."

The person who has trusted Jesus Christ has not only become acquainted with truth; he or she has the Truth living inside!

Unless we understand and live the truth within the context of this vital relationship with God, it will ultimately lead to legalism. That is why it is so important to teach that truth resides within the person of God, the very person who wants to reside within us.

Jesus prayed, "And I will ask the Father, and He will give you another Helper, that He may be with you forever; that is the Spirit of truth. . . ." (John 14:16–17, NASB). Apart from the Spirit of truth, the Holy Spirit, we cannot hope to live a life pleasing to God. "But when he, the Spirit of truth, comes, he will guide you into all truth" (John 16:13, NASB).

We need to teach our young people that when they trust Christ, God's Holy Spirit actually enters their life (Rom. 8:9; 1 Cor. 3:16). It is the Holy Spirit that claims and seals them for God, not the following of commandments (Eph. 4:30; 2 Cor. 1:21–22). That isn't to say He doesn't want us to follow His commands, it simply means obedience is a result of our relationship with God, not the cause of it.

I have used the following steps to explain and lead my children into a Spirit-filled life. Perhaps it will help you guide your youth to allow God the Holy Spirit to take charge of their lives.

1. Confess our sin (1 John 1:9). The Holy Spirit cannot fill and lead us when we choose to live independently from God. Whenever we realize we are living contrary to God's commands, we must agree that our own way is wrong. By faith, we can claim God's love and the forgiveness for disobedience He has promised us. Remember: we are completely forgiven because Christ paid the ultimate price for our sin through His death.

2. Trust God to fill us and lead us by his Spirit. God calls us to respond to His love by allowing Him to be Lord of our lives and fill us with His Spirit. Being filled with the Spirit means that He is directing our lives and giving us His power to resist temptation, gain courage, make right choices, and deal with everything that happens in our lives each day.

What must we do to be filled with the Holy Spirit?

First, we must present every area of our lives to God (Rom. 12:1–2). We must ask God to help us surrender every area of our lives to Him—activities, friends, desires, etc.—and tell Him we want to depend on Him to lead us in each area.

Secondly, we must ask the Holy Spirit to fill us. God commands us to be filled with the Holy Spirit (Eph. 5:18). Asking to be filled is a clear step of obedience.

Thirdly, we must believe that He fills us when we ask Him to. The Holy Spirit is a free gift to be received. God has promised to answer if we pray and express our request to be filled (1 John 5:14–15).

3. Keep walking in the Spirit. Trusting God to fill us with His Spirit doesn't mean that we will never again blow it through lack of faith or disobedience. But we can live more consistently day after day if we apply these simple principles.

First, when we blow it, we must confess our sin quickly and turn back to God. We must then ask Him to fill us again with His Spirit and trust Him to do so.

Secondly, we must build our faith through the study of God's Word and through prayer (Rom. 10:17).

Thirdly, we must be prepared for spiritual conflict against the world (1 John 2:15–17), the flesh (Gal. 5:16–21), and Satan (1 Pet. 5:8–9), and respond to the conflict by relying on God's Spirit working in us and through us.

The greatest thing you can do for your children, students, grandchildren, or friends is to introduce them to the Person of truth and teach them how to live in the power of the Spirit of truth. We cannot expect our youth to always make the right choices. But by diligently teaching the truth, we can help them "become mature, attaining to the whole measure of the fullness of Christ" (Eph. 4:13).

Coming to Terms with the Truth

JAMES MILFORD KNOCKED on his son's bedroom door as he poked his head into the room. Philip sat on the floor at the end of his bed; he held a video game controller in his hand. James glanced from Philip to the small television screen, where some amorphous creature navigated a maze of mysterious dangers and obstacles.

"What's this game called?" James asked as he sat on the floor next to his son and crossed his legs with a grunt.

Philip shrugged. "The Kingdom of Nobo," he answered.

James nodded as if he understood. He watched the screen for a while. His foot felt as if it were already going to sleep. He unfolded his legs and crossed them again.

"Can we talk for a minute?" James asked.

Philip didn't take his eyes off the screen. He shrugged.

James waited, watching his son now, not the video game.

After a few moments, Philip glanced at his father. "You want me to turn the game off?" he asked.

James nodded.

"Just let me save this game," Philip said. He punched several buttons, and finally the screen went dark.

"I wondered if you might want to go do something, just the two of us," James said.

Philip blinked.

"I thought maybe we could go to that miniature golf course in the Far Hills Plaza."

Philip shrugged. "You mean now? Tonight?" he asked.

"You got something else planned?"

"No." Philip laid his head back against his bed. "I just don't feel like it."

James began to feel irritated, but he tried to stuff it down and keep it from surfacing in his voice. "You're still mad at me."

Philip shrugged.

James swallowed. "Can I be honest?" He looked seriously at his son. "I guess I'm still a little bit mad at you. But I don't want to be. And I know I've waited a long time to say this." He breathed deeply. "I'm sorry, son. For yelling at you the way I did. For some of the things I said."

Philip eyed his father suspiciously, but said nothing.

"And I was wondering if you'd do me a favor."

Philip turned his head and faced his father. Curiosity showed in his face.

"I want you," James began, "to help me control my temper better. I really don't like it that I yell at you and Sara so much. Would you remind me, when I start to yell at you or your sister, that we had this conversation?"

The boy looked wonderingly at his father for a long time. Finally, he shrugged. "Whatever," he said.

James stood. His knees cracked as he walked to the doorway.

"Dad?"

James turned back at the sound of his son's voice. Philip still faced the blank television screen. "Why can't you be this way all the time?"

The father pondered his son's question in silence. He stood rooted to the spot where he had turned to respond to his son's voice. After a long silence, he asked, "What do you mean?"

Philip still faced away from him. James could not see his expression.

"I mean, why do you have to be so different when you're around other people?"

"Different? How?"

"You turn into a preacher."

"What do you mean?"

"You turn into a preacher. It's like you act all different. And we have to act different too. I can't mention that I play Dungeons and Dragons. We can't talk about the movies we see. We have to put up a good show for the people at church."

"Now, that's not true," James protested.

"It is too." Anger crept into Philip's voice. He pushed himself off the floor and stood to face his father. "We have to be the perfect family!"

"But we're not!" he shouted. "Tell the truth, Dad," he continued. "When you yelled at me on the way home from school after I got suspended, were you mad because of what I did or because it embarrassed you?"

The man opened his mouth to speak, but quickly closed it again.

"Tell the truth," his son admonished again.

James wrestled for control. He wanted to argue with his son, to prove he was wrong. But as he looked in his son's eyes, he saw that Philip already knew the truth. He took two steps forward, and halted directly in front of Philip. He put a hand on each of his son's shoulders.

"I'm—I'm sorry," he said.

□ □ □

Brittney Marsh crept into the bathroom across the hall from her room and shut the door slowly and quietly behind her. She turned the brass lever above the doorknob to lock the door. She leaned her head against the door for a moment before switching the light on.

She pulled the box, which was about the size of a box of cake mix, from under her blouse. She sat down on the side of the bath-tub and, with trembling hands, withdrew the contents of the box and began reading the instructions.

She was seized with panic. She read the directions three or four times, referring to the simple drawings in the margins, before she comprehended what she was supposed to do. Tears began to cloud her sight. She tore a length of tissue from the roll beside the toilet, dabbed her eyes, and wiped her nose. Then, with a whimpering sigh, she began following the instructions.

When she had completed the procedure, she sat on the toilet seat, with the lid closed, marking off five minutes on her watch. Her knees vibrated up and down as she shook her legs nervously. She glanced from her watch to the home pregnancy test and back again, then repeated the exercise, ten, twenty, thirty times or more. She convinced herself several times that the test must be broken, or outdated; *maybe,* she thought, *I didn't do it right. What if it doesn't work?* she wondered. *What will I do then?*

Her period was more than a week overdue.

□ □ □

Geena Santoro hurried her friend, Beth McConnell, into the airport terminal.

"I'm so nervous," she told Beth. "Why am I so nervous?"

"You'll be fine," Beth said. "No matter what happens, you're doing the right thing."

A booming voice on the intercom system announced flights to Baltimore and Winston-Raleigh.

"Is that me?" Geena asked. "Am I late?" She giggled loudly, then blushed. "I'm sorry. I always do that when I'm nervous; I laugh like a turkey."

"You're not late," Beth said as soothingly as she could. She smiled at her friend.

They checked Geena's bags and proceeded through the metal detector without incident. They came to a "T" in the terminal and faced a choice between turning to the left for terminal A or to the right for terminal B.

"What gate?" Beth asked.

"What?" Geena asked.

"What gate do we want?"

"Oh," Geena answered. "I don't know." She laughed again, sounding more like a chicken than a turkey this time. "I wasn't really listening when the man at the counter told me. What do we do now? I don't have to go all the way back to the ticket counter, do I?"

Beth rolled her eyes and shook her head. She plucked Geena's ticket from her hand and glanced at the gate number, handwritten in magic marker on the paper ticket sleeve.

"Gate B9," she announced.

Geena laughed again at her own foolishness; her cackle turned the heads of several people in the terminal. She shifted her heavy purse to her other shoulder and fell into step beside her friend.

Nearly twenty minutes later, Beth and Geena faced each other at Gate B9.

"Don't worry about a thing. I'll stop in every other day to check the house and water your flowers."

"Thanks, Beth," Geena said. An earnest expression replaced the smile on her face. "I don't know what I'd do without you."

"Now, don't go down there with high expectations," Beth warned. "A reconciliation would be nice, but it's probably not going to happen."

"Oh, I know that. I know I can't change the past. I'll just be happy to do a little something about the future."

A tear glistened at the corners of Geena's eyes. She hugged her friend, showed her ticket to the flight attendant, and walked down the ramp to the plane.

Beth waved until Geena was out of sight.

□ □ □

A sudden knock on the door nearly caused Brittney to throw her home pregnancy test across the tiny bathroom.

"Yes?" she called through the door. Her heart beat rapidly.

"Matt's on the phone." It was her mother's voice.

"Tell him I'll call him back."

"Are you all right?" her mother called. "You've been in there for quite a while."

"I'm fine," Brittney answered. "I'll be out in a few minutes."

She craned to hear her mother's footsteps retreating down the hall. She breathed a sigh of relief, and once again consulted the test she balanced on her knees. A minus sign had appeared.

Negative. Relief washed over her with such force, she nearly cried out. *It's negative*, she exulted. *I'm not pregnant.* She leaned back against the toilet tank and restrained the tears that welled in her eyes.

Oh, thank You, Lord. Thank You, God. Thank You. She poured out her relief in a monotonous prayer of thanks.

She heard her mother's soft footsteps pass the door again, and she scrambled into action. She stuffed the contents of the test back into the box and closed it. She began to stuff the box under her blouse again, then thought better of it. *Mom might stop me in the hall,* she reasoned. She pulled the wastebasket out from under the bathroom sink and squirreled the box away at the bottom, making sure it was hidden from sight before she pushed the wastebasket back under the sink.

She splashed cold water on her face and hurriedly dried her face and hands. She inhaled deeply; then, with one hand on the doorknob and the other on the lock, she unlocked the door and opened it in one motion.

No one was in the hall.

She dashed into her room, closed the door, and dialed Matt's number.

□ □ □

Late that night, Pastor James Milford sat behind his desk in his small study at home. His wife and two children had gone to bed hours ago. He sat motionless, recalling his conversation with Philip.

He's right, he admitted. He replayed every moment of his confrontation with Philip. *I was mad because I knew there would be no way to keep Philip's suspension a secret from the congregation. I was thinking about what people would think, what they would be saying, what I would say to them.*

He closed his eyes. The only light in the room shone onto his desk from a tiny green-shaded lamp, a gift from a previous church. Books lined the wall behind him; an old, beaten couch occupied the wall across from him. A tiny electric alarm clock occupied a corner table beside the couch, loudly ticking off the seconds.

He shook his head, his eyes still closed. *I can't believe it. Philip is right. I was less upset about the fact that Philip had lied, and cheated, and pushed his teacher, than I was about how it would look. That's why I started shouting at him, because I was afraid he'd sullied my reputation.*

He leaned his elbows on his desk, and placed his face in his hands. "Oh, God," he said. "I was more worried about me than I was about him. And I was angry because he'd offended me, not because he'd offended You." He opened his eyes and stared at the opposite wall.

He continued to pray with his eyes open. "Your heart was breaking for Philip," he said. "And I couldn't see how he'd hurt You, how he'd hurt himself by doing what he did. I was so wrapped up in how he'd hurt me." He sat up straight in the chair. "And how I could put the best face on it for my congregation."

An idea had occurred to him suddenly. He tested it, turning it around in his mind the way a housewife judges a melon.

"Oh, Lord," he said in a whisper of realization. *I've been so stupid.* His mouth hung open. He placed his right hand flat against his chest as if to feel his heartbeat. He recalled the time that the family had returned from vacation much earlier on a Sunday evening than they had expected; he had insisted that they pull the car into the garage and leave the lights off in the front rooms of the house so no one would know that they had been back in town during the evening service.

He planted his left elbow on the arm of his chair and buried his face in his hand. He sat, unmoving, as the clock on the table counted the passing moments. He occasionally muttered, "Oh, God," or "Dear Lord," as he struggled to come to terms with his inconsistency. "Have mercy upon me, O God," he prayed, reciting the psalm from memory, "according to thy lovingkindness." He faltered after a few verses, and quickly opened his Bible on the desk in front of him and continued praying, speaking aloud as he read the words from Psalm 51.

He prayed, with his head in his hands, for a long time. His words eventually subsided, though his lips still moved.

Finally, after the hands on the tiny alarm clock had passed 2:00 A.M., he reached for a pencil and legal pad. He began writing.

Pastor James Milford stood in the pulpit of Westcastle Community Church. A crowd of about 175 worshipers had just finished singing the hymn, "Holy, Holy, Holy." A visible shifting occurred throughout the congregation as the crowd prepared for the sermon of the morning.

In one smooth gesture, he scooped his Bible from the pulpit, and balanced it in his left hand. He carefully and neatly arranged the yellow sheets of paper from his late-night study session on the pulpit.

"A couple weeks ago," he began, "I stood in this pulpit and made a confession. I told you that I had been remiss in my responsibilities as a father. I declared to you that our children are not adopting our values and morals, and I shared my conviction that it's not the fault of the culture, nor the government, the schools, the media—but of parents, like me, who have failed to take charge of their children's moral and spiritual education."

Milford adjusted his glasses. "God has not left me alone since that day. He has—gently but firmly—continued to speak to me, and lead me to repentance."

He looked around himself doubtfully, then glanced at his notes as if he had lost his place. He closed his eyes and slid his thumb and index finger under his glasses to rub his eyes.

Suddenly, he stepped to the side. His tall, forty-year-old frame stiffened.

"I have some things to confess this morning," he said. "I don't much care for pulpit confessions. But I have not been completely

142

faithful or truthful with you." He gestured, with his Bible, to his family. His voice was soft, but it did not waver. "My family is not perfect—far from it. They are the people I love most in this world, but my children sometimes disobey me, and I often disappoint them. That's probably not shocking news, but I have been so intent on making myself and my family look good before God's people, that I have not been totally honest with you. I have stopped short of lying to you, but I have stopped short of telling you the whole truth too. And I have been teaching my children to stop short of total honesty as well."

"There are some things about me," he said, "that, if you knew them, would cause you to judge me harshly." He began to relate the details of his conversation with Philip, and his subsequent spiritual struggle in his study at home. "I have actually told my children, 'Don't let on about this at church.' I've asked them, 'What if your Sunday school teacher knew you acted this way?'"

"I am not talking about sinful actions. I am not talking about unChristian behavior. I'm talking about value judgments and parenting decisions that my wife and I have made for our family, and have subsequently tried to hide for fear that God's people might not understand. 'My brethren, these things ought not so to be!' Should a pastor feel constrained to keep things from his brothers and sisters in the church for fear that they will judge him and his family too harshly? Should the church be a place where we must look a certain way and talk a certain way in order to please men, while we offend God himself by our lack of honesty?"

He licked his lips and swallowed. A lone cough sounded in the back of the sanctuary.

"I realized late last night that I have been telling my children one thing with my lips, and teaching them something else entirely with my actions. I've been trying to teach them honesty while involving them in my efforts to present a less-than-honest picture to this congregation. And I have been trying to tell others that God is truth while I have been living a lie."

The eyes of many in the congregation stared at the floor or the walls. Some people exchanged awkward looks. Few still looked at the pastor.

He raised the black Bible in his hand. "Last night," he said, "I confessed all this to God, and received His overwhelming mercy. He has created 'a pure heart' and renewed 'a steadfast spirit within me.' He has restored to me 'the joy of His salvation' and granted me 'a willing spirit, to sustain me.'

"I have determined from this day, with God's help," he declared with authority, "to live a life of honesty and transparency before God and before you."

He set the open Bible on the pulpit, and led his congregation in prayer.

□ □ □

Gary Marsh approached a small clot of people gathered at the corner of the parking lot after the service. Andy Porter was speaking as Gary arrived.

"I'm sorry, but I had guests with me this morning. Can you imagine what they thought? What kind of an impression are they going to have of our church now? It's embarrassing to have him go off in a sermon like that."

"It just ruins the mood of the whole service," Marjorie Henry said. "Services used to be so enjoyable here."

"Well, this morning just does it for me," Gary offered. "I have no desire to come to church anymore. I figure if the man wants to get stuff of his chest, fine—in the proper place. But I come to church to hear the Word of the Lord, not the sniveling confessions of a man who can't keep his son in line."

He left the group, then, and joined his wife and daughter, who waited for him in the car.

PART 3

THE
APPLICATION
OF
TRUTH

10

What's the Truth about Sex?

BRITTNEY CLIMBED THE STAIRS to the second floor. She had expected to find her mom in the living room or kitchen; it was Saturday afternoon, and she had just arrived home from her high school soccer game. She hoped to borrow a few dollars from her mother so she could go to the mall with some friends.

She thought she heard her mother's voice coming from the bedroom. *Must be talking on the phone,* she thought, knowing that her father was putting in some overtime today.

The bedroom door was slightly open; Brittney placed a hand on the door and pushed, as she leaned into the room and called her mother softly, being careful not to interrupt the conversation.

Her mother was not on the phone. She sat on the edge of the bed, with a wad of tissues in her lap and a white trash bag at her feet. Her face was splotched and red, and she choked off a sob as she saw Brittney enter the room.

"Mom, what's wrong?" Brittney asked.

Penny wiped her face hurriedly and scrambled to gather up the tissues that littered the bed and floor beside her.

Brittney sat beside her mother. "What's wrong?" she repeated.

Her mother turned her head then, and looked at Brittney like a wounded animal. Her eyes conveyed a mixture of pain and panic that scared Brittney.

Penny reached into the plastic bag at her feet. "I found this," she said, her words punctuated with emotion, "when I was emptying the wastebaskets this morning." She pulled out the home pregnancy test Brittney had used last Saturday night.

Brittney kicked herself inwardly for not getting the evidence out of the house. She opened her mouth to speak, but met her mother's pained expression only with silence.

"Oh, Brittney," her mother cried, and launched into a new round of sobs. Mother and daughter sat wordlessly for many long moments, until Penny stifled her emotions, licked her lips, and straightened her back.

"I thought—" she began. She clenched her jaw as she struggled to gain control. "I thought you said you always used protection." The words were spoken matter-of-factly, with pain, but no bitterness.

"I do," Brittney replied quickly. "Well," she added reluctantly, "not always."

Her mother nodded seriously. "Why didn't you tell me?" Her voice was different already. Controlled. Concerned. Like a mother inspecting a bump on a child's forehead.

Brittney lowered her eyes and stared at the floor. She shrugged. "I don't know," she answered. Her voice quivered. "I was just so scared."

Penny stretched an arm around her daughter, pulling her close. After a few moments had passed, Penny asked, "Was it positive, or negative?"

Brittney reached across her mother's lap for a tissue. "Negative," she said, as she wiped her eyes.

Penny drew a deep breath. She squeezed her daughter's shoulders. "Are you sure?"

"Yeah. *Now* I am."

Penny cocked her head and looked at her daughter's face. She smiled. "Never thought you'd be so glad to start, did you?"

Brittney returned her mother's smile, and laid her head on Penny's shoulder.

After a few moments, Penny spoke again. "You know how you felt when you were worried that you might be pregnant?"

Brittney nodded. "It was awful. My hands wouldn't stop shaking."

"You think that's what true love feels like?"

Brittney didn't move. "What do you mean?"

"Well, you felt scared, you felt alone; you had to sneak into the bathroom and go through that experience by yourself. Are those the kinds of feelings you expect true love to produce?"

Brittney didn't answer.

"See, Brittney, those are exactly the kinds of things God wants you to avoid. That's one of the reasons He tells us to 'flee sexual immorality,' because He'd rather have you and your husband taking a pregnancy test together, waiting hopefully for the result, instead of trembling in fear by yourself as you take it."

A few more moments of silence passed.

"Does Matt know?"

Brittney nodded without removing her head from her mother's shoulder.

"How did he react to all this?"

"I don't know. He's glad I'm not pregnant, but he's seemed kind of weird lately."

"It might have scared him too."

"Yeah, I guess." A melancholy note sounded in Brittney's voice.

■ THE TEST OF TRUTH ■

Have you ever watched a portrait painter at work? He sits his subject five to ten feet away, poses the person, then sits before a blank canvas. He begins to sketch an outline, staring carefully at his subject, then glancing at the canvas, then quickly returning his gaze to his subject. He mixes colors on his palette, then applies the brush to the canvas, referring constantly to the live subject. Occasionally he will speak to the subject; "lift your chin," he will say, or "turn your head this way." Seldom does he take his eyes off the subject—the original—of his painting.

The portraitist who fails to refer frequently to his subject will produce an unsuccessful portrait. And, while he may possess impressive technique and expertise, if he does not capture the image of the subject, his portraits will most likely disappoint—because they do not reflect the original.

The same is true when it comes to helping your kids make moral judgments in the area of sex. In order to help them determine what makes sex right, you must employ the Test of Truth, which asks, *How does it compare to the original?* We do that, of course, by constantly referring, through precept and principle, to the person of God himself, the very author of sex.

☐ PRECEPT

In biblical terms, sexual immorality is all extramarital (including premarital) sex. God has spoken through the law, and He has made His standard clear: sexual involvement outside of marriage is wrong.

The precept is clear:

"Abstain from . . . sexual immorality" (Acts 15:29).
"Flee from sexual immorality" (1 Cor. 6:18).
"We should not commit sexual immorality" (1 Cor. 10:8).
"But among you there must not be even a hint of sexual immorality . . . because these are improper for God's holy people" (Eph. 5:3).
Put to death, therefore, whatever belongs to your earthly nature: sexual immorality [and] impurity . . ." (Col. 3:5).
"It is God's will that you . . . should avoid sexual immorality" (1 Thess. 4:3).

150

God has reinforced the standard repeatedly. The inhabitants of Sodom and Gomorrah were destroyed because of their "grievous" sin, which included rampant sexual immorality. King David's sexual sin with Bathsheba was answered with the judgment of God; David suffered unspeakable pain and grief as a result of his immorality. The apostle Paul attributes the death of twenty-three thousand Israelites to their "sexual immorality" (1 Cor. 10:8).

"These things occurred as examples," the Bible says (1 Cor. 10:6), to communicate that "the precepts of the Lord are right" (Ps. 19:8). Over and over again, God has emphasized the precept, "avoid sexual immorality" (1 Thess. 4:3).

☐ PRINCIPLE

God's law forbidding sexual immorality is not predicated on a desire to squelch our freedom or squash our fun. It is based upon a universal and eternal principle; the "negative" command expresses a positive principle. The biblical command to "flee sexual immorality" is based on at least three fundamental principles: love, purity, and faithfulness.

The biblical standard of sex is one of love:

> For the commandments, "You shall not commit adultery," "You shall not murder," "You shall not steal," "You shall not bear false witness," "You shall not covet," and if there is any other commandment, are all summed up in this saying, namely, "You shall love your neighbor as yourself." Love does no harm to a neighbor; therefore love is the fulfillment of the law (Rom. 13:9–10, NKJV).

The word *love* is like a line drawing in a coloring book; it has no content. The law gives content to love; the commandments fill in the picture.

According to the Bible, love is evident when the happiness, health, and spiritual growth of another person is as important to you as your own. The Word of God records the command, "love your neighbor *as* yourself;" it doesn't command us to love our neighbor *more* than ourselves. We are to love *God* more than we love ourselves, but we are to love our neighbor, or our mate in marriage, *as* we love ourselves.

The problem, however, is that our youth are working from a faulty concept of love. For example, 46 percent of our youth say that they will be more likely to have sex outside of marriage if they are in love with the other person. In fact, 77 percent of our youth who have already had sexual intercourse—and 78 percent of those who regard premarital sex as morally acceptable—say that "love" would make them more likely to have sex.

In the minds of our young people, love is definitely the greatest determining factor in the decision to engage in sex. It is a greater determinant than whether they intend to marry the person. It is a greater determinant than if they could be sure a pregnancy would not result. It is a greater determinant than whether they could be sure a parent wouldn't find out, greater even than if they felt their parents wouldn't object to them having sex.

In the minds of our youth, love makes sex "right." They believe that true love makes sex perfectly moral—even beautiful. I happen to believe they're right—love *is* the biblical standard for sex. The problem, as stated before, is our youth's counterfeit standard of love—one that says love permits sex without boundaries, outside God's definition of love.

Brittney Marsh, for example, believes that her love for Matt makes sexual involvement OK; because she loves him, she reasons, it is right to express that love sexually. Her mistake is in accepting a contemporary counterfeit of "true love." True love, as defined by God, sets clear boundaries for sex. The principle of true love requires that the happiness, health, and spiritual growth of another person be as important to us as our own before love makes sex right.

I often announce to youth audiences that I believe "love makes it right." That statement is invariably greeted with strange looks, especially on the adult faces in the audience. So I go on quickly to clarify the principle of "true love."

"Do you," I say, "expect true love to produce intimacy? Do you expect it to result in a closeness and connectedness, a bonding of two people?"

The crowd inevitably responds with nods of approval.

"Do you," I continue, "expect true love to be giving, and trusting—a love that wraps its arms around you and says, 'No matter what, I will love you?'"

Again, heads will nod, and people will smile warmly in agreement.

"Do you," I proceed, "envision true love to be secure and safe, loyal, and forever?"

Without exception, crowds will agree to that principle of "true love."

Ephesians 5:28 helps us understand the biblical principle of love even better: "So husbands ought to love their own wives as their own bodies; he who loves his wife loves himself." What does it mean to love our own body as Scripture commands? The next verse explains: "For no one ever hated his own flesh, *but nourishes* and *cherishes* it, just as the Lord does the church" (emphasis added).

You see, God's principle of love means to value the happiness, health, and spiritual growth of another person as much as you do your own happiness, health, and spiritual growth.

The biblical standard of sex is one of purity: "Marriage should be honored by all, and the marriage bed kept pure, for God will judge the adulterer and all the sexually immoral" (Heb. 13:4). God's standard of sex demands that the sexual relationship be kept pure and beautiful. God designed sex to be enjoyed in a husband-wife relationship, for procreation (Gen. 1:28), for spiritual unity (Gen. 2:24), and for recreation (Prov. 5:18–19). It's meant to form an unbroken circle, a pure union: two virgins entering an exclusive relationship. That circle, that union, can be broken even *before* marriage, if one or both of the partners has not kept the marriage bed pure by waiting to have sex until it can be done in the purity of a husband–wife relationship.

The biblical standard of sex is also one of faithfulness. "Love and faithfulness meet together," the Bible says (Ps. 85:10). In practical terms, this means that the biblical standard of sex requires a commitment of two people to remain faithful to each other. That is why marriage is central to biblical sexuality, because it binds two people together in a lifelong commitment. If the act of love is to produce the emotional, physical, and spiritual intimacy it is designed to produce, it must be committed, it must be faithful.

God's precepts regarding human sexuality are grounded upon the principles of biblical love, purity, and faithfulness. Those principles, in turn, reflect the person of God himself.

☐ PERSON

Those principles are right because they are from God—they reflect His nature and character. They pass the test of truth; they reflect the "original."

God is love. "The one who does not love does not know God, for God is love. By this the love of God was manifested in us, that God has sent his only begotten Son into the world so that we might live through Him" (1 John 4:8–9, NASB). Love is not simply what God does; it is who He is. And by His nature, He views the happiness, health, and spiritual growth of others more important than himself. That is what motivated Him to send His own Son to suffer and die for us. God's kind of love "always protects, always trusts, always hopes, always perseveres" (1 Cor. 13:7).

God is pure. "Everyone who has this hope [of glory] in him purifies himself, just as he [God] is pure" (1 John 3:3). God has continually strived to communicate His purity to His people: He demanded the use of pure gold in the construction of the tabernacle; He prescribed pure incense for use in worship; He required pure animals for sacrifice; He commanded pure hearts (Matt. 5:8), pure religion (James 1:27), and pure relationships (1 Tim. 5:2). As the prophet Habakkuk said, God's purity is such that even "[his] eyes are too pure to look on evil" (Hab. 1:13).

God is faithful. "Know therefore that the LORD your God is God," Moses told the Israelites. "He is the faithful God, keeping his covenant of love to a thousand generations of those who love him and keep his commands" (Deut. 7:9). Now that's faithfulness! God keeps His covenant to a thousand generations. As Paul told Timothy, even "if we are faithless, He (God) remains faithful, for He cannot deny Himself" (2 Tim. 2:13, NASB). In other words, God cannot be unfaithful, because faithfulness is not something He does; it is something He is. He cannot "deny Himself," He cannot contradict His own nature, He cannot be something other than what He is.

Because God is pure, sexual impurity is an offense against Him. Because He is faithful, sex outside of a marriage commitment is an affront to Him. King David, who sinned with Bathsheba, later repented; he confessed to God, "Against you, you only, have I sinned and done what is evil in your sight" (Ps. 51:4). Was David ignoring the fact that his sin had affected other people, resulting in the death of Bathsheba's husband, Uriah, and of the baby Bathsheba bore David? No, he was acknowledging the fundamental fact that when he sinned with Bathsheba, he sinned against the Lawgiver. His act was wrong because it offended God's purity and violated God's standard of love, purity, and faithfulness.

The Test of Truth, then, grounds the virtue of chastity—biblical love, sexual purity, and faithfulness—in the nature and character of God. Brittney's relationship with Matt contradicts God's character. Their sexual relationship is not loving, because they are not considering each other's happiness, health, and spiritual growth as important as their own. Their sexual involvement is not pure, because it is not being enjoyed in the context for which God designed it. It does not fit God's standard of faithfulness, either, because it exists outside the lifelong, exclusive commitment of marriage. Her sexual activity, then, is wrong, not simply because her parents disagree with her, but because she violated God's declaration that sex was to be enjoyed within the confines of a loving, faithful, and pure relationship of marriage. We can then say that chastity—biblical love, sexual purity, and marital fidelity—is right for all people, for all times, for all places.

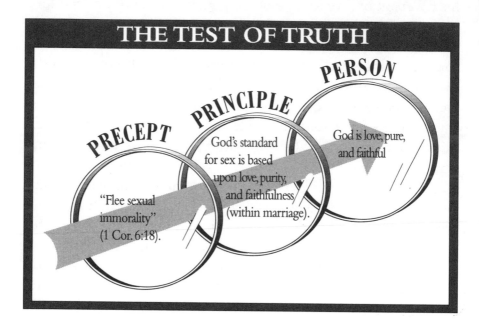

THE TEST OF TRUTH

PRECEPT

"Flee sexual immorality" (1 Cor. 6:18).

PRINCIPLE

God's standard for sex is based upon love, purity, and faithfulness (within marriage).

PERSON

God is love, pure, and faithful

■ THE EVIDENCE OF TRUTH ■

No matter what the Test of Truth says, however, some people—many of our kids included—would claim that "moralizing" will not make a bit of difference in the sexual behavior of youth. In fact, a *USA Weekend* poll reveals that less than one in eleven teens (8 percent) believe that preaching "premarital sex [as] immoral" would be an effective means of persuading teens to say no to sex. Thirty-eight percent tend to believe that "the most effective thing to say to teens to persuade them not to have sex" would be telling them about the health risks (such as getting AIDS), and 33 percent think the most effective abstinence message would be warning about the disadvantages of an unplanned child.[1]

Appealing to morals will do little to persuade a generation that lacks moral convictions regarding sex before marriage. But if we can show them that truth actually works in the real world—if we can expose them to the Evidence of Truth—then we increase the chances that our youth will acknowledge the truth and reconsider their actions.

Brittney Marsh is typical in this regard. She cared less about the right and wrong of her actions than she did about what would fulfill her hunger for love, her craving for attention. With the help of her mother, she is beginning to understand that moral behavior is not only right, but also provides for her deepest longings and protects from her deepest fears. She's beginning to realize that moral choices are not only right (that is, they conform to God's character); they are also the surest path to pleasure and fulfillment (they correspond favorably to reality), because they protect and provide for her.

☐ 1. PROTECT FROM GUILT AND PROVIDE FOR SPIRITUAL REWARD

God's standards for sexual behavior protect from guilt. Because God defines right and wrong, when we transgress His standards, we will invariably suffer guilt. Do you remember the girl who wrote me and confessed that she "always felt bad" after a sexual encounter? She was describing the effects of guilt. And though Brittney Marsh denied feeling guilty, when she admitted that she sometime felt "sad" as a result of her sexual encounters, she was describing the effects of guilt.

One of the participants in our "Write Your Heart Out" Essay Contest (part of the national "Why Wait?" campaign) described the guilt that results from sexual immorality, saying it "begins to rob a person of a healthy self-image . . . which decreases his ability to experience the transparency needed to cultivate an intimate relationship. . . . [It] can . . . leave him feeling 'grimy.'"[2]

God's standards for sexual behavior provide for spiritual rewards. The blessing of a clear conscience and an unhindered walk with God are inestimable. It is an immeasurable blessing to be able to stand before an altar and proclaim the singular devotion of your body to your mate and to God. The sexual relationship between a husband and wife is not only pleasurable, it is sacred; "The body is not meant for sexual immorality," the Bible says, "but for the Lord, and the Lord for the body" (1 Cor. 6:13). Sexual purity and faithfulness are pleasing to God and rewarding to the marriage partners.

□ 2. PROTECT FROM UNPLANNED PREGNANCIES AND PROVIDE FOR A HEALTHY ATMOSPHERE FOR CHILD-REARING

God's standards for sexual behavior protect from unplanned pregnancies and abortions. Every day in America, 2,795 teenage girls get pregnant and 1,106 have abortions. Those girls who carry their babies for the full term often face overwhelming difficulties; many drop out of school, many experience physical problems, many feel left out of "normal" teen activities because of their responsibility to a child.

Those girls who abort their children are not delivered from such consequences; abortion produces traumatic results too. Dr. Anne Catherine Speckard, of the University of Minnesota, reports the following long-term (five to ten years later) consequences of abortion:

- 81 percent reported *preoccupation* with the aborted child
- 73 percent reported *flashbacks* of the abortion experience
- 54 percent recalled *nightmares* related to the abortion
- 23 percent reported *hallucinations* related to the abortion

Dr. Speckhard's study reported that 72 percent of the subjects said that they held no religious beliefs at the time of their abortions, and 96 percent said that, in retrospect, they regarded abortion as the taking of life or as murder.[3]

God's standards for sexual behavior provide for a healthy atmosphere in which to raise a child. God's plan for every newborn is to be nurtured and loved by a man and a woman who love each other exclusively and are committed to each other for a lifetime. This is not to suggest that single parents do not perform bravely and admirably in their efforts to raise children. Nor does it ignore the fact that some children of unmarried parents have overcome significant odds to achieve great things. But the evidence overwhelmingly shows that, as Barbara Dafoe Whitehead writes, "The social arrangement that has proved most successful in ensuring the physical survival and promoting the social development of the child is the family unit of the biological mother and father."[4]

God's standard of purity, love, and faithfulness for sex had the protection of every newborn child in mind. Obedience to God's precept based on His love, purity, and faithfulness can create an atmosphere of love and security for a child that can leave a lifelong positive imprint on a child, spiritually, emotionally, psychologically, and even physically.

☐ 3. PROTECT FROM STDS AND PROVIDE FOR PEACE OF MIND

God's standards for sexual behavior protect from sexually transmitted diseases. Every day in America, 4,219 teenagers contract a sexually transmitted disease. The World Health Organization estimates that, by the year 2000, over twenty million men and women will be infected with the deadly AIDS virus. Every year there are four million new cases of chlamydia, a million new cases of pelvic inflammatory disease, over a million cases of gonorrhea, a half-million cases of herpes, and over 100,000 cases of syphilis. According to the Minnesota Institute of Public Health, "there are twenty sexually transmitted diseases which are not prevented by contraception."[5] Yet *not one* of those incidents has occurred between two mutually faithful partners who entered the relationship sexually pure . . . because God's standards for sexual behavior protect from sexually transmitted diseases.

God's standards for sexual behavior provide for peace of mind. I have personally never entered the "marriage bed" with the slightest worry or fear. I have never had to interrupt an intimate moment with my wife to think about "protection." I have never once awaited the results of a blood test to determine whether I have contracted a sexually transmitted disease. My sex life has been characterized by peace of mind. Why? Because I have followed God's standard of love, purity, and faithfulness before marriage and in marriage. I have complete peace of mind, that my relationship with my wife is free of disease, free of the "ghosts" of past partners, and free of "emotional baggage" as a result of a past immoral relationship.

☐ 4. PROTECT FROM SEXUAL INSECURITY AND PROVIDE FOR TRUST

God's standards for sexual behavior protect from sexual insecurity. The power of sexual interaction is a force a person may have to deal with for years after the sexual contact. God created the sexual experience to give us the most unforgettable, vivid, and often-recalled memories we will ever have. As a result, sexual immorality can produce haunting effects. Stacy and Paula Rinehart, in their book, *Choices*, describe one man's discovery of this fact:

> One young husband admitted that his relationship with his new wife wasn't what he had hoped it would be. "It's really my fault," he admitted. "Before we were married I had several physical relationships with girlfriends. Now, whenever I kiss my wife or engage in love play, my memory reminds me that this girl could kiss better than my wife, that girl was better at something else and so forth. I can't concentrate on loving my wife with all that I am—there have been too many women in my life to be wholly committed to one."[6]

Because sexual immorality is not exclusive, it creates insecurity and jealousy, and hinders sexual freedom and self-expression.

God's standards for sexual behavior provide for trust. Sexual purity and faithfulness before marriage contributes to an atmosphere of trust within marriage. That trust provides peace of mind for both partners when they are apart; each knows that the other is worthy of trust. Why? Because, in the period before their marriage, they proved their character, their maturity, and their self-control.

That's why premarital sexual activity can be such a source of distrust in a marriage. "If he couldn't control himself before marriage," the wife reasons, "what makes me think he will control himself in marriage?" "She 'played around' before she met me," the husband figures. "What's to stop her from playing around now?" Indeed, their fears seem justified; a study of 100,000 women put it like this: "Premarital sex . . . does not necessarily lead to extramarital sex—it simply increases the odds."[7]

☐ 5. PROTECT FROM EMOTIONAL DISTRESS AND PROVIDE FOR
    TRUE INTIMACY

God's standards for sexual behavior protect from emotional distress. The emotional costs of sexual immorality are immeasurable. One teen explained the effects of her sexual involvement in these words:

> . . . Having premarital sex was the most horrifying experience of my life. It wasn't at all the emotionally satisfying experience the world deceived me into believing. I felt as if my insides were being exposed and my heart left unattended . . . I know God has forgiven me of this haunting sin, but I also know I can never have my virginity back. I dread the day that I have to tell the man I truly love and wish to marry that he is not the only one, though I wish he were . . . I have stained my life—a stain that will never come out.

Another girl described her experience this way:

> After you've done it, you're really attached to that guy. It's as if he's your life; you feel really vulnerable. [When the relationship ended, I felt] really awful. I can't describe it. About a week after we had

sex, we broke up because I found out he was dating other girls. It really hurt.

Those who heed God's standard are protected from the consequences sexual immorality (whether premarital or extramarital) breeds: suspicion, disappointment, sorrow, stress, emptiness, and many other destructive emotions.

God's standards for sexual behavior provide for true intimacy. One woman wrote the following description of the blessing of true intimacy:

> Last July, God gave me the most wonderful man in the world to be my husband. I had asked for Prince Charming, and the Lord gave me *much more* than that. He gave me someone I can share my deepest feelings with, someone I can talk to God with, someone I know will always love me and be faithful to me, someone I am glad I waited for.
>
> On our wedding night, I experienced sex for the first time, and it was with my husband. I wouldn't have wanted to share my first time with *anyone* else. I had no riches or jewels to offer my husband, but he asked for none. All he wanted was me, and that is just what I had to give him—all of me, untouched, his alone. That meant a great deal, and we both knew it.

God's standard for sexual behavior provides a degree of intimacy that only exists within marriage. "For this reason," God said, "a man will leave his father and mother and be united to his wife, and they will become one flesh" (Gen. 2:24).

God's design for sexual intimacy protects from many dangers, and provides the best climate for the enjoyment of spiritual rewards, peace of mind, trust, intimacy, and many other benefits, to be enjoyed in a life-long relationship of love, purity, and faithfulness.

God's standard for sexual relations is, indeed, meant to produce intimacy; after all, God Himself recognized that "It is not good . . . to be alone" (Gen. 2:18). True love, purity, and faithfulness are intended to result in a closeness and connectedness, a bonding of two people; after all, God Himself decreed, "For this reason a man will leave his father and mother and be united to his wife, and they will become one flesh" (Gen. 2:24). When our behavior conforms to God's absolute truth, we can experience all the benefits of His protection and provision:

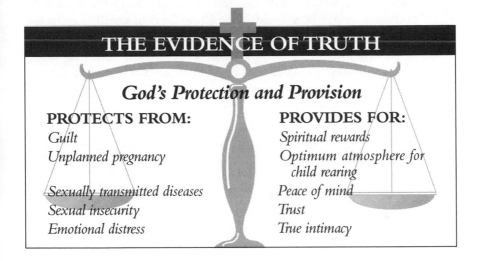

THE EVIDENCE OF TRUTH

God's Protection and Provision

PROTECTS FROM:
Guilt
Unplanned pregnancy

Sexually transmitted diseases
Sexual insecurity
Emotional distress

PROVIDES FOR:
Spiritual rewards
Optimum atmosphere for child rearing
Peace of mind
Trust
True intimacy

■ THE APPLICATION OF TRUTH ■

A battle is raging within our culture, and our youth's moral purity is at stake. Our young people need to hear the truth. They need to see the evidence. And they need help applying the truth "when [they] sit at home and when [they] walk along the road, when [they] lie down and when [they] get up" (Deut. 6:7).

Parents, pastors, teachers, and youth leaders can apply the truth in various ways (the modern equivalents, perhaps, of tying phylacteries to our hands and foreheads). Here are some suggestions on how to apply what we have been dealing with in this chapter with your younger children and teenagers.

■ **Celebrate anniversaries.** Wedding anniversaries are ideal times to let children know how faithfulness and purity has protected and provided for you in the areas discussed above. Make your anniversary a family celebration. Let your children know how much marital fidelity means to you. Tell them what the marriage commitment has done for your relationship. The more they see how your love, faithfulness, and purity has benefited your lives and theirs, the more impact it will have on them.

Don't underestimate the ability of younger children (six, five, or four years old, for example) to understand the principles of biblical love, sexual purity, and marital fidelity. You have an excellent opportunity to build a foundation for their sexual chastity by helping them understand these principles. You can explain your love for your spouse by describing how your spouse is as important to you as your own body. You can explain your faithfulness in the form of promise-keeping. You can explain marital fidelity by saying, "that is why I only live with your (mother or father) and with no one else." Teach them early of your commitment to each other and how you are exclusively devoted to each other. Your modeling and teaching will pay off when their hormones start raging.

Pastors and youth workers, take advantage of your anniversary (or that of a mature couple in the church). Have your spouse come into the youth group for a faithfulness and purity celebration. Explain how those principles have brought provision and protection into the marriage.

- **Take full advantage of weddings**. Go to weddings as a family and use those occasions to celebrate God's principle of faithfulness and purity. Make sure your children understand its significance. Take time prior to and following the ceremony to emphasize the commitment the couple is making and their promise to be faithful for a lifetime. Get a copy of the marriage vows and read it together with your younger children. Teenagers may not respond favorably to reading it together, but you can make it exciting to a child or pre-teen. Weddings are an ideal time to reinforce the principles of love and sex within the marriage commitment—and how that reflects the character of God.

   Youth workers and pastors, you have an excellent opportunity during wedding ceremonies to emphasize the relationship between God's precepts, principles, and His person.

- **"Use" the four-letter word**. We live in a culture that is becoming bolder and more flagrant in its use of profanity and vulgarity. An obscene four-letter-word for the sex act is used regularly in our society these days, and it is invariably used in a derogatory or denigrating manner. Some years ago, I decided to use the opportunity presented by hearing or seeing that offensive word to place sex in its proper context with my children. I described such an occasion, when my son and daughter were traveling with me one day, in the *How to Help Your Child Say No to Sexual Pressure* book:

> Before long, as so commonly happens with kids, they got into a little argument. In the middle of their spat, my angelic, eight-year-old Sean said to his sister, "F___ you!"
>
> How would most parents respond in that situation? Would they say things like: "Shut up! That's nasty. Dirty. Filthy. I'm going to wash your mouth out with soap if you ever say that again"? Often that's what you would expect, right?
>
> However, I saw Sean's words as a golden opportunity to teach.
>
> So I said, "Son, where did you learn that word?"
>
> "On the school bus," he answered.
>
> "Do you know what it means?" I said.
>
> "No," he said.
>
> "Can I explain it to you, then?" I said.
>
> "Yeah!" he answered. "What is it?" He was dying to know.
>
> And for the next forty minutes. I had a fabulous opportunity to teach my son and daughter about the sanctity, the beauty, and the purpose of sex. It was an opportunity for which I am extremely grateful, an experience I'll never forget—nor, I suspect, will they.

Our society has become so debased that that offensive word appears in graffiti, on the airwaves, in our classrooms and in our workplaces. We can't avoid it; but we can use such opportunities to explain to our youth why that word—which degrades something God intended to be beautiful—is so offensive, and in so doing teach them something about the sanctity of sex in the context of a faithful and pure relationship of marriage.

■ **Use opportunities presented by TV, news, and current affairs.** Take every opportunity to correct the warped portrayals of love and sex in the "entertainment" media and news.

When you and your kids see something on television or in the movies that contradicts God's standard for love and sex, discuss the benefits and consequences of obeying God's command. You may be surprised how insightful your youth are in detecting the benefits and consequences of people's actions once they begin to see life through the "lens" afforded by the Test of Truth and the Evidence of Truth. I believe you will be amazed at how quickly young people see the specific protection and provision God gives in result of living under the principles of His commands.

By continually modeling and teaching how to process life choices through the Test and Evidence of Truth with your children and teenagers, you will be equipping them to discern right from wrong.

As you apply the truth of love and sex in everyday life, you will reinforce to your children and teenagers that chastity—biblical love, sexual purity, and marital fidelity—is right for all people, for all times, for all places.

■ **Take advantage of the resources.** Families, churches, youth groups, and Christian schools need all the help they can get to shore up the crumbling foundations of our young people. And there are many resources you and your church can obtain to help in this battle of the sexual purity of our kids.

The "Why Wait?" Campaign has produced numerous books, single video tapes, audio tapes, video series, etc. to help you. In the *"Why Wait?"* book we have documented some twenty-eight physical, spiritual, emotional, and relational reasons to save sexual involvement until marriage, all presented in the context of God's loving provisions and protections, to help you lead your youth to the conclusion that God has their best interest at heart when He says, "Flee sexual immorality." Other ministries like Focus on the Family are providing excellent resources for the church, Christian schools, and the family. Take advantage of the resources. Go to your local Christian bookstore, order ministry catalogs, find out what your denomination offers—you may be surprised just how many excellent tools there are available to help you teach your children the biblical perspective of love and sex. (A list of products and ministry resources can be found on page 327.)

What's the Truth about Honesty?

PHILIP MILFORD DROPPED TO HIS KNEES and laid his cheek on the ground. He closed one eye, then opened it and closed the other. He lifted his head and peered at the hole in the ground, about five feet away.

"How long does it take," his father protested, "to line up a putt?"

Philip tossed his dad an annoyed look, and struck a stance beside the ball. He drew back slowly on the putter in his hands, swung forward, and, with a firm tap, propelled the golf ball into the eighteenth hole. The ball disappeared with a hollow clunk.

"Yes!" Philip pumped a fist into the air. He flashed a triumphant smile. "That's a two, Dad."

Pastor Milford recorded Philip's score and then began tallying the totals for the game.

"What's the score?" Philip asked when his father finished.

Pastor Milford feigned disgust and handed his son the scorecard.

"I beat you!" the boy cried. "Forty-nine to forty-one! I smeared you!"

A smile broke across James Milford's face, and he wrapped an arm around his son's neck.

"I guess you did," the man said. "But you got lucky."

"Lucky, nothing," Philip answered, laughing. "I smeared you."

James Milford laughed, too, and tried to remember the last time he and Philip had laughed together.

Later that week, Pastor Milford treated Philip and his daughter, Sarah, to ice cream cones at the Freez Whip. He dug into his pocket for change and pulled out a handful of coins and slips of papers.

Philip snatched a pale green card from his father's cupped hand and unfolded it.

"This is the scorecard from our game!" He turned to his little sister and showed it to her. "See? I beat him bad."

James Milford paid the cashier and rolled his eyes at his son. An idea suddenly occurred to him.

"What if I told you," the pastor suggested, "that you didn't really win that game of putt-putt?" "No way." Philip crunched on the chocolate sprinkles that coated his chocolate cone and waved the card. "I wiped the floor with you."

"What if I told you I doctored the scorecard to let you win?"

Philip's expression changed. "No way!" he protested.

"What's the difference? You wanted to win, didn't you?"

"Yeah, but . . ." The boy's face flushed.

Pastor Milford adopted a reassuring tone. "Don't get upset, Philip. I didn't doctor the scorecard. You won fair and square."

His son still wore a puzzled expression, but the anger had disappeared. Nine-year-old Sarah looked on, rapt with attention.

"It would have upset you," the father continued, "if I'd cheated for you." It was a statement, not a question.

"Yeah," Philip admitted. "I wanted to beat you."

"But you still would have won."

"It wouldn't have been the same."

"Why not?"

Philip thought for a moment. "Because it wouldn't have been real," he said finally. "It wouldn't have meant anything."

His father nodded. "Right. Cheating would have robbed you of the satisfaction and sense of accomplishment you got from beating me fairly. And it would have ruined your confidence the next time we played." The trio finished their cones, threw their napkins in the trash, and left the tiny restaurant together.

James Milford stopped on the sidewalk in front of the Freez Whip. He glanced back and forth between his son and his daughter as he spoke. "You see, like I've told you both before, honesty is right because God is true; honesty is part of His nature. But I also want you to realize that part of the reason God wants us to be honest is because He knows dishonesty is no fun; it robs us of a lot of good things."

Philip rolled his eyes. "I know, Dad. I'm not stupid, you know."

Sarah gripped her father's hand as they walked toward their car.

"Oh, I know that," he said, smiling as he answered his son. "That's my point."

□ □ □

Pastor James Milford has begun applying the Test of Truth and the Evidence of Truth to standards of honesty. He is attempting to show his children why honesty is right and dishonesty is wrong.

The research indicates that one of the areas in which our youth struggle most is the area of honesty. Two of every three (66 percent) say they have lied to a "parent, teacher, or other older person" within the last three months. Slightly fewer—six in ten (59 percent)—say they have lied to a friend or peer within the last three months. More than one-third (36 percent) admit that they have cheated on an exam or other evaluation within that same three month period, and nearly one-sixth (15 percent) say they have recently stolen money or other possessions.

What has caused our children to adopt a lifestyle of deceit and dishonesty? Why do they seem to think that *dishonesty* is the best policy? Because they have embraced a "man-centered" view of truth, one that relies on human ideas—rather than divine standards—of truth and morality. Our research shows that over half of our youth (52 percent) are struggling with this issue; they tend to believe that "lying is sometimes necessary."

Our young people have bought into a counterfeit. They see deceit as an "easy" way to get ahead. They view dishonesty as a means of impressing their peers and gaining approval from their parents. They're not even convinced it's wrong, and they seldom see the negative consequences of deceit, nor the positive results of honesty. That's why they need to hear and understand the Test of Truth and the Evidence of Truth.

■ THE TEST OF TRUTH ■

"Honesty is praised," wrote Juvenal, the first-century Roman poet and satirist, "and starves." It is extolled by everyone as a virtue (though practiced, it often seems, by few).

But why is honesty praised? Why is it a virtue? What makes it right?

In order to determine that—according to the Test of Truth—we must ask, *How does it compare to the original?* We must measure it against the nature and character of God, the Source of truth. If we wish to gauge whether something (in this case, honesty) is right or wrong, we must trace it through precept to principle and, ultimately, to God Himself.

☐ PRECEPT

Thousands of years ago, God descended to a remote mountain in the Sinai peninsula and issued these commands:

> You shall not steal.
> You shall not give false testimony against your neighbor (Ex. 20:16–15).

In the course of His revelation to Moses, God reiterated, amplified, and applied those precepts:

> Do not steal.
> Do not lie.

170

Do not deceive one another.

Do not swear falsely. . . .

Do not defraud your neighbor or rob him (Lev. 19:11–13).

God made it abundantly clear to His people—by precept—that lying, cheating, and stealing were wrong.

God repeated the lesson throughout history. The Old Testament book of Joshua records how the Lord's anger burned against Israel because Achan stole plunder from Jericho; God said to Joshua, "They have stolen, they have lied, they have put them with their own possessions" (Josh. 7:11). Joshua, following God's instructions, discovered the crime, and Achan was stoned, and his home and family destroyed.

Over a thousand years later, a husband and wife teamed up to lie to the church, attempting to deceive the church leaders into thinking they were more generous than they were. The apostle Peter confronted Ananias (and later his wife, Sapphira), saying, "You have lied to the Holy Spirit. . . . You have not lied to men but to God" (Acts 5:3–4). Husband and wife both dropped dead at Peter's feet.

The dishonesty of Achan was an affront to God because it transgressed His precepts. Ananias and Sapphira sinned against God because they broke His law. But that is not the end of the story.

☐ PRINCIPLE

God's negative commands against lying, stealing, and cheating reflect a positive principle. This principle serves, like an umbrella, to protect all who stay within its boundaries.

That principle, of course, is honesty, the quality of being truthful, transparent, and trustworthy. In many ways, honesty is defined by what it will not do.

Honesty will not lie. "Therefore," the Bible says, "each of you must put off falsehood and speak truthfully to his neighbor" (Eph. 4:25).

Honesty will not cheat. "Do not be deceived," Paul warned, ". . . swindlers will [not] inherit the kingdom of God" (1 Cor. 6:10).

Honesty will not steal. It is the honest person's goal "not to steal . . . but to show that [he] can be fully trusted" (Titus 2:10).

"The Lord detests lying lips," Solomon wrote, "but he delights in men [and women] who are truthful" (Prov. 12:22).

But the principle of honesty does not possess intrinsic value; it is a virtue because it springs from the nature and character of God.

☐ PERSON

When my daughter Kelly was in fourth grade, several students in her class swiped an object off the teacher's desk while the teacher was out of the room. The children only wanted to play with the object, but it soon broke, and they returned it to its previous place on the teacher's desk.

When the teacher discovered the damage, she asked one of Kelly's classmates what had happened. The girl yielded to the pressure of the group and lied. Then the teacher asked Kelly. Kelly explained matter-of-factly what had happened.

The next day I took Kelly out for breakfast at the Rong Branch Cafe, a local restaurant, and I told her she'd done the right thing, in spite of any pressure or harassment she may get from her classmates.

"Honey," I then asked, "why is lying wrong?"

"Because the Bible says it's wrong," she answered.

"Why does the Bible say it's wrong?"

"Because God commanded it."

"Why did God command it?"

"I don't know," she admitted.

I took her hands in mine and locked eyes with her. "Because God is truth, Kelly. Truth comes from His nature, and whatever is contrary to God's nature is sin."

A moment ago I mentioned Achan, the Israelite warrior who took plunder from Jericho. Achan's action was offensive to God, not only because it transgressed God's law, but because it was contrary to God's nature. The deception of Ananias and Sapphira was a violation against God's character.

Honesty is right (and dishonesty wrong) because God is true. Truth is not something God does, nor is it something He possesses; it is a part of who He is. In the wilderness of Horeb, Moses sang, "He is the Rock, his work is perfect . . . a God of truth and without iniquity, just and right is he" (Deut. 32:4).

He is the "God who does not lie" (Titus 1:2). When God speaks a promise, Paul says, you may count on it, because "it is impossible for God to lie" (Heb. 6:18).

Though honesty may go begging on earth, as Juvenal said, there is an eternal, universal standard of truth that will not waver or change; "God must be true," the Bible says, "though every man be proved a liar" (Rom. 3:4, Revised English Bible).

Because God is true, lying is an offense against His nature. Because God is true, cheating is an affront to Him. Because God is true, stealing is an insult to Him. God is true, and there is nothing false in Him. It is His nature, therefore, that defines honesty as moral, and dishonesty, fraud, and theft as evil.

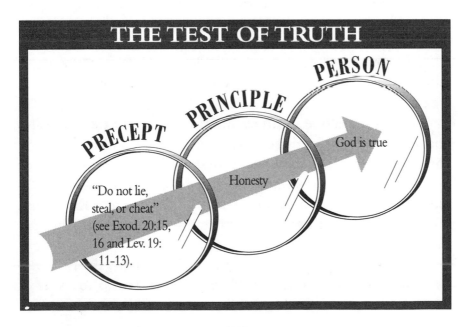

The Test of Truth grounds the virtue of honesty in the nature and character of God. Honesty is good and right—objectively and absolutely—because God is true. Dishonesty is evil and wrong—objectively and universally—because it is contrary to God's character. That is what makes dishonesty wrong—and honesty right—for all people, for all times, and for all places.

■ THE EVIDENCE OF TRUTH ■

The Test of Truth may help Philip Milford recognize that an objective standard for right and wrong exists, and that standard—God Himself—clearly says that Philip's cheating and lying are wrong. But Philip also needs to be walked through the Evidence of Truth (which his father began to do in their conversation at the ice-cream store).

Philip cheated because he had accepted several notions (which the Evidence of Truth will expose as counterfeits). He saw cheating as an easy way of getting ahead in school; he figured it would save him the trouble of studying, give him an edge on his fellow students, and pay the added bonus of making his father proud of him. When he was caught, of course, he compounded his problem by trying to lie to his father, because again he saw dishonesty as a possible way out of his problems. He thought it would be easier to lie than to face his father's anger. In each of his assumptions, of course, Philip was wrong—but not just because he got caught.

Philip is not alone in his assumptions. The research indicates that two out of every three (66 percent) of our children employ dishonest means to achieve their desires. That proportion holds true even among our youth who profess to have a personal relationship with Jesus Christ. Our youth are buying into the notion that lying and cheating are legitimate ways to get ahead; they are accepting the counterfeit that says dishonesty is the best policy.

James Milford has begun to help his children apply the Evidence of Truth (always in concert with the Test of Truth) to issues of honesty and integrity, exploring the answers to the question, *How does it correspond to reality?* In other words, he's investigating with his teenage son whether dishonesty achieves the things he thinks it will, and he's striving to impress on both Philip and Sarah a strong appreciation for the fact that honesty reflects God's nature and character. He is also working on his relationship with them and striving to be an example to them, while he helps them see that God's standards of honesty, far from holding them back in the world, can actually protect them and provide for them.

☐ 1. PROTECT FROM GUILT AND PROVIDE FOR A CLEAR CONSCIENCE

God's standards of honesty protect from guilt. In Edgar Allan Poe's classic short story, "The Telltale Heart," the narrator of the story tells how he killed a man, dismembered his body, and buried the remains beneath the floorboards of his room. But the clever concealment of his crime was ruined when three policemen inquired at his room. His guilt made him imagine he heard his victim's heart beating beneath the floor. In a rage, he confessed, and pointed the police to where the corpse was hidden.

"Their heart is deceitful," Hosea said of his countrymen, "and now they must bear their guilt" (Hos. 10:2). Guilt is among the most powerful of emotions, and it will cling to the dishonest heart like a python, choking the life out of its victim. "My guilt has overwhelmed me," confessed the psalmist David, "like a burden too heavy to bear" (Ps. 38:4). The burden of guilt deprives the dishonest soul of maximum enjoyment, satisfaction, and fulfillment.

The young man or woman who heeds God's standard of honesty will be protected from the burden of guilt. When you're honest, you don't always have to be looking over your shoulder. Of course, one's conscience can be seared by repeatedly doing wrong (1 Tim. 4:2). But even so, the consequences are always desctructive (Prov. 14:12).

God's standards of honesty provide a clear conscience, and an unbroken relationship with God. "Lord, who may dwell in your sanctuary?" asked the psalmist David. "Who may live on your holy hill? He whose walk is blameless and who does what is righteous, *who*

175

speaks the truth from his heart" (Ps. 15:1–2). Dishonesty cannot help but damage a person's walk with God, but the man or woman who "speaks the truth" will reap the reward of "clean hands and a pure heart" (Ps. 24:4) toward God.

☐ 2. PROTECT FROM SHAME AND PROVIDE FOR A SENSE OF ACCOMPLISHMENT

God's standards of honesty protect from shame. When Florence Griffith Joyner crossed the finish line of the women's 100-meter race in the '88 summer Olympic games in Seoul, Korea, she laid claim to the title of "the world's fastest woman." In those same Olympic games, another runner finished first and broke a world record. But Ben Johnson's victory was short-lived. He didn't know "Flo-Jo's" feeling of exhilaration and satisfaction, because a post-competition drug test revealed that Johnson's achievement was illegally aided by drugs. He was stripped of his medal and left Korea the next morning, in disgrace.

A habit of honesty can protect a person from the embarrassment and shame that results when their deception is discovered. After his teacher confronted him in the hallway about his cheating, Philip Milford protested, "I'm not going back in there where everybody will be staring at me." Stricken with shame, he was embarrassed to face his classmates.

God's standards of honesty provide a sense of accomplishment that the dishonest heart will never enjoy. Pastor Milford realized that he could use their miniature golf game to drive this point home. He told Philip, "Cheating would have robbed you of the satisfaction and sense of accomplishment you got from beating me fairly." Solomon said, "A fortune made by a lying tongue is a fleeting vapor and a deadly snare" (Prov. 21:6), not only because it entraps the person in a cycle of dishonesty, but also because its reward is short-lived; it evaporates like fog.

If Philip had not been caught cheating, he may have shown his test paper to his father, hoping for his approval, but he could have taken no genuine pride in his performance—because he had not earned it. His hunger for praise and approval would have continued unabated.

☐ 3. PROTECT FROM THE CYCLE OF DECEIT AND PROVIDE FOR A REPUTATION OF INTEGRITY

God's standards of honesty protect from entrapment in a cycle of deceit. To repeat Solomon's wise words, "A fortune made by a lying tongue is a fleeting vapor and a deadly snare" (Prov. 21:6). It is a snare because every lie breeds more lies, every deceit leads to more deceit. Like a person who paints himself into a corner, the dishonest heart is soon trapped by its own duplicity.

Richard Nixon's presidency was not destroyed by the Watergate break-in; it was ruined by the lies he told to cover it up. Then he ordered others to lie, and created more lies with the help of his aides. Eventually, the cover-up, not the break-in, cost him his presidency.

Adherence to God's standard of honesty saves a person from being snared in the web of their own deceit.

God's standards of honesty provide a reputation for integrity. Early in my relationship with Dottie, I told her, "I have something to say to you, and you don't need to respond, but I need to say it. I believe I'm in love with you." She began laughing.

"I don't think you heard me right," I said, very seriously. "I said I think I'm in love with you."

She pulled out a letter she had received from a Campus Crusade staff member. The author of the letter explained that she had heard Dottie was dating me. "Josh has a reputation for dating a lot of women," the letter read. "So be very careful. I don't want you to be hurt." The following paragraph, however, probably saved my relationship with my future wife. "But one thing that is true about Josh," it read; "He'll always be honest with you. He won't lead you on, and you'll always know where you stand with him."

I have been grateful ever since that the writer of that letter regarded me as a man of integrity. That is one of the blessings of heeding God's standard of honesty. "A good name is more desirable than great riches," the Bible says, "to be esteemed is better than silver or gold" (Prov. 22:1).

☐ 4. PROTECT FROM RUINED RELATIONSHIPS AND PROVIDE FOR TRUSTING RELATIONSHIPS

God's standards of honesty protect from ruined relationships. Several years ago, I sponsored a series of events called "fishbowls." Ten to fifteen teen volunteers came in and sat in a circle in the center of the room; they were surrounded by adults, who were permitted only to listen and observe. One of the objects was to let parents see firsthand the extent of the crisis our youth were facing.

In one such session, a fifteen-year-old girl started crying. "I'll never trust my mother again," she said.

I asked her why, and she explained, "I asked my mom two years ago if she and Dad had waited until marriage to have sex, and she said 'yes,' they had waited. The other day I found her diary and read it, and I found out she didn't wait. I found out she lied to me." Through tears of bitter disappointment, she vowed, "I'll never trust her again."

On another occasion, I was in England speaking to a group of youth directors. In the question-and-answer period following my talk, the subject turned to sexually transmitted diseases. One youth director approached me after the session and said he had told his wife he was a virgin when they were married. They had been married five years, and he'd recently learned from his doctor that he had Human Papilloma Virus (HPV). Since she had been a virgin at the time of their marriage, the disease was, of course, proof positive that he had lied to her for five years. He had to go home and tell his wife the belated truth; it turns out she also had HPV. That was over three years ago, and to this day, their relationship has not recovered.

There is nothing that will bring down a relationship any faster than deceit and dishonesty. God knew that—He invented relationships. The very foundation of relationships is built upon trust, and trust simply can't survive in the atmosphere of deceit.

God's standards of honesty provide for trust in relationships. On my first date with my wife, Dottie, I decided to buy a newspaper from a machine as we were coming out of a restaurant. I put my quarter in to get a paper; the paper came out, and so did my quarter. I asked Dottie to wait a minute. I took the quarter into the restaurant and gave it to the cashier before continuing our date.

I found out later that that incident had a profound effect on Dottie. She figured that if I could be trusted over the price of a newspaper, I was probably trustworthy in other areas. My honesty on that seemingly insignificant occasion won the respect of the woman who would become my wife, and laid a solid foundation of trust in our relationship.

I tell my children, "If you tell the truth all the time, I can believe you all the time. But if you only tell the truth some of the time, I can't believe you any of the time."

Solomon wrote, "Many a man proclaims his own loyalty, but who can find a trustworthy man . . . a righteous man who walks in his integrity [?]" (Prov. 20:6–7, NASB). The wise king also extolled the importance of trust in his song to the godly wife: "An excellent wife, who can find? . . . The heart of her husband trusts in her" (Prov. 31:10–11, NASB). As we have said, the element of trust is indispensable in building any successful, lifelong relationship. It undergirds marriage vows and business agreements with a reassuring, fortifying element. A strong foundation of trust will improve and enrich the quality of your relationships, providing something that money can't buy, and dishonesty can't achieve.

Once again, when our behavior conforms to God's standards, we can experience all the benefits of His protection and provision (see graphic, next page).

Philip didn't understand that when you accept a fake, there are consequences. He bought into the notion that lying and cheating

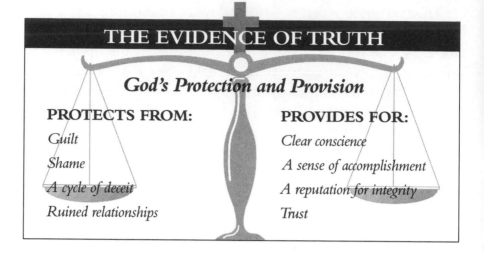

THE EVIDENCE OF TRUTH

God's Protection and Provision

PROTECTS FROM:

Guilt

Shame

A cycle of deceit

Ruined relationships

PROVIDES FOR:

Clear conscience

A sense of accomplishment

A reputation for integrity

Trust

are sometimes justified. But a thoughtful investigation of the Evidence of Truth about honesty reveals that his behavior didn't accomplish what it was supposed to. Instead of making things easier for him, his actions complicated his life. Full of guilt and shame, Philip had no true sense of accomplishment. Instead of making his father proud, he undermined their relationship. Instead of impressing people, he hurt his own reputation. Predictably, the counterfeit did not deliver what Philip thought it promised.

■ THE APPLICATION OF TRUTH ■

Many of our parents and grandparents practically cut their teeth on stories of Abraham Lincoln and George Washington that reinforced the value of honesty. Many of today's youth have never heard such moral tales. But we can still impart the value of honesty to today's youth.

■ **Play the "what if" game on trips with your family or youth group.** Ask youth to imagine how the world would be different if everyone in the world were absolutely honest (we wouldn't have to lock things up, chain things down, or install alarm systems, for example). Guide them from there into a discussion of how honesty protects and provides for us, to reinforce the evidence of the truth of honesty.

180

You may be surprised what a fun discussion like that will do. The next time your child locks a door, chains down a bicycle, or hears an alarm system go off, he or she will be reminded of the value of honesty. Use times like that to remind them that God is a true God, full of truth, and that when we are honest we honor Him as a God of truth.

■ **Use shopping trips to reinforce God's standard of honesty.** Let younger children pay the store cashier or insert the money in the vending machine, and take a moment to briefly discuss the Test of Truth and the Evidence of Truth with them. Guide older youth in a discussion of how stores must often compensate for shoplifting by raising prices and how that thwarts God's ideal.

■ **Give an "honesty bonus."** Try to "catch" your children being honest, so you can reward them. It need not be an heroic display of honesty; it could simply be paying a cashier the correct amount, or admitting that a chore has been neglected. Make it a habit to dispense appreciation and perhaps occasionally a small reward—such as one night of extended curfew or a one-time "bonus" in weekly allowance—to say, "I noticed your honesty."

■ **Use television, news, and current affairs to teach honesty.** Newscasts are full of practical illustrations of the consequences of dishonesty and the benefits of honesty. Discuss a news item or current event at school, work, or in the community that is negatively affected by dishonesty or benefited by honesty.

There are times, for example, when you and I prohibit our son or daughter from going somewhere alone or at night, and it often causes disappointment. Use such an opportunity to reinforce the high cost of dishonesty; if everyone were living by the principle of honesty, parents wouldn't have to be so protective.

It is not practical, of course, to expect to talk to our young people every day about honesty, sexual purity, or any other issue. If we seize every opportunity, however—when we sit at home, when we walk along the road, when we lie down and when we get up—we can continually reinforce the truth that living according to God's objective and absolute standards is both right and rewarding.

12

What's the Truth about Family?

GEENA SANTORO'S DAUGHTER met her at the airport with a wide smile.

"Your hair!" Geena exclaimed, as they hugged.

"Do you like it?" Melissa stepped back from her mother and lifted a hand self-consciously to her hair.

"It's so short," Geena stared at her daughter, trying to get used to her appearance.

"I got so tired of my hair, I finally decided to whack it all off. Do you like it?"

"Well, you're so beautiful, you'd look good even if you were bald," she said. Immediately, a thought occurred to her. "But don't get any ideas," she added. Her eyes widened and her distinctive laugh echoed through the terminal.

The two women claimed Geena's suitcase at the baggage carousel, and in less than an hour, they sat at Melissa's kitchen table, sipping tea.

Geena looked around the stark apartment. Stacks of boxes cluttered the tiny living room, which contained no furniture. The kitchen boasted a table and chairs, and the bedroom contained a single bed, empty bookshelf, and night stand.

"I still have stuff I need to pick up from Don," she explained. "I just haven't had time to get it from him. I've got a job," she announced cheerily.

Geena ignored her daughter's statement. "What about Don?" she asked.

The smile disappeared from Melissa's face. "What about Don?" she returned.

Geena's lips drew a thin, stern line across her face.

"I think the landlord is letting him stay in the house until he finds something else," Melissa answered. "Look, Mother, I know you're upset, but we went through all this on the phone, remember? Don and I just weren't meant to be together."

Geena leaned across the table. "You *married* him, Melissa!"

"Like you married my father?"

Geena straightened as if she had been punched in the jaw. A tense minute passed, in which neither woman spoke. Finally, without a word, Melissa arose from the table and left the room.

As she sat alone in the kitchen, her hands wrapped around a warm cup of tea, Geena shook her head. *I never could make her behave. She always had a mind of her own, and once she made it up, there was just nothing anyone could do.* She smiled ruefully.

She scooted her chair back from the table, and placed her teacup and saucer on the kitchen counter before leaving the room. She found her daughter sitting on the bed, her back against the wall. Geena leaned against the wall beside the dingy bedroom window, and gazed into the courtyard below. Scraggly bushes lined the pavement, and a child's tricycle lay abandoned on its side, its owner nowhere in sight.

"I didn't come here to argue with you," she told Melissa. *I never won an argument with you anyway,* she remembered. "I came because I wanted to be with you, and spend time with you, and let you know how important you are to me."

She turned away from the window and faced her daughter. "I've realized, Melissa, that I'm not responsible for you. It took God—and a real good friend—to help me understand that I'm responsible *to* you, but not *for* you. I want to be faithful to you, I want to show you a good example, I want to have a great relationship with you, and I want to be here for you to support you in all the tough choices you have to make."

Tears welled in Melissa's eyes. "I really need to know that Mom, and so does this one." Melissa patted herself just below the waistline.

Geena's eyes widened and her mouth dropped open.

Melissa nodded in answer to her mother's unspoken question. "I'm pregnant. Due in December."

"Oh, Melissa!" Geena exclaimed. "A Christmas baby!" She embraced her daughter and held her tight. The two women cried together.

Throughout the afternoon, Geena grilled Melissa about symptoms, obstetricians, and other details about her pregnancy. The dinner hour arrived before they had given a thought to food; they sipped coffee together and discussed dinner plans.

"Melissa," Geena finally ventured. "Does Don know about the baby?"

Melissa nodded and set her coffee mug down on the table. "I told him yesterday," she said.

"Does that change anything?" Geena asked cautiously.

"Not really. Of course, it changes a lot of things financially. But it doesn't mean we'll be getting back together, if that's what you mean."

Melissa seemed to read her mother's expression. "I know, Mother, it's not going to be easy raising a child alone. But I'm determined to make a good home for my child."

"I know you will, dear," Geena began, "but raising a child without a father . . . you know how hard it was not having your father around."

"Look, Mom, I'm going to love my child and it is going to love me, and we're going to be a great family with or without

Don. People do it all the time these days. I'm even thinking about having another single parent mother sharing my apartment—it will help with the load of single parenting."

Geena's expression wasn't reassuring to her daughter.

"Face it—it's not a perfect world, Mother. I'm not going to run out and get a man just because my child may need a father." She shrugged nonchalantly. "If it gets too bad, I'll just call 'Rent-a-Dad.'"

"'Rent-a-Dad?'" Geena asked. Her mouth hung open.

Melissa laughed. "I was kidding, Mother."

Geena sighed loudly. "You never know these days. They have so many new things nowadays, I thought that was just one I hadn't heard of yet."

Melissa laughed again. "You're a trip, Mom. Speaking of new things, how about going shopping? This place could use a few new things."

"That sounds great," Geena replied. She gathered the coffee mugs and rinsed them out in the sink. "I want to stop by the baby department. I want to be the first to get my grandbaby a new outfit."

□ □ □

Geena Santoro is finding out that it is important to develop and maintain a good relationship with her grown daughter. Melissa's concepts of marriage and family are already formed, of course, but if Geena can assimilate new ideas of truth and family, perhaps her daughter can too.

Our youth are growing up in a society which has attempted to reinvent marriage and redefine the family. Eighty percent of the children in the post-World-War-II generation grew up in "intact" families (two biological parents married to each other). By contrast, only 50 percent of the children born in the 80s could expect to grow up in an intact family. "If current trends continue," writes Barbara Dafoe Whitehead, "less than half of all children born today will live continuously with their own mother and father throughout childhood. . . . [and] an increasing number of

186

children will experience family breakup two or even three times during childhood."[1]

Like Melissa, the majority of our youth—churched youth— have bought into a counterfeit view of marriage and family. Over half of our youth define marriage and family in fluid, nebulous terms; eight in ten (79 percent) regard divorce as a potential way out of a loveless marriage, and seven in ten (69 percent) define family as "those who deeply care about you, or [whom] you deeply care about," "people living together," or "people sharing the same goals and values," definitions that require no commitment, no risk.

That's not to say that Melissa and her child will not be a family; single-parent homes are still families, but they are broken families. Nor is it to say that divorce destroys all traces of family togetherness; but it does create damage—for children *and* adults— that is not easily repaired—if ever. That may seem harsh, but it is impossible to completely avoid the tragic consequences of a broken marriage and family. There are steps a single parent can take to limit or repair the damage divorce causes, and we will cover them later in this chapter.

The best line of defense, of course, is in preventing such family tragedy in our lives and in our children's lives. And we do that by equipping ourselves and our youth with God's truth about marriage and family. If our youth possess strong moral convictions regarding marriage and family, those convictions can affect their decisions and make for better marriages and stronger families.

■ THE TEST OF TRUTH ■

A *Newsweek* magazine story responded to the "family values" debate in the 1992 U.S. presidential election with a fold-out cover that trumpeted: "*Whose* values? *Whose* family? *Who* makes the choices?" *Newsweek's* desperate questions echo Stephen L. Carter's dilemma: where are the "settled rules by which to determine . . . truth" in the areas of marriage and family?

Such "settled rules" do in fact exist, and we—and our youth—can discover them by applying the Test of Truth, by asking, *How does it compare to the original?*, by tracing attitudes and behaviors through precept to principle, and, ultimately, to the nature and character of God Himself.

☐ PRECEPT

In the first days of human life, in the dewy dawn of the Garden of Eden, God devised a wonderful plan for humanity. "It is not good for the man to be alone," He declared. "I will make a helper suitable for him." So God created them male and female, a man and a woman, suited for each other physically, emotionally, intellectually, and spiritually.

After relating the story of humanity's first appearance on the world stage, God's Word then adds one of the earliest precepts of Scripture:

> For this reason a man will leave his father and mother and be united to his wife, and they will become one flesh (Gen. 2:24).

God went on, in His Word, to further explain and amplify that first precept regarding marriage. Jesus, speaking specifically of the marriage commitment, added, "What God has joined together, let man not separate" (Mark 10:9). The apostle Paul, under the inspiration of the Holy Spirit, wrote, "To the married I give this command (not I, but the Lord): A wife must not separate from her husband. . . . And a husband must not divorce his wife" (1 Cor. 7:10–11).

God issued specific precepts regarding the family as well. He included the command to "Honor your father and mother" (Ex. 20:12) in the Decalogue. He instructed parents to train their children (Deut. 4:9), and teach them the fear of the Lord (Deut. 31:13). He commanded a loving, giving, respectful relationship between husbands and wives (Eph. 5:21–33). He instructed children to obey their parents, and fathers not to exasperate their children (Eph. 6:1–4).

Any study of God's precepts concerning marriage and the family will reveal that God intended our marital and familial relationships to be strong, loving, and lasting relationships.

☐ PRINCIPLE

Like all of God's precepts, His commandments regarding marriage and the family are intended to reflect a universal and eternal principle. The principle behind God's commands for marriage and family is unity. God's design for a husband and wife is evident in the words of Genesis 2:24: "a man will . . . be *united* to his wife, and they will become *one* flesh. God did not come up with that idea just to make for nice wedding ceremonies; in God's eyes, unity is the central element of the marriage relationship.

Similarly, God designed the family as a unity; an unbroken circle of strong, loving, lasting relationships; the primary unit of human society (Num. 1, e.g.); a hedge against loneliness (Ps. 68:6); a defense against poverty and affliction (1 Tim. 5:4–8); and an environment for child-rearing and education (1 Tim. 3:4).

God values unity. "How good and pleasant it is when brothers live together in unity!" the Bible says (Ps. 133:1). Jesus reminded His disciples of His desire to bring all people—not only the Jews—into His kingdom, so that there would be "*one* flock and one shepherd" (John 10:16). Scripture records Jesus' prayer that His disciples "may be *one*" (John 17:21), and God's Word advises His children to "Make every effort to keep the *unity* of the Spirit" (Eph. 4:3).

God's precepts concerning marriage and family are not thrown out willy-nilly, like a child creating a spatter-painting on a spinning wheel at the county fair; they are part of a positive, purposeful design, a design that is meant to reflect a principle: unity.

☐ PERSON

For century upon century, faithful Jews have begun their daily prayers by reciting the *shema*, the phrase Moses spoke to the Israelites after delivering the Ten Commandments to them:

Hear, O Israel: The LORD our God, *the LORD is one* (Deut. 6:4).

Those words are sacred to a Jew. Those are the words, written in Hebrew on tiny slips of paper, that orthodox Jews bind to their arms and foreheads in phylacteries, and attach outside the doors of their homes in a little box or cylinder called a *mezuzah* (in literal obedience to Deut. 6:8–9).

The *shema* reveals the singularity of God. There is no other God. "See now," God says in his Word, "there is no god besides me" (Deut. 32:39). "Before me no god was formed," He declares, "nor will there be one after me" (Isa. 43:10).

But the *shema* does not only refer to the singularity of God; it also testifies to His unity. Long before Jesus Christ was revealed to men and women as the Son of God, long before the Holy Spirit was given to the Church at Pentecost, God revealed Himself as a mysterious unity. Even the Hebrew Scriptures intimate the concept of a plural Godhead—yet within the Godhead existed also perfect unity. The Christian Scriptures reveal that God is Father, Son, and Holy Spirit (2 Cor. 13:14). Yet the *shema* makes it clear that God is not a partnership. He is not a conglomeration. He is not a committee. He is a *unity*: "Hear O Israel: The Lord our God, *the Lord is one*" (Deut. 6:4).

He cannot be separated. He cannot be divided. Unity is not something He strives for; it is not even something He achieves. It is something He *is*. "I and the Father are one," Jesus said. "Understand that the Father is in me, and I in the Father" (John 10:30, 38).

Unity is part of God's nature and character. He is one. And it is that unity that He wishes us to reflect in our marriages and family relationships. When the Bible says that a man and woman shall "be united . . . and . . . become one flesh" (Gen. 2:24), it is saying that marriage should reflect God's nature. When parents obey the divine command to "be fruitful and increase in number" (Gen. 1:28), the family should also reflect the unity that God values.

The test of truth grounds "family values" in the nature and character of God. Because God is one, disunity in a marriage or family is displeasing to Him. Because God is one, broken marriages and families do not reflect His standards. Because God is one, His nature defines marriage and family in lasting, lifelong terms. We can then say that unity in marriage and family is right for all people, for all times, for all places.

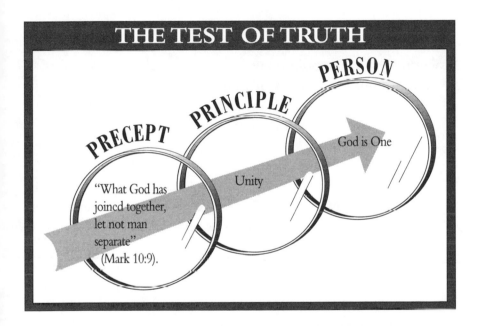

THE TEST OF TRUTH

PERSON

PRINCIPLE

PRECEPT

God is One

Unity

"What God has joined together, let not man separate" (Mark 10:9).

■ THE EVIDENCE OF TRUTH ■

God ordained the institutions of marriage and family not only to reflect His unity, but also, as I have said before, because He knew some things we didn't; He wanted to protect us and provide for us.

The research shows that less than half of our kids (48 percent) can say that they want "a marriage like that of my parents," and eight in ten (79 percent) see divorce as a viable solution to marital problems, regardless of whether children are involved. Less than half (47 percent) see the family as a crucial element of American society.

Yet, at the same time, 90 percent of our young people avow that "God intended marriage to last a lifetime." These numbers suggest that most of our children desperately need to understand how the Evidence of Truth supports God's standards for marriage and the family.

☐ 1. PROTECT FROM DISILLUSIONMENT AND PROVIDE FOR FULFILLMENT

God's standards for marriage and family protect from disillusionment. Brokenness and disappointment invariably result from attempts to short-cut biblical standards of marriage and family. Our youth who live together outside of marriage are setting themselves up to be disappointed—even if they "intend" to marry later.

One woman wrote:

> I wish I could tell every young adult in America that you truly will reap what you sow. Cohabitation may seem wonderful initially (sin is so deceiving!), but eventually it creates more problems than you can imagine.
>
> I lived with my boyfriend for two years before we got married. I knew I was breaking my parents' hearts, as well as my Heavenly Father's heart! My boyfriend was not a Christian, but I figured I could change him if we moved in together.
>
> The "this-is-yours, that-is-mine" mentality that enabled us to "successfully" live together completely unraveled once we got married. We had become too separate and too selfish, making it nearly impossible to become "one flesh." The honeymoon was over before the wedding day ever arrived.[2]

Notice that the author of that letter was a professing Christian when she moved in with her boyfriend! She hoped to evangelize him by living with him outside of marriage. Like too many of our children, she accepted a counterfeit (cohabitation) for the real thing (marriage).

In his 1993 book, *The Future of the American Family*, George Barna says, "Cohabiting has increased 1888 percent among eighteen- to twenty-four-year-olds in the last three years." Many of those cohabiting couples see living together as a sort of "trial marriage." But they are deceived.

"The National Survey of Families and Households," conducted by University of Wisconsin researchers, reveals that two-fifths of couples who live together break up within 1.3 years—before they get married. Those who *do* marry after cohabiting are 50 percent more likely to divorce than those who don't cohabit before marriage. In other words, the "conventional wisdom" that views cohabitation as a trial marriage is flat-out wrong; living together does not prevent mistakes nor increase one's chances of building a successful marriage. Quite the opposite.

Moreover, compromising biblical standards can be physically dangerous—especially to women. A Justice Department study reported that cohabiting women are sixty-two times (520 percent) more likely to suffer from assault as wives. Apparently, says religion columnist Michael McManus, "Men respect wives [more than they do] live-in lovers."

God's standards for marriage and family provide for fulfillment. Married life is not necessarily easy. Husbands and wives argue, dishes get dirty, laundry piles up, children struggle at school— family life can be complex and exhausting. But when a man and woman are "united . . . and . . . become one flesh" (Gen. 2:24), they can experience a unity that can weather the storms and bring intimacy and fulfillment in their relationship.

☐ 2. PROTECT FROM PARENTAL INATTENTION AND PROVIDE FOR
PARENTAL INVOLVEMENT

God's standards for marriage and family protect from parental inattention. I do most of the traveling in my family. I fly off to distant cities and foreign lands, while my wife keeps the home and family running smoothly. Not long ago, however, the tables were turned; Dottie went on an extended trip and I was left at home. It was my responsibility to not only keep up with my work, but to make sure my children got to school on time, to ferry them to sports events, to make sure they were fed, had clean clothes, and had their homework done. Some days, it seemed I had forty children (instead of four) and that I would never have enough time for them all.

That is the very situation many single parents must deal with daily. They strive not only to provide economically for their children, but to run a home, attend parent-teacher meetings, and, if any time is left, to read their little ones a story at the end of the day. Divorced parents who are remarried face incredible obstacles as well; some must squeeze all their parenting into weekends, or a few months out of the year. Ultimately, no matter how hard a parent tries, the child of a broken family usually gets less of his parents' attention and affection, simply because there are not enough hours in the day for one parent to be both mother and father. Nor can one parent be two places at once, giving attention to more than one household of children or step-children.

Children of broken families suffer in various ways from this inattention. Barbara Dafoe Whitehead writes:

> Not only do children experience a loss of parental attention at the onset of divorce, but they soon find that at every stage of their development their parents are not available in the same way they once were. "In a reasonably happy family," [Judith] Wallerstein observes, "the child gravitates first to one parent and then to the other, using skills and attributes from each in climbing the developmental ladder." In a divorced family, children find it "harder to find the needed parent at needed times."[3]

As much as a parent may strive to overcome such effects of family disruption, they cannot completely negate them. As I have stated before, God's standards are like an umbrella, and when— for whatever reason—we move out from under that umbrella, we no longer benefit from its protection. The more we can help our youth understand the Evidence of Truth, therefore, the more they will understand why a lifetime commitment of marriage is in the best interests of parents and children.

God's standards for marriage and family provide for greater parental involvement. Those ten or twelve days in which I had to manage my home and family while my wife was away not only renewed my appreciation for her, but revived my gratitude for God's wisdom in providing "a helper suitable for [each of us]" (Gen. 2:18).

My wife's contribution to our family does not only provide two more hands, making it possible for me to take Katie to a concert while she helps Heather with her homework; she can answer questions that I cannot, and offer a perspective that I lack. That is part of God's wise plan. Our union enables us to be much more involved with our children—what they're doing, what they're thinking, what they're feeling, what they're planning—than either of us could manage alone. When we help our kids see the specific roles that each parent plays in their lives, they can better understand why God intended married partners to remain married.

☐ 3. PROTECT FROM EMOTIONAL INSECURITY AND PROVIDE FOR EMOTIONAL STABILITY

God's standards for marriage and family protect from emotional insecurity. A 1988 study by the National Center for Health Statistics revealed that children in single-parent families are two to three times as likely to experience emotional and behavioral problems than children of two-parent families. They are more likely to drop out of high school, to use drugs, and to get in trouble with the law. Girls in single-parent families are more likely to be sexually active, and are more likely to become pregnant as teens, and to give birth outside of marriage.

Judith Wallerstein, director of the California Children of Divorce Study, reported that children whose parents have divorced suffer the emotional effects for years after the event. More than a third still experience moderate or severe depression five years after the breakup. Ten years later, many continued to struggle, wander, or falter through life. Even fifteen years later, many of the subjects of Wallerstein's study exhibited the effects of the childhood trauma of divorce.[4]

Novelist Pat Conroy has said that "each divorce is the death of a small civilization." No one feels that loss more keenly than children. God wanted to protect our children from the emotional insecurity that results from divorce when he said, "What God has joined together, let man not separate" (Mark 10:9).

God's standards for marriage and family provide for emotional stability. Children need to know there are certain things they can always count on. They need stable and constant patterns in their lives. They need that sense of security that says "God's in His heaven, all's right with the world."

Adherence to God's standard for marriage and family provides that kind of stability. It fosters feelings of consistency and permanence. It helps them to know who they belong to, who belongs to them, who they can trust, and what their lives will be like tomorrow. That sense of belonging—a feeling of being accepted by other people, a sense of being part of a relationship, the realization of being loved for who we are—is among the most basic human needs. A marriage and a family that are founded on God's standard of unity provide for the emotional stability of children *and* adults, a blessing longed for by many of our friends and loved ones in our society—and in our churches.

□ 4. PROTECT FROM RELATIONAL PROBLEMS AND PROVIDE FOR HEALTHY ROLE MODELS

God's standards for marriage and family protect from relational problems. Research reveals that many children of broken marriages and disrupted families face severe relational problems, not only as children, but throughout their lives. Many find it difficult to achieve intimacy in a relationship, to build long-lasting love relationships, or to form a solid marriage. Some even find it hard to hold a steady job. Most of these studies invariably conclude that these children suffer from "adolescent alienation"—a relational disconnectedness from adults.

Such difficulties are not due only to marital separation and divorce, but also to the events that led to and followed the break-up. Divorce is not an isolated event; it is generally preceded by disagreements, arguments, even unfaithfulness. And it is often followed by new boyfriends or girlfriends, live-in partners, step-parents, and new "siblings." All of these, combined with the absence of one natural parent from the household, can create a breeding ground for a child to feel alienated that results in relational confusion and distress. Many children carry such scars well into their adulthood.

God's standards for marriage and family provide for healthy role models. An intact family of a husband and wife who display a loving, giving, respectful relationship provides an invaluable resource for children. When my daughter Kelly was much younger, I said to her, "Kelly, do you know that I love your mother?"

"Yeah," she answered. "I know it."

"How do you know?"

"Because you always tell her."

"What if I lost my voice and couldn't tell her? How would you know then?"

"Because you always kiss her."

"What if I got chapped lips and couldn't kiss her? Then how would you know?"

Kelly thought for a moment. "Because of the way you treat her," she answered.

That's the answer I was looking for, because it told me that I was modeling a loving relationship between a man and a woman. My children will benefit for the rest of their lives from my wife's model of womanhood; she has given my daughters a model to strive for, and my son a model to look for in a woman. Dottie and I together have modeled what a loving, respectful male-female relationship should look like.

197

God's standard of unity in marriage and family relationships extends His gracious protection and provision to those who heed it:

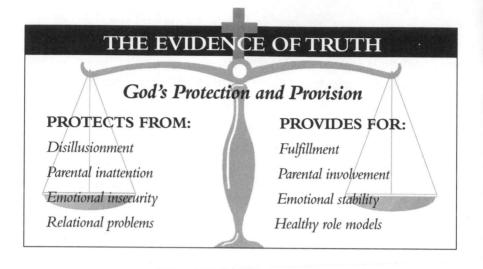

THE EVIDENCE OF TRUTH

God's Protection and Provision

PROTECTS FROM:

Disillusionment

Parental inattention

Emotional insecurity

Relational problems

PROVIDES FOR:

Fulfillment

Parental involvement

Emotional stability

Healthy role models

■ IS THERE AN ANSWER FOR MELISSA? ■

As sociologist Don Popenoe says (in the cautious language of the social scientist):

> In three decades of work as a social scientist, I know of few other bodies of data in which the weight of evidence is so decisively on one side of the issue: on the whole . . . two-parent families are preferable to single-parent and stepfamilies.[5]

The evidence *is* overwhelming, and we may be able to make a convincing case to a young person not yet married. But what about people in situations like Geena's or Melissa's? Are there any answers for those trying to raise children in a single parent home? Regardless of whether the situation has been caused by divorce or from the death of a spouse, a single parent faces a daunting task.

There are some answers. There are positive steps a single parent can take. God said He was "a father to the fatherless and a judge for the widows" (Ps. 68:5, NASB). God loves those who are without parents or spouses too. And there is another living model of unity that can provide some answers for those from broken families.

Scripture instructs husbands to "love your wives, just as Christ also loved the church and gave Himself up for her. . . . He who loves his own wife loves himself; for no one ever hated his own flesh, but nourishes and cherishes it, just as Christ also does the church, because we are members of His body" (Eph. 5:25–30, NASB). God's will is for His unity to be expressed in the family; but He has also chosen to reveal His oneness in the institution of the church—His body. Just as a man and woman shall leave mother and father and become one flesh (Eph. 5:31), so Christ has become one with the church—His body.

Paul the Apostle said, "This mystery is great," when referring to the oneness of Christ and the church. The person who trusts Christ as Savior is adopted into a living family, a family that is intended to reflect the unity of God Himself. Jesus Christ promised to send the Holy Spirit, so that we may experience unity; so that "all of [us] may be one . . . [that we may] be brought to complete unity" (John 17:21, 23).

The single parent who becomes involved in the local body of Christ, a local church, can experience—and expose his or her children to—a living, thriving family that can compensate, in some ways, for the loss of a husband, wife, father, or mother. "For by one Spirit we were all baptized into one body, whether Jews or Greeks, whether slaves or free, and we were all made to drink of one Spirit . . . God has so composed the body, giving more abundant honor to that number which lacked, that there should be no division in the body, but that the members should have the same care for one another. And if one member suffers, all the members suffer with it; if one member is honored all the members rejoice with it. Now you are Christ's body, and individually members of it" (1 Cor. 12:13; 24–27, NASB).

Do you see God's plan? He wants each of us to suffer when another suffers—to rejoice when another rejoices. He wants us to "bear one another's burdens." A vibrant, caring body of believers can be a support through the tough times, and can enable parent and child to experience God's unity as well.

If you're a single parent, you and your child may have felt the disillusionment, emotional insecurity, and disconnectedness that often comes from being orphaned and widowed by divorce or the death of a spouse. Find a caring church—a vibrant body of believers—and immerse yourself and your child in that fellowship. I know multitudes of broken families that have found a great degree of healing, emotional stability, and an overwhelming sense of belonging as they have experienced the oneness that the unity of the body provides.

■ THE APPLICATION OF TRUTH ■

Our children desperately need to see the values of marriage and family in terms of the Test of Truth (which grounds the virtue of unity in the nature and character of God) and in light of the Evidence of Truth (which confirms that marital and familial unity and stability is the safest and surest route to happiness and fulfillment for parents and children alike). But how do we apply the truth to our youth? What can we do to get the message across?

- **Encourage your youth's involvement in youth group.** A healthy and vibrant youth group is an important part of a young person's life—especially for a child from a single-parent home. Meet with your church youth worker and share the progress of your child's spiritual and emotional growth. Ask your youth worker what you can do to better support your child and the entire youth group. Youth workers need you and you need them. Let them know of good programs and resources that are available (see Resource Section on page 327.)

- **Take advantage of adult small group studies and meetings.** Join a small group that is biblically based, one that focuses on helping you in your parenting responsibilities. Some churches have single-parent small groups. Ask your group leader what programs and courses will be covered over the next twelve months. Make them aware of the excellent parenting studies that are available (see Resource Section on page 327). Of course, this book is part of a parent video series; it is an excellent way to begin a church-wide emphasis on instilling biblical values within our youth.

- **Pull out your wedding album.** You may be surprised at how fascinated your children are—even teenagers—by the story (and pictures) of your wedding. Pull out the wedding photos and use them as a way to share your deep convictions about marriage, the vows you made to your spouse, and how that commitment stands today. Sharing stories of your courtship and marriage—and how honoring marriage has resulted in God's protection and provision in your life—will reinforce your child's convictions on marriage and family.

- **Talk of your children's births.** Whether you are five, fifteen, or fifty, hearing about the details of the day you were born is always fascinating. Use that fascination to provide your child a greater sense of belonging. Emphasize to your children the fact that they came from the union of your love for your mate. Explain how they have inherited distinct characteristics and features from each of you. The more they have a sense of their heritage, the more connected they will feel to the unity of the family.

- **Openly communicate your love to your spouse.** Take advantage of every opportunity to let your children know how much you love your mate. Be affectionate with each other around them. The more you show them how much you are devoted to your mate, the more secure they will feel. Kisses, roses, special dates, favorite meals—there are a hundred and one ways to openly demonstrate before your children how you love each other. My kids love it when I involve them in helping me plan a special meal or surprise that demonstrates my love and appreciation for my wife; their participation also increases their awareness of—and confidence in—our loving commitment to each other.

- **Use opportunities presented by television, news, and current events.** Use movies or news events of divorces or pending marriages as topics of discussion. Rather than condemning a person who has suffered a divorce, talk about the protection and provision they will be missing. If you know the person, discuss how you and your children can be supportive and helpful. Using current events can be an ideal way to discuss the negative consequences of violating God's standard of unity in marriage and family and a good way to point out the positive rewards of living in obedience to that standard.

God's truth about marriage and family is absolute—it is for all people, for all times, and for all places. Take the time to diligently teach the Test of Truth and the Evidence of Truth about marriage and family "to your sons (and daughters) and talk of them when you sit in your house and when you walk by the way and when you lie down and when you rise up . . . And you shall do what is right and good in the sight of the LORD, that it may be well with you . . ." (Deut. 6:7, 18, NASB). Instill God's value of marriage and family in your children and they will reap rewards for generations to come.

13

What's the Truth about Other Truths?

PASTOR JAMES MILFORD opened his front door. Penny Marsh stood alone on the step.

"Come in, Penny," he said. He stepped aside, and she entered the room. A crowd of people lined the couch and chairs; several sat on the floor, and Geena Santoro stood in the doorway between the living room and dining room.

The pastor closed the door and turned to face the crowd.

"I hadn't realized this group had grown so large," he said. The worship attendance at Westcastle Community Church had dwindled since Pastor Milford had related his discovery of the Test of Truth and the personal renewal he had been undergoing since coming to terms with his own inconsistencies. But this group, which had been meeting weekly to discuss their efforts to equip their children with biblical values, had grown from eight to between twenty and thirty parents.

"I want to thank you all for agreeing to meet here today," Pastor Milford continued. "I explained to some of you on the phone that just yesterday we moved my father-in-law out of a nursing home and into the spare bedroom, and Diane didn't want to miss this meeting, but she didn't want to leave him just yet, either.

"We'll have a lot of adjustments to make in the next few weeks, and we're going to be strapped financially, but we decided we could best fulfill our responsibility to Dad by having him be a part of our household. And I've only recently begun to realize how much my son and daughter can benefit from the daily influence of a godly grandfather. Frail though he may be, he may help our family counter the culture more successfully than we have in the past."

Betty Todd spoke up. She sat on the end of the couch. "I think you'll find that your children will learn a lot about family, too, and family responsibility. My Buster helped take care of my mother the last couple years of her life; I think he learned a lot through the experience."

Pastor Milford smiled and nodded at Betty. He clapped his hands together and asked if anyone in the group wished to share their experiences of the past week. He explained to the two or three newcomers to the group that they ordinarily spent much of their time discussing how they have been trying to teach the Test of Truth and the Evidence of Truth to their children, and what results, if any, they have seen.

"I just got back Thursday from visiting Melissa," Geena Santoro said. "I never thought *I'd* be tired of talking, but I'm so glad I went." She exchanged smiles with her friend, Beth McConnell, who sat on a folding chair beside the piano. "I even had lunch with Don." She began to relate, with characteristic energy, the details of her visit and Melissa's pregnancy, prompting numerous smiles and bursts of laughter with her effusive personality. She finished seriously, however, with a sigh of resignation. "I don't think they'll ever be reconciled, but I feel a little better about Melissa. And I think I helped her make connections with a wonderful little church that might help her through it all; they even have a small group for single parents, so I'm excited about that. I'd like to ask prayer that she and the baby will be able to experience and appreciate God's unity in the future . . . better than she has in the past."

Pastor Milford nodded. With no announcement or fanfare, several in the group closed their eyes; DeVonne Davis began praying aloud. Her prayer was followed quickly by an impassioned prayer by Doug Withers. By the time the people in the crowded room lifted their heads and opened their eyes, the room seemed to crackle with electricity.

Pastor Milford, sitting cross-legged on the floor by the front door, waited for a few moments before speaking. He drew a deep breath. "Philip and I have come a long way already in our relationship. Little by little, he's opening up to me and beginning to trust me.

"And Diane and I have been trying to use every opportunity to communicate the Test of Truth and the Evidence of Truth to him. We watched the Braves play the Cubs on TV together the other night, and the umpire made a call that Philip didn't agree with." He smiled broadly. "He was jumping up and down in the middle of the family room as if *he'd* been called out at home. When he calmed down, I asked him if he realized why he'd gotten so indignant. He said, 'no.'

"I said, 'You thought the umpire made the wrong call, didn't you?'

"He said, 'He did! The catcher never tagged him.'

"'So what?' I said. That's when the lights came on in his eyes, and he saw what I was getting at.

"'Because it's not fair, that's why,' he answered. Then he went on to explain to me, just like I've explained to him, why injustice is wrong. I had to help him identify some of the biblical precepts forbidding injustice, but after that he identified the principle of justice and took it right back to the nature of God, identifying injustice as wrong because God is just.

"We spent the rest of the game munching on chips and salsa and relating the Evidence of Truth to justice. It was wonderful."

One of the group asked how Philip was responding.

Lines of concern wrinkled the pastor's brow. "He understands," he said, pointing to his head. "He can process the Test of Truth and the Evidence of Truth almost as well as I can. He can see it pretty clearly now—which is a big change from a month or two ago—but I'm still waiting for him to show me that he's willing to make right choices."

"Sometimes our kids will go their own way no matter what," Beth McConnell said.

"I have some really good news to report." Every head in the room turned to Penny Marsh, who had been sharing a hassock with Diane Milford. "I've been really desperate to help Brittney," she started, "and I've pretty much had to do it alone; Gary's really struggling with all this stuff. Anyway, some things have happened recently that have really helped Brittney to see that God's standards are really for her good, and I've just constantly been pointing out to her the good things God wants to give her.

"We were up until three in the morning one night talking about her relationships and what she wants, what she's looking for in a man, what God wants for her . . ." Penny rifled through her purse and withdrew a tissue; she had started crying.

"Anyway," she said, dabbing her eyes and fighting to control her emotions, "to make a long story short, she broke up with her boyfriend this week. She said she wants to wait for God's best for her!"

She dabbed her eyes again, and her voice trembled, but she smiled when she spoke. "You know what's funny? I am so glad, in a way, that we've gone through this with Brittney, because now I'll be able to really help Lauren and Michael—they're eleven and seven—develop some good, strong values." Her eyes welled with tears again. "I haven't been this hopeful about my kids in years."

Diane Milford stretched an arm around Penny's shoulder and pulled her close.

Without warning, one of the group launched into prayer again, a prayer of praise to God for what He was accomplishing in and through each person in the room. That first prayer was followed by several others; prayer after prayer focused on God, and His nature: His glory, His mercy, His love, His purity, His unity. The prayers were punctuated with tears, occasional laughter, and songs of praise and worship. Minute after minute ticked by on the clock, and still the praying continued, with no one squirming, no one checking a watch; every mind in the room was caught up in the Spirit of God, in submitting to Him and worshiping Him, in reverential fear and love.

The spoken prayers and singing stopped, and the group lingered in silence that seemed charged with the presence of God. Finally, Geena Santoro broke the silence.

"God, I want to thank You for what all this has done for me." Her eyes were moist, but her quiet voice did not waver. "It's given me a new vision of You, a new reverence for you. All this has helped me recognize that You are as the Source of everything, You are the Source of all that I have, of everything good. And it's made me realize how far I had drifted from You, how my thinking—and living—had shifted away from You, and how much I need You. I need Your purity, I need Your holiness, I need Your faithfulness— I need You so much in my life. *I need You.*" She stopped, and then repeated those three words with a burning intensity. *"I need You."*

□ □ □

Geena and the others at Westcastle Community Church have begun applying the Test of Truth and the Evidence of Truth to the values of chastity, honesty, and family. But they have begun to go beyond those areas, applying the truth to other biblical values as well. James and Diane Milford, for example, used the opportunity presented by a bad call in a baseball game to discuss the biblical value of justice with their son, Philip. They have also discovered, as Geena related, that when we begin to apply ourselves and our lives to the truth, we may also recover a biblical "fear of the Lord," a renewed vision of the God who is our Source.

■ MORE BIBLICAL VALUES ■

What other biblical values should we communicate to youth? We should teach them to value chastity, and honesty, and unity in marriage and family; but are there other values to which we should apply the Test of Truth and the Evidence of Truth?

The four "Cardinal Virtues" formulated by the medieval church were prudence, justice, temperance, and fortitude. William J. Bennett categorized the stories and essays in his bestseller, *The Book of Virtues*, according to a list of ten virtues. Linda and Richard Eyre's excellent book, *Teaching Your Children Values*, cited more than a dozen values (some of which are expressed in complementary pairings, such as "fidelity and chastity") that parents should pass on to their children.

For the purposes of this book, we will show the Test of Truth and the Evidence of Truth at work through five more biblical values (in addition to the three—chastity, honesty, and family unity—we have already covered in previous chapters) that form the basis of character and the backbone of society. These values will not be dealt with as extensively as we have treated the values of chastity, honesty, and family unity. Nonetheless, using the Test of Truth and the Evidence of Truth to teach these values to our children will equip them to make right choices in many important areas.

■ WHAT'S THE TRUTH ABOUT LOVE? ■

Love, it has been said, is the universal language. It is extolled everywhere, by everyone, as the pinnacle of virtue. "What the world needs now," Dionne Warwick sang, "is love, sweet love." The Beatles claimed, "All you need is love." Michael Bolton contended, "Love is a wonderful thing." It is, of course, a wonderful thing. But why? Why is love a virtue?

■ THE TEST OF TRUTH ABOUT LOVE ■

☐ PRECEPT

An accomplished rabbi once posed a question to Jesus that many rabbis before him had debated. "Teacher," he said, "which is the greatest commandment in the Law?"

208

"'Love the LORD your God',"Jesus answered, "'with all your heart and with all your soul and with all your mind.' This is the first and greatest commandment. And the second is like it: 'Love your neighbor as yourself'" (Matt. 22:37–39).

The greatest precept in the law, according to Jesus, is the command to love. He even went so far as to say, "Love your enemies and pray for those who persecute you, that you may be sons of your Father in heaven" (Matt. 5:44–45).

The precept is clear; love—for God, for our spouses, for our neighbors, even for our enemies—is commanded. "This is the message we have heard from the beginning," according to the apostle John. "We should love one another" (1 John 3:11).

☐ PRINCIPLE

Like all precepts, these commands point to a principle: love for God and love for others. The principle is larger than the precept. We might dodge or circumvent the precept by clever maneuvering, the way we might take advantage of a loophole in the tax law; but we cannot avoid the principle. Regardless of whether a specific precept addresses a certain decision or behavior, the principle of love for God and others dictates whether our actions are right or wrong, because love is a principle God values.

☐ PERSON

Ultimately, of course, love is a virtue not simply because it is commanded, nor even because it is a principle God values, but because God is like that. The precept and the principle both point to the person of God Himself. "God is love" (1 John 4:16b). He loves us "with an everlasting love" (Jer. 31:3). He loves us so much that He gave His son to die for us (John 3:16). He loves us so much that, while we were still sinners—displaying enmity toward God—Christ died for us (Rom. 5:8). He is the kind of God who loves even those who curse Him, because love is His nature. It is not something He does, it is something He is.

There can be no disputing the fact that love is a virtue, because the Test of Truth grounds love in the nature and character of God. We can then say that love for God and others is right—for all people, for all times, for all places.

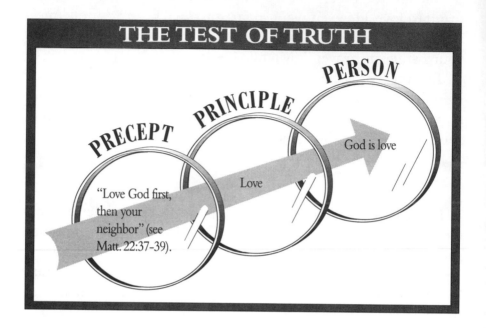

THE TEST OF TRUTH

PRECEPT · PRINCIPLE · PERSON

"Love God first, then your neighbor" (see Matt. 22:37-39).

Love

God is love

■ THE EVIDENCE OF TRUTH ABOUT LOVE ■

Few people would argue with the notion that love is right. Yet many harbor hatred in their hearts, or nurse grudges, or keep an eternal flame of resentment burning against someone who has slighted them or hurt them—and they justify such behavior as being perfectly reasonable! But the Evidence of Truth is nowhere clearer than in this area.

☐ 1. PROTECT FROM STRIFE AND PROVIDE FOR PEACE

God's standards of love protect from strife and provide for peace. I grew up hating my father. Everyone in our small town knew about my father and his drinking. My teenage buddies made jokes about him, and I laughed, too, hoping my laughter would hide my pain. Sometimes I'd go out to the barn and find my mother lying in the manure behind the cows, beaten so badly she couldn't get up. Sometimes when he came home in a drunken stupor, I would drag him out to the barn, tie him to a stall, and leave him there to "sleep it off." As a teenager, I would tie his feet with a noose that ended around his neck, hoping he would choke himself while trying to get free.

My hatred for my father was consuming; it filled my life and robbed me of peace. Not long after becoming a Christian, though, I not only reconciled with my father, I helped him trust Christ for salvation. Fourteen months later, he died of a heart attack, but I had learned what love can do, even in the most desperate situation. Fourteen months of loving my father did much more for me than twenty years of hating him had ever done.

☐ 2. PROTECT FROM SELF–CENTEREDNESS AND PROVIDE FOR FULFILLMENT

God's standards of love protect from self-centeredness and provide for fulfillment. I know a woman who evaluates every conversation, every relationship, every event of her life in terms of how it affects her. She suffers from what I call "I disease." Though she has some friends and acquaintances, she has not really learned to love any of them. She loves only herself. And it shows.

Dr. S. I. McMillen, in his book, *None of These Diseases*, quotes an internationally known psychiatrist, Alfred Adler, as saying:

The most important task imposed by religion has always been, "Love thy neighbor . . ." It is the individual who is not interested in his fellow man who has the greatest difficulties in life and provides the greatest injury to others. It is from among such individuals that all human failures spring.[1]

The person who loves God and others expresses interest in the ideas and pursuits of others, often enjoys giving as much as receiving, and finds joy in sharing with others and caring for them. Such a person naturally tends to be more appreciated and successful than the self-centered individual.

☐ 3. PROTECT FROM SPIRITUAL BARRENNESS AND PROVIDE FOR SPIRITUAL BLESSING

God's standards of love protect from spiritual barrenness and provide for spiritual blessing. The first-century writings of John the Apostle bluntly state, "Anyone who does not love remains in death. Anyone who hates his brother is a murderer, and you know that no murderer has eternal life in him" (1 John 3:14b–15). Such strong language communicates the tragic spiritual consequences God wants to protect us from; that is why He commands us to love. He wants to protect us from the barrenness of an unloving soul and provide the spiritual blessings that spring from "the most excellent way" (1 Cor. 12:31) of love.

These are, of course, not the only Evidences of Truth, but they do indicate God's protection and provision through obedience to the command to love one another.

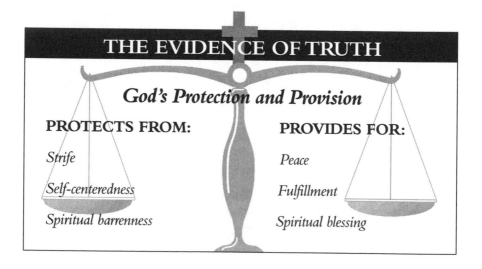

THE EVIDENCE OF TRUTH

God's Protection and Provision

PROTECTS FROM:

Strife

Self-centeredness

Spiritual barrenness

PROVIDES FOR:

Peace

Fulfillment

Spiritual blessing

■ THE APPLICATION OF TRUTH ABOUT LOVE ■

We may be tempted to think that love will come naturally to our youth—that they will inevitably develop familial love, romantic love, or love for God. But healthy love, like any other value, must be taught; its value must be traced back to the nature of God by using the Test of Truth, and its benefits must be shown through the Evidence of Truth. There are, of course, many practical ways to do this, a few of which follow.

- **Display love for God in your family.** Before your younger children leave for school, ask them, "How can we show our love for God today?" Interpret church traditions and sacraments as means of expressing love for God. Remind your youth occasionally, when the offering plate is passed during worship, that your giving is one way you show love for God.

- **Model love in front of your children.** Young people learn what love should look like from their family; give them positive models of romantic love, parent-child love, brother-sister love, love for neighbors, love for "enemies," etc. Point out to them the ways you show your love for them, your spouse, an elderly neighbor, a co-worker.

- **Recognize and reinforce loving habits,** and interpret them to your youth as reflections of God's nature. Learn to use statements like, "You remind me of God when you show love to your brother," or "The way you treated Mrs. Sparks made me think of God's love."

- **Rent the movie, "Fiddler on the Roof," and watch it with your children.** Discuss the different kinds of love displayed in the movie. Ask how it differs from the ways your family expresses love. Pause the tape after the song, "Do You Love Me?" and ask what they think the message of the song is.

- **Evaluate prime-time television depictions of love (romantic and otherwise) with your teenage children.** Guide them through the Evidence of Truth to determine if the "love" depicted on the screen accomplishes what true love ought to accomplish.

213

■ WHAT'S THE TRUTH ABOUT JUSTICE? ■

How do you react when another driver races to the head of a long line of traffic and noses ahead of you in line? How do you feel when your boss takes credit for your ideas? What do you think when your bank slaps a penalty on you for an overdraft caused by their mistake?

If you're like most people, you react by saying, "That's not fair!" You—and everyone who appeals to what is fair and what is unfair—are appealing to a standard of justice that you think everyone ought to know and accept. That's what Philip Milford did when he protested the umpire's call in the baseball game he watched with his father; he appealed to the value of justice.

■ THE TEST OF TRUTH ABOUT JUSTICE ■

☐ PRECEPT

The Bible abounds with precepts like, "Defend the cause of the weak and fatherless; maintain the rights of the poor and oppressed" (Ps. 82:3), "Give everyone what you owe him" (Rom. 13:7), and "Masters, provide your slaves [employees] with what is right and fair" (Col. 4:1). The Law of Moses contained detailed commands to treat strangers and foreigners fairly, to provide for orphans and widows, even to return stray animals to one's enemies. These precepts—specific, practical applications of truth—can be summed up in what has been called "the Golden Rule": "Do to others as you would have them do to you" (Luke 6:31).

☐ PRINCIPLE

Such behavior is basic morality, reflected in the principle of justice. God instructed the ancient Israelite judges, "Follow justice and justice alone, so that you may live and possess the land the Lord your God is giving you" (Deut. 16:20). Justice—treating everyone fairly—is the principle behind the Golden Rule, and the other precepts mentioned above. The precepts illustrate the fact that justice is a principle God values.

☐ PERSON

But ultimately, justice is not simply a virtue because God commands it, nor even because God values it; it is a virtue because it reflects the person of God Himself. Justice is not something God does; it is something He is. He is a just God. "God is just," Paul wrote (2 Thess. 1:6). "He is the Rock," Moses sang, "his works are perfect, and all his ways are just" (Deut. 32:4). "The Lord works righteousness and justice for all the oppressed" (Ps. 103:6). "Morning by morning he dispenses his justice" (Zeph. 3:5). We ought to be fair because God is fair; we ought to be just because He is just. The Test of Truth grounds the virtue of justice in the nature and character of our just God. We can then say that justice (treating everyone fairly) is right—for all people, for all times, for all places.

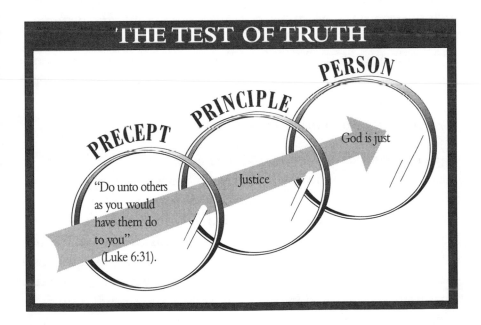

THE TEST OF TRUTH

PRECEPT — "Do unto others as you would have them do to you" (Luke 6:31).

PRINCIPLE — Justice

PERSON — God is just

■ THE EVIDENCE OF TRUTH ABOUT JUSTICE ■

Justice is shown to be right because it reflects the original; it corresponds to the nature and character of God Himself, who is just. But the Evidence of Truth—a look at how justice works in the "real world"—supports the Test of Truth.

☐ 1. PROTECT FROM REVENGE AND PROVIDE FOR A CLEAR
      CONSCIENCE

God's standards of justice protect from revenge and provide for a clear conscience. In the desert culture of Moses' day, an injustice committed by an individual would often be avenged against his entire family, resulting in a bitter and destructive blood feud. The precepts of the Pentateuch were designed to protect God's people from such consequences and provide them with a conscience and dignity that served as a beacon to the surrounding cultures.

The same can happen today. The person who treats someone else unfairly often invites revenge and retaliation; the man or woman who behaves justly toward other people will often avoid such repercussions. Many bitter family feuds and tragic disagreements could be avoided by obeying the biblical standard to "deal with each other justly" (Jer. 7:5). Those who "do justly" also enjoy the benefit of a clear conscience toward other men and women.

☐ 2. PROTECT FROM GUILT AND PROVIDE FOR PEACE

God's standards of justice protect from guilt and provide for peace. I once knew a man who had treated a co-worker unfairly and disrespectfully. The man thrived, and continued to gain power and influence, while the co-worker toiled away in relative obscurity. But the unjust man became a prisoner of his own injustice; he went to great lengths to avoid his victim, and when they did cross paths, he found himself unable to look his co-worker in the eye. That man was haunted by the guilt and shame for what he did, while his "victim" worked serenely and happily at his job until

216

he retired. While injustice always hurts the victim in one way or another, it also frequently exacts a terrible toll on the one who commits the injustice.

☐ 3. PROTECT FROM DISHONOR AND PROVIDE HONOR

God's standards of justice protect from dishonor and provide honor. My wife was once elected to represent her peers in a professional situation that required honesty and integrity because, it was unanimously decided, "she's never treated any of us unfairly." A reputation for fairness brings honor. People respect a just man or woman, and just behavior pleases God Himself, "for the LORD loves the just" (Ps. 37:28).

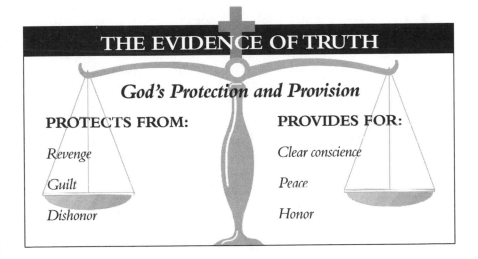

THE EVIDENCE OF TRUTH

God's Protection and Provision

PROTECTS FROM:

Revenge

Guilt

Dishonor

PROVIDES FOR:

Clear conscience

Peace

Honor

■ THE APPLICATION OF TRUTH ABOUT JUSTICE ■

Parents, pastors, teachers, and youth workers are surrounded with daily opportunities to model, teach, and reinforce justice to our youth.

■ **Be an example of fairness to the young people in your life.** Take care to treat each child fairly; if that does not mean you always treat them uniformly, help them understand how treatment that is "different" can still be "fair." Require that they treat their siblings and friends fairly.

- **Seize every opportunity to point out to youth how everyone expects to be treated fairly.** Baseball games, court trials, inspection stickers on gas pumps and merchants' scales, lines at banks and grocery stores—these are all daily reminders of the value of justice in our interaction with other people. Help young people understand such things as evidences that there exists an objective standard of justice that is absolute (it is right for all people, for all times, for all places).

- **Help younger children understand how such simple skills as taking turns, sharing toys, and waiting in line reflect God's nature**—because they help us treat other people fairly.

- **Use news of court trials and congressional hearings to stimulate discussions with your older children and explore their concepts of justice.** Remember to pursue the value of justice through the Test of Truth and the Evidence of Truth.

- **Be open and reasonable when your child protests your family rules (such as dating restrictions, curfews, etc.).** Use such opportunities to discuss the justice or injustice of family rules, what might happen if the rule were abolished, and how their appeal to justice reveals that they accept justice as an objective moral standard. Employ the Test of Truth to help them see *why* justice is right, and the Evidence of Truth to help them see its benefits.

■ WHAT'S THE TRUTH ABOUT MERCY? ■

"The quality of mercy is not strained," said Portia to Shylock, in Shakespeare's play, *The Merchant of Venice.* "It droppeth as the gentle rain from heaven upon the place beneath."[2]

Many individuals and cultures agree that mercy is a virtue; it is like gentle rain from heaven. But *why* is it right to be merciful? What makes mercy a virtue?

218

■ THE TEST OF TRUTH ABOUT MERCY ■

☐ PRECEPT

The Hebrew prophet Micah warned his fellow countrymen that their empty religious exercises fooled neither God nor man. "He has shown you, O man, what is good. And what does the Lord require of you? To act justly and to love mercy and to walk humbly with your God" (Micah 6:8). Micah boiled God's law into three simple precepts, and the command to "love mercy" was among them. Micah saw his people's failure to heed those simple precepts as a sure road to destruction and captivity, a road that ended in the fall of Jerusalem (586 B.C.) and the Babylonian captivity.

The prophet Isaiah commanded, "Share your food with the hungry, and . . . provide the poor wanderer with shelter—when you see the naked . . . clothe him, and [do not] turn away from your own flesh and blood" (Isa. 58:7). The author of Hebrews instructed Christians to "Remember those in prison as if you were their fellow prisoners, and those who are mistreated as if you yourselves were suffering" (Heb. 13:3). James issued the precept to "look after orphans and widows in their distress" (James 1:27).

☐ PRINCIPLE

Such Scriptural precepts—and many others prescribing forgiveness, compassion, and caution in pronouncing and exacting punishment—were given to reflect a principle of mercy. The precepts, such as that administered through the prophet Zechariah, made it clear that God values mercy: "This is what the LORD Almighty says: 'Administer true justice; show mercy and compassion to one another'" (Zech. 7:9).

☐ PERSON

But the divine precepts to "love mercy" and "show mercy" are not right because they reflect a principle; they are right because

219

they come from God—they reflect His nature of mercy. Micah extolled God as One who "delight[s] to show mercy" (Micah 7:18). David testified that "his mercy is great" (1 Kings 3:6). The mercy of God was supremely shown in the revelation of Jesus Christ, who accepted the Samaritan woman, who delivered the daughter of a Canaanite woman from demon possession, who healed lepers, who spoke blessing to the woman caught in adultery, who pronounced forgiveness for those who crucified Him, who died so that we might escape judgment. As Shakespeare's Portia said, "Mercy . . . is an attribute [of] God Himself; And earthly power doth then show likest God's when mercy seasons justice."[3]

We can then say that showing compassion and mercy is right—for all people, for all times, for all places.

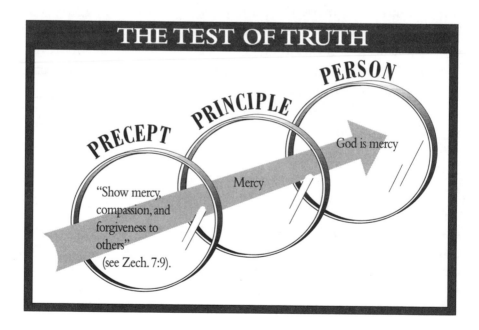

THE TEST OF TRUTH

PRECEPT

"Show mercy, compassion, and forgiveness to others" (see Zech. 7:9).

PRINCIPLE

Mercy

PERSON

God is mercy

■ THE EVIDENCE OF TRUTH ABOUT MERCY ■

The test of truth, then, determines that mercy is right—it is a virtue—because it reflects the nature and character of God Himself, whose "mercy endures forever" (Ps. 107:1, NKJV). The

Evidence of Truth reveals that mercy is not only right; it is also beneficial.

☐ 1. PROTECT FROM WANT AND PROVIDE FOR BLESSING

God's standards of mercy protect from want and provide for blessing. Shakespeare's Portia said that mercy "blesses him that giveth, and him that takes."[4] Mercy not only benefits the person who is shown mercy, but the person who shows mercy as well. The unmerciful person must bear the shame of an ungracious spirit; the man or woman who shows mercy, on the other hand, enjoys the inner rewards that come from being thanked, from being appreciated, from being warmed by the response mercy brings—even when it is unnoticed.

Jesus said, "Give, and it will be given to you. A good measure, pressed down, shaken together and running over, will be poured into your lap. For with the measure you use, it will be measured to you" (Luke 6:38). The motivation to show compassion and mercy should not be "to give in order to get," but showing mercy will, nonetheless, reap great rewards. On the other hand, Jesus' words bring a warning as well. A person who measures out little or no mercy will reap what he sows. The man or woman who does not sow compassion and mercy will reap a life of emptiness and want. That want may not be a lack of material things—some of the most merciless individuals I know are wealthy people—but the promise cuts both ways: the merciful will reap blessing; the merciless will experience want.

☐ 2. PROTECT FROM RETRIBUTION AND PROVIDE FOR LENIENCY

God's standards of mercy protect from retribution and provide for leniency. Jesus said, "Blessed are the merciful, for they will be shown mercy" (Matt. 5:7). I believe He not only meant that the merciful would receive mercy from God, but from others as well. He told a story that illustrates the beatitude, about a servant who owed the king a monstrous debt that would certainly have landed him in prison; the king showed him mercy, however. After his debt was erased, this servant went out, collared a man who owed him a paltry sum, and had him thrown in prison. When the king learned of this, he summoned his servant and said, "Shouldn't you have had mercy on your fellow servant just as I had on you?" The king was so angry, he regretted having shown the man mercy, and had him thrown into prison. Had the king's servant been merciful, he would have avoided retribution. That's often how mercy works. Those who fail to show mercy often invite retribution on themselves; those who show mercy to others make it easier for people to be lenient on them.

☐ 3. PROTECT FROM UNFORGIVENESS AND PROVIDE FOR FORGIVENESS

God's standards of mercy protect from unforgiveness and provide for forgiveness. Jesus said, "For if you forgive men for their transgressions, your heavenly Father will also forgive you. But, if you do not forgive men, then your Father will not forgive your transgressions" (Matt. 6:14–15, NASB). That's pretty clear, isn't it? If we hold back from forgiving others, we won't find forgiveness ourselves, because we are clinging to the sin of unforgiveness (not

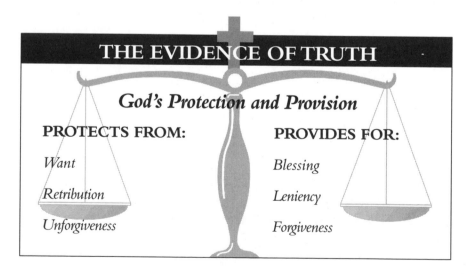

THE EVIDENCE OF TRUTH

God's Protection and Provision

PROTECTS FROM:	**PROVIDES FOR:**
Want	*Blessing*
Retribution	*Leniency*
Unforgiveness	*Forgiveness*

forgiving another). Until we repent and turn away from our spirit of unforgiveness, we cannot accept God's forgiveness.

When we live in harmony with God's standard of mercy, we will be protected from an unforgiving heart and will be rewarded with forgiveness from God.

■ THE APPLICATION OF TRUTH ABOUT MERCY ■

We can help youth acquire the biblical value of mercy by teaching the Test of Truth and the Evidence of Truth at every opportunity, "when [we] sit at home and when [we] walk along the road, when [we] lie down and when [we] get up" (Deut. 6:7).

- **Model mercy.** Go out of your way to help others. Find church, class, or family projects that will help a young person experience the rewards of showing mercy to others.

- **Discuss with older youth how Christ's atonement satisfied God's justice *and* mercy.** Use that example as an opportunity to teach that justice does not preclude mercy, nor vice versa. Ask, "how can we be fair *and* merciful with each other?"

- **Parents, communicate mercy to your children every time you must correct them** by tempering discipline with an opportunity for restitution—in order to teach mercy. For example, you might say, "Susie, you took your brother's Walkman without permission and through carelessness lost it. What you've done is wrong and unfair to your brother. But if you're willing to apologize to your brother and buy him a new tape player, I'll consider the matter closed."

- **When a child or teenager struggles with unforgiveness, explain the value of mercy and the consequences of unforgiveness.** Help them understand that unless they are willing to let go of their unforgiving spirit, they will not be able to receive or take hold of forgiveness for themselves. A good way to illustrate this to a child is have them hold onto a basketball in both hands fully around the ball. Show them a dollar bill or a five dollar bill. Then tell them you will give them the money if they can reach out and hold both ends of the bill while their hands—not their arms or wrists—are fully wrapped around the basketball. Of course, no one can hold two ends of a bill if their hands are firmly wrapped around a basketball. But that's the point: we can't receive forgiveness unless we let go of our unforgiveness. When you've made your point, show mercy yourself—give them the money anyway.

- ** **Use literature and the media to reinforce the value of mercy to your children.** For example, *Les Miserables* is a classic depiction of the tension between justice and mercy. The Lerner and Loewe musical, *Camelot,* presents some excellent opportunities to discuss justice and mercy, as do some police dramas and court dramas on television.

- ** **Discuss with youth whether they would rather *receive* justice or mercy.** Ask them to explain why. Ask if they would rather *give* justice or mercy, and ask them to explain that answer as well.

■ WHAT'S THE TRUTH ABOUT RESPECT? ■

Aretha Franklin's rendition of the Otis Redding song, "RE-SPECT," became a smash hit in 1967 with its assertive refrain spelling out the word and enjoining the listener to "find out what it means to me." Part of the reason for the song's popularity is men and women's universal longing for respect. Comedian Rodney Dangerfield made a career off his trademark line, "I don't get no respect."

Everyone wants to receive respect: children, adults, parents, politicians, comedians, singers, actors, and athletes. But many of us—including our children—are less adept at giving it. If treating others with respect is a virtue, it seems to be one that is fast disappearing from our culture—particularly among our youth.

■ THE TEST OF TRUTH ABOUT RESPECT ■

☐ PRECEPT

The first commandment with a promise, according to the Bible, is the precept, "Honor your father and your mother" (Ex.

20:12). The Word of God abounds with similar precepts to "honor [the king], for he is your lord" (Ps. 45:11), "show respect for the elderly" (Lev. 19:32), and "honor one another above yourselves" (Rom. 12:10). Paul advised Timothy that "the elders who direct the affairs of the church well are worthy of double honor" (I Tim. 5:17), and Paul directed the church at Rome to "submit . . . to the governing authorities" (Rom. 13:1). The Bible also includes precepts about how husbands and wives, children and parents, masters and slaves, are to treat and honor each other.

☐ PRINCIPLE

The over-arching principle behind all those precepts is respect. The Bible makes it clear that we ought to "Show proper respect to everyone" (1 Pet. 2:17). It often seems these days that children lack proper respect for their parents, men lack respect for women, students lack respect for their teachers, and Christians lack respect for church leaders.

But we are not only to show respect *to* individuals, but also respect *for* authority. God has established an authority system—of government, parents, teachers, and church leaders—that we are commanded to respect (see Romans 13, for example). The individual who respects God will also respect those He allows to exercise positions of authority on earth. Precept after precept points to the principle of respect as a quality God values. We please God when we show proper honor and respect to others and to those in authority.

☐ PERSON

Respecting others is right because there is something respectable about each of us that comes from the very nature of God himself. God is Spirit and in Him is life, the Bible says (John 4:24 and John 1:4), and it is that part of His nature that every human being shares with Him, for "the LORD God . . . breathed into his nostrils the breath (the *ruach*, "spirit") of life, and man became a living being" (Gen. 2:7). Humans are made in the image of God (Gen. 1:26–27); they are immortal spirits, created with dignity and purpose. Every human being, therefore, is worthy of respect, because he or she is created in the image of God. Every man, woman, and child on earth ought to be treated respectfully, because he or she is a reflection of the God who gives life and breath to all people.

Additionally, God is God; He is above all, there is no higher power and there is no greater being. ". . . When God made the promise to Abraham, since He could swear by no one greater, He swore by Himself" (Heb. 6:13, NASB). And when we are commanded to respect and obey those in authority over us, we are acknowledging God's authority over all. "For there is no authority except from God, and those which exist are established by God" (Rom. 13:1, NASB). We can then say that showing respect for other human beings and for those in authority is right—for all people, for all times, for all places.

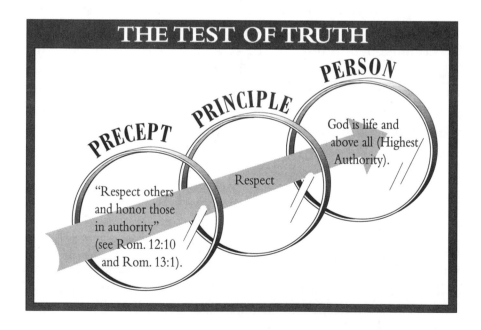

THE TEST OF TRUTH

PERSON — God is life and above all (Highest/Authority).

PRINCIPLE — Respect

PRECEPT — "Respect others and honor those in authority" (see Rom. 12:10 and Rom. 13:1).

■ THE EVIDENCE OF TRUTH ABOUT RESPECT ■

The Test of Truth shows us that respect for others and for those in authority is right because it corresponds to the original; it reflects the nature of God as God (no one greater or above Him) and of Him who is Spirit, and of Him who is the essence of life. However, the Evidence of Truth shows us how respect plays out in reality—what it provides for and protects from.

☐ 1. PROTECT FROM SELF–DISPARAGEMENT AND PROVIDE FOR SELF–ESTEEM

God's standards of respect for others protect from self-disparagement and provide for self-esteem. An attitude of respect for all human beings because they are made in the image of God reminds me that I, too, am made in the image of God. As I treat others with respect, I will remind myself that I possess intrinsic worth. This is not a license for sinful pride, but obedience to the biblical admonishment, "Do not think of yourself more highly than you ought, but rather think of yourself with sober judgment, in accordance with the measure of faith God has given you" (Rom. 12:3). We are neither to think more highly of ourselves than what we really are nor less than what we really are. I believe God's standard of respect requires us to see ourselves as God sees us—no more or no less. This will guard us from self-disparagement and provide us with a healthy self-image.

☐ 2. PROTECT FROM HARMFUL RELATIONSHIPS AND PROVIDE FOR HEALTHY RELATIONSHIPS

God's standards of respect for others protect from harmful relationships and provide for healthy relationships. Respectful treatment of others creates a solid foundation for relationships. A person who respects himself and others will neither tolerate nor inflict abuse. Respect for others will enhance communication and enrich relationships.

It will create an atmosphere of mutual trust and affection in inter-personal relationships.

☐ 3. PROTECT FROM OFFENSE AND PROVIDE FOR ATTRACTIVENESS

God's standards of respect for others protect from offense and provide for attractiveness. I know a fifteen-year-old boy I'll call Brett (not his real name). I met him several years ago, and found him to be a likeable, often funny young man—until I saw the way he treated his mother. He was rude to her. He called her names and made comments designed to hurt her. He displayed a total lack of respect for the woman. I explained that he offended me when he spoke to his mother that way, and I let him know that his disrespectful attitude, far from impressing others, made him look ridiculous and repulsive. God's standard of respect for others protects from that kind of offense. On the other hand, a truly respectful boy, girl, man, or woman makes himself or herself attractive to others; such a person is a pleasure to be around.

☐ 4. PROTECT FROM CONDEMNATION AND PROVIDE FOR PRAISE

God's standards of respect for others protect from condemnation and provide for praise. But remember, God's standard of respect also includes respect for those in authority. The authority relation-ships that exist, for example, between parent and child, employee and employer, and citizen and government are established by God. And God's Word says, "Therefore he who resists authority has opposed the ordinance of God; and they who have opposed will receive condemnation upon themselves" (Rom. 13:2, NASB). When we fail to honor those in authority we suffer condemnation.

The reverse is true when we respect authority by living accord-ing to God's commandments because we live free of condemna-tion and enjoy the praise of those in authority. "For rulers are not a cause of fear for good behavior, but for evil. Do you want to have no fear of authority? Do what is good, and you will have praise from the same" (Rom. 13:3, NASB).

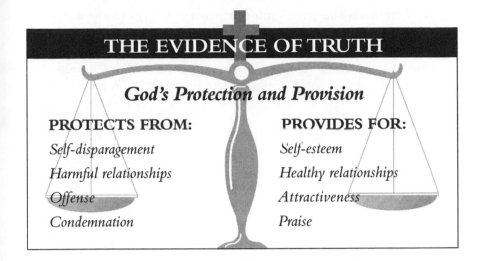

THE EVIDENCE OF TRUTH

God's Protection and Provision

PROTECTS FROM:	PROVIDES FOR:
Self-disparagement	Self-esteem
Harmful relationships	Healthy relationships
Offense	Attractiveness
Condemnation	Praise

■ THE APPLICATION OF TRUTH ABOUT RESPECT ■

Aretha Franklin is not the only one who values respect; God does, and we should too. But how do we help our youth develop the value of respect? How do we instill in them a respect for themselves, for others, and for authority?

■ **As in other areas, example is the most powerful tool for teaching respect.** Evaluate yourself in this regard. How do you treat your own parents? How do you speak about others in the presence of young people? How do you show respect for your spouse? Your superiors? Leaders in the church? Co-workers? Traffic laws? City ordinances? Determine to model respectful attitudes and actions to the youth in your life.

■ **Treat youth with respect.** Many adults consider respect to be a one-way street; but youth are made in the image of God too. Don't "talk down" to young people. Ask their opinions, and *listen* when they respond.

■ **Congratulate children or teenagers when you see or hear them acting respectfully.** Explain to them why you value that kind of behavior (relating it, through precept and principle, to the person of God himself).

229

■ **Parents, teach your children practical ways to show respect for people.** Explain manners—such as opening the
door for someone, or addressing elders as "sir" and "ma'am"—
as ways of communicating respect, and honoring the God-
given worth of another person and of those in authority.

■ WHAT'S THE TRUTH ABOUT SELF–CONTROL? ■

"Man cannot live without self-control," said Isaac Bashevis
Singer, and yet it seems so many in our society, churches, classrooms,
and homes do. The 60s motto, "let it all hang out," has become a
way of life for many people. To many, self-control is a vice; they
see it as evidence of repressed desires and outdated ideals.

■ THE TEST OF TRUTH ABOUT SELF–CONTROL ■

☐ PRECEPT

Yet God has given specific precepts that command self-control.
Jesus applied the command against adultery to "anyone who looks
at a woman lustfully" (Matt. 5:28). The Bible forbids obscenity,
foolish talk, or coarse joking (Eph. 5:4). God, in His Word, has
issued precepts against anger, rage, malice, and slander (Col. 3:8),
and against drunkenness (Eph. 5:18) and greed (Col. 3:5).

☐ PRINCIPLE

The principle behind all these precepts is that of self-control.
The reason God says, "be self-controlled" (1 Pet. 1:13, 5:8) is
because God values self-control. He wishes for us to control our
urges and desires (through the power of His Spirit) rather than be
controlled by them.

☐ PERSON

But ultimately, the reason self-control is a virtue is because God
is like that Himself. He delays His wrath (Isa. 58:9); "The Lord is

slow to anger" (Num. 14:18). God responded slowly and patiently to the repeated provocation of the Israelites in the wilderness; "They rejected my laws and did not follow my decrees," He said, "Yet I looked on them with pity and did not destroy them or put an end to them in the desert" (Ezek. 20:16–17). Jesus epitomized self-control when He stood before the ridicule and torture of Roman and Jewish officials and "made no reply" (Mark 15:5). When we exhibit self-control, we behave like God. We can then say that self-control is right—for all people, for all times, and for all places.

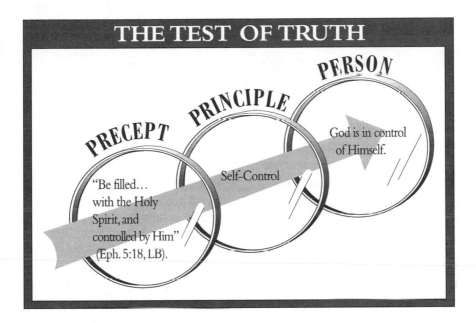

THE TEST OF TRUTH

PERSON

PRINCIPLE

PRECEPT

God is in control of Himself.

Self-Control

"Be filled... with the Holy Spirit, and controlled by Him" (Eph. 5:18, LB).

■ THE EVIDENCE OF TRUTH ABOUT SELF–CONTROL ■

Self-control is right, then, because "God is like that." But our youth can be helped to appreciate not only its rightness, but also its wisdom.

☐ 1. PROTECT FROM EXCESSES AND PROVIDE FOR ENJOYMENT

God's standards of self-control protect from excesses and provide for enjoyment. The man or woman who develops self-control is less susceptible to overindulgence and excesses. Likewise, the self-controlled individual is more able to enjoy health and other benefits, as illustrated in the experience of Dr. S.I. McMillen, author of *None of These Diseases*:

> I recall a certain New Year's Day. My wife and I arose refreshed and happy, and we thoroughly enjoyed a breakfast of grapefruit, cereal, ham and eggs. At noon we enjoyed to the full a New Year's dinner with all the luscious trimmings. But not so the other two couples who visited us. They had seen the New Year in with drinks and had spent the entire morning holding their heads, swallowing aspirin, and fighting severe nausea.[2]

Self-control can heighten the enjoyment of such things as recreation, music, art, food, sex, sight, and conversation. The lack of self-control can lead to all types of excesses.

Of course, most compulsive and addictive behavior cannot be remedied by simply urging a person to "straighten up and get some self-control." There are often various and complex reasons for addictive behavior. This is not in any way an excuse for not dealing with such behavior, but overcoming addiction is often a long and painful road to recovery.

Furthermore, self-control—like any value—cannot be flawlessly (or even consistently) accomplished without the power of the Holy Spirit. A well-disciplined person can bring many areas of his life into control, but if we are to live pleasing to God in every aspect of our lives, we must lead a Spirit-filled life.

☐ 2. PROTECT FROM CONTEMPT AND PROVIDE FOR RESPECT

God's standards of self-control protect from contempt and provide for respect. I know an intelligent, capable man who is an accomplished executive. He once enjoyed the respect of many of his co-workers and employees. But any time this man gets around alcohol—at the office Christmas party, business receptions, conventions—he drinks until he becomes a foul, loathsome fool. His lack of self-control in such instances not only colors his employ-ees' attitudes toward him; it also limits his advancement within the organization. The self-controlled individual, on the other hand, often wins the respect and admiration of others who see self-control as a virtue and an indication of character.

☐ 3. PROTECT FROM SELF–DOUBT AND PROVIDE FOR SELF–ESTEEM

God's standards of self-control protect from self-doubt and provide for self-esteem. I have struggled with my weight in recent years and, while I am still learning self-control in that area, I have discov-ered that every success at disciplining myself to eat healthier and lose weight makes me believe that I can accomplish my goals and makes me feel better about myself. That is the effect that self-control has on us; mastery over our own urges and desires (with the Holy Spirit's help, of course) boosts confidence and instills a healthy self-esteem.

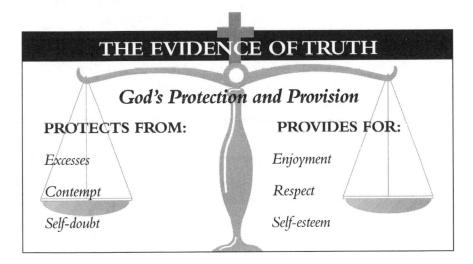

THE EVIDENCE OF TRUTH

God's Protection and Provision

PROTECTS FROM:

Excesses

Contempt

Self-doubt

PROVIDES FOR:

Enjoyment

Respect

Self-esteem

■ THE APPLICATION OF TRUTH ABOUT SELF–CONTROL ■

The Test of Truth grounds the virtue of self-control in the nature and character of God; the Evidence of Truth can extol its benefits. Parents, grandparents, teachers, youth leaders, and pastors who wish to influence youth must be open to every opportunity to apply the Test of Truth and the Evidence of Truth.

- **Be open and honest about your efforts to develop self-control.** Enlist the help of others in your family, church, or youth group. I once gave my son permission to remind me about my desire to develop self-control in my eating habits; he never abused that privilege, and his reminders (often just his presence) helped me discipline myself.

- **Seize every opportunity to help youth see God as a God who is self-controlled.** Explore biblical examples of God's self-control; doing so can help you appreciate "old" stories in a "new" way, as you meditate on God's self-control in the events surrounding the ten plagues, the Noahic flood, Sodom and Gomorrah, David and Bathsheba, the prophet Jonah, and Jesus calming the storm on the Sea of Galilee.

- **Help children look beyond such things as piano lessons or savings accounts as opportunities to develop self-control** (such examples also provide great openings for communicating the Evidence of Truth).

- **Praise youth (and other adults) when they exhibit self-control.** Commend a child who controls his anger on the playground; compliment a teen who spends money wisely; congratulate a friend for refusing an extra helping at the dinner table. Identify such behavior to your youth as examples of self-control, and point out to them why it is a quality God values.

These five biblical values (love, justice, mercy, respect, and self-control) do not exhaust the range of virtues that we can help youth develop. Many more, such as patience, kindness, gentleness, and faith, can be addressed, using the Test of Truth and the Evidence of Truth. In fact, parents or youth leaders may wish to launch a family or class project to help youth use the Test of Truth and the Evidence of Truth to evaluate these and other values on their own.

14

Making it Right

BRITTNEY MARSH CLOSED HER LOCKER and spun the lock with her right hand, cradling her school books to her chest with her left arm. She whirled around to head down the hall toward the doors and almost ran into Matt.

"You scared me!" she said in a scolding tone.

Matt wore a serious expression. "Can we talk?"

She nodded and began walking slowly down the hall. Matt fell into step beside her.

"I still don't understand why you broke up with me," he said.

"I told you," she said. "I don't want to . . ." She looked around carefully. "I don't want to do those things anymore."

"But why not?" A sharp edge entered his voice. "I thought we were in love."

She stopped beside the flagpole. Bright impatiens and pansies circled the pole. "I thought so, too," she said, resting her chin on the tops of the books she hugged to her body.

"So I don't see what the problem is," he said, thrusting his face close to hers and speaking in a low, urgent tone. "I love you, Brittney. I just want to show you how much I love you."

She turned to look at him. "Can you show your love for me by waiting?"

"Huh?"

"Can you show how much you love me by waiting to have sex until we're married?"

"What are you talking about?" he said. "You're fifteen! You can't get married for . . . for *years!*"

Brittney nodded.

"You can't be serious!" He searched her eyes, but she did not flinch. "Is it about that pregnancy thing?"

She looked around them with a panicked expression. He lowered his voice. "Is that what this is all about? Hey, I was just scared, that's all. I wasn't ignoring you. I would have been right there for you."

She turned and began walking slowly up the sidewalk, away from the school. Matt circled her and stood in front of her, blocking her progress. "Look, Brittney," he said. His tone was softer now. "I love you. I miss you." He placed his hands on her arms and leaned his head close to hers. He kissed her neck.

She closed her eyes. He moved her hair and kissed her again. "I want us to be together, like we were," he whispered. "I love you, Brittney, what's wrong with that?"

She opened her eyes and stepped back from him. "It's wrong," she answered. Her dark eyes shone with understanding. "It's wrong; because our kind of love wasn't willing to wait, our love wasn't pure. Love is supposed to be a certain way, Matt, and what we've been doing isn't the way it's supposed to work."

"Huh?" he said.

"I was lying to my parents and sneaking around behind their backs. I don't believe in that kind of stuff anymore, but that's what our 'love' made me do. And when I had to take that pregnancy test, I was scared—not just of being pregnant, but about whether you would stick around or not. That's not the kind of love I'm looking for."

"We can change all that," he said. "We—"

"No," she said. "Because it would still be wrong. See, I've had some kind of twisted idea about what makes something right or wrong, but I've been learning that my problem has been trying to figure those things out myself, instead of looking to God for those kinds of things."

"God? What's God got to do with this?" Matt persisted.

"A lot," Brittney responded. "I can't explain it as good as my mom can, but I know that something is right if it's like God. If it's not like God, it's wrong, and that means it's not going to make me happy. And I'm not going to have sex with anyone unless it includes a love that is pure and committed to me for a lifetime in marriage. That's what's right, Matt."

Matt stared at Brittney with a look of disbelief. "I don't know where you're getting all this, Brittney, but are you really going to let someone else decide what's right for you?"

She shrugged. "Yeah. Because He knows a lot more than either one of us."

■ THOSE WHO MOVE BOUNDARY STONES ■

Brittney Marsh is beginning to apply the truth to her own life . . . and she's learning to share the truth with others in her world. She may not always say the right thing, or express herself exactly the way she wants, but she is starting to take a stand for truth in a world of counterfeits. She's beginning to understand the value of moral boundaries in a world that is constantly striving to change those boundaries.

The Old Testament prophet Hosea announced God's judgment against Judah's leaders, saying:

Judah's leaders are like those who move boundary stones. I will pour out my wrath on them like a flood of water (Hos. 5:10).

Judah's leaders have their counterparts in our age and culture. There are many today who would move the boundary stones.

They wish to change the boundaries between what is acceptable and what is not, what is good and what is evil, what is right and what is wrong.

What used to be called sexual perversion is now simply one's sexual preference. What once was termed "living in sin" is now an "alternative lifestyle." What people once called obscene is now called art. A culture that once acknowledged God as the Judge of good and evil now looks to mere men and women to divide right from wrong.

But we are not powerless to counter the culture and begin turning the tide. Truth, after all, is on our side, and we are on the side of truth. We *can* pass on biblical values to our children in the midst of a "perverse and crooked generation." We *can* counter the culture and reinforce the crumbling foundations in our homes and churches. We *can* take a stand against the madness of a culture that is in rebellion against God. There are steps we can take to make it right in our homes, in our churches, and in our community.

■ MAKE IT RIGHT IN YOUR HOME ■

James and Diane Milford, Geena Santoro, Penny Marsh, and others have begun to explore ways to make it right in their homes and families. They have begun building better relationships. They have recognized the effects of their own example. They have begun teaching the Test of Truth and the Evidence of Truth to their children as they attempt also to lead their children to a knowledge of the Person of Truth, Jesus Christ Himself.

If you desire to make it right in your home—to counter the culture and pass on biblical values to your children—you must begin with yourself.

Allow *the Holy Spirit of God to identify and correct ways in which your own world view—and actions—have departed from the "faith of our fathers."* Geena Santoro wrestled with her view of marriage, and how that affected her daughter; James Milford came to terms with the inconsistency between his teaching and his life; Penny Marsh recognized that her (and her husband's) lack of a cohesive view of truth and morality had poorly equipped their daughter to resist counterfeit pleasures. Similarly, if you wish to make it right in your home, ask the Holy Spirit to show you anything that would hinder you in equipping your children with strong moral and ethical convictions.

Assimilate the Test of Truth and the Evidence of Truth yourself. Conduct a personal Bible study of the precepts of God, and trace them through the eternal principle back to the person of God himself; be open to Evidences of Truth as you read your newspaper or watch the evening news and share them with your husband or wife. Conduct an extended personal study of what the Bible means when it commands us to "fear God." Review this book often, and take advantage of the additional resources listed in the back. Conduct a study of this book with the help of the video series that accompanies it with friends and study other books together. Seek to make the Test of Truth and the Evidence of Truth so much a part of your thinking and acting that it becomes second nature; inscribe them upon your heart (Deut. 6:6).

Affirm the truth with your children. Before sharing the truths about sex, honesty, family, love, respect, mercy, etc., I suggest writing out your goals for each of your children along with the test and evidence for each of these truths you wish to share. I've discovered that committing a goal to paper motivates me further to its fulfillment, because writing it brings the goal down out of the clouds and makes it visible, concrete, like etching my name in wet cement. Similarly, I find that my mind can wrestle with an idea or concept for weeks, but it often becomes much clearer to me when I force myself to write it out before I explain it to someone else.

Write your thoughts in a journal or diary; discuss your discoveries with your family. Talk about them when you sit at home and when you walk along the road, when you lie down and when you get up (Deut. 6:7). Seize every opportunity to affirm your convictions about truth and morality with your family.

The "Right from Wrong" Campaign is continuing to create helpful resources for you and your family. Plans include a series of videos and picture books for younger children and a book for teenagers. These resources are designed to help you better communicate biblical values through the Test of Truth and Evidence of Truth method in your own home. Take advantage of these resources by asking your local Christian bookstore for the "Right from Wrong" material for children and youth. Plans are to release these resources by mid-1995.

Add to these things the pointers found in our chapter on "Teaching the Truth." Enrich your relationship with your children and others you wish to influence. Be an example, a model they can imitate. Share the truth "with great patience and careful instruction" (2 Tim. 4:2). And lead those under your influence to a personal knowledge of the Truth, Jesus Christ.

■ MAKE IT RIGHT IN YOUR CHURCH ■

Pastor James Milford is an example of what can happen when members of the Body of Christ begin holding each other accountable for sharing the truth in their families.

Expose *your church to the "Right from Wrong" Campaign.* The "Right from Wrong" Campaign is a long-term effort in cooperation with forty to fifty denominations and para-church ministries. It is a grassroots effort designed to help you and your local church better reach your goal of passing on your values to the next generation.

Parents, get this book in the hands of your pastor and youth worker. Pastors and youth workers, meet with the church staff and make this book available to them. Urge your congregation to initiate a church-wide emphasis on "Right from Wrong"—an emphasis among adults, teenagers, and younger children. Obtain the "Right from Wrong" catalog, listing the resources available for use in the church (to receive a catalog, write to the address in the resource section of this book).

Empower *your church to communicate the "Right from Wrong" message simultaneously to adults, teens, and children.* Pastors, use *Right from Wrong* to spur your sermon planning; construct a series of messages that will utilize the material in this book, address the current crisis of truth, and equip God's people to counter the culture.

Plan prayer campaigns to prepare for and kick off a church-wide emphasis on turning the tide of relativism and immorality in our homes and communities. Enlist neighboring churches in the effort; form prayer chains or concerts of prayer in cooperation with other churches (each church assuming responsibility for one hour out of six, for example).

Take advantage of the many available resources. This book is the centerpiece of the "Right from Wrong" campaign, but a multitude of resources have been designed for church use that break down the "Right from Wrong" material into digestible lessons and makes it more applicable to various age groups. Current plans include release of the following by mid-1995:

- **"Right from Wrong" video series to equip parents**—a multiple-session course using this book as its companion guide. It will include a "live" Right from Wrong Video Seminar, a leader's guide with activity sheets, and a creative video preview to enable you to generate church-wide interest in the entire "Right from Wrong" emphasis. The series will offer a survey of the book's message for parents, and will be designed to foster a support-group atmosphere for building each other up in the faith and meeting the challenge to pass on our values to our children.

- **Single videotapes for parents**. Videotapes suitable for parents to view at home and tapes for parents to use at home with their children will be produced.

- **Audio tapes for parents**. Audio tapes will be made available so that the "Right from Wrong" message can be absorbed while commuting to work or working in the garden.

- **Video series for youth**. A multiple-video program for students will translate the essence of this book into a relevant and captivating message to youth. It is designed to empower our young people with a biblical perspective of truth and a fresh vision to take a stand and counter the culture. The series is not only designed to instill biblical convictions within our youth, but will include an outreach strategy for "telling the world the truth."

- **A "Right from Wrong" book for youth**. A companion book to the youth video series will be made available in early 1995 that will continue the stories of Brittney Marsh, Philip Milford, and other teenagers from the small community of Westcastle. This book, the third in the PowerLink Chronicles, will instruct youth on how to know the truth and reject the counterfeits in life, and will inspire and challenge junior-high and high-school students to take a Daniel-like stand in a Babylonian-type culture.

- **Children's church video series**. A multiple-part video series is planned to instruct younger children in biblical values from the Test of Truth and Evidence of Truth perspective. These highly entertaining videos will be perfect for use in children's church, Sunday school classes, or vacation Bible school.

- **Children's picture books and chapter books**. Picture books will be directed to younger children; chapter books will be aimed at eight- to eleven-year-olds. These books will complement the children's video series.

These and other resources to be released are part of an orchestrated effort to assist you and your local church in your efforts to counter the culture. Look to your local Christian bookstore as your "Right from Wrong" resource center and obtain these and other resources, then conduct a church-wide emphasis to help rebuild the crumbling moral foundations of our society.

As Francis Schaeffer wrote:

We need . . . a generation of radicals for truth and for Christ. We need a young generation and others who will be willing to stand . . . [against] the humanistic, secular consensus which is the dominant destructive force of our day.[1]

■ MAKE IT RIGHT IN YOUR COMMUNITY ■

Much of this book has dealt with ways to communicate biblical, objective standards of truth and morality in our families and in our churches. That is where we must begin. However, we must also be prepared to make it right in our communities.

If the culture has turned sour, it may be because the seasoning hasn't been doing its job! Jesus calls us to be salt; He calls us to counter the processes that would spoil and contaminate our society. We cannot expect a fallen world to light itself; we must be the light (see Matt. 5:13–15). We have too often wondered why our culture has become so rotten, while many have abrogated involvement in education, politics, and the media.

We cannot retreat into an intellectual "no-fly zone." Our youth will face questions and challenges from educators, from the media, and from their own friends and neighbors. We must teach and model how to counter the culture in our own communities.

☐ HOW TO COUNTER THE CULTURE

In April 1980, an elite group of U.S. servicemen were dispatched on a secret mission to rescue Americans who had been held hostage for about six months in Iran. The military equipment employed the latest technology; the participants were highly trained experts; the planners were accomplished strategists. The mission ended in failure, however, due to what can only be termed a tragedy of errors. Multiple equipment failures, a swirling dust cloud, and other factors resulted in the deaths of eight servicemen.

Many good ideas have failed because of poor execution. If we are to help rebuild the crumbling foundations of morality in our communities, we must heed Jesus' admonition to be "wise as serpents but harmless as doves." We must plan, prepare, and perform with wisdom and careful forethought.

I suggest five steps, drawn from my own experience and observation of others, that can effect positive change in our communities.

☐ 1. CHOOSE YOUR ISSUES WISELY

There seem to be hundreds of things happening in our communities that can bristle the hair on our necks. But we can hardly speak out on every issue; we would soon exhaust ourselves and our resources. We would also probably gain a reputation that could cripple our future effectiveness. If we wish to be effective in re-establishing a moral foundation in our communities, I suggest we begin by selecting an issue that clearly violates the average parent's sense of morality.

People *are* waking up to the madness all around us. Newspapers report it: "Drugs Sold by Children," "Violence Erupts in Our Classrooms," "Crime Takes Over Our Streets." The most unlikely voices are being raised to protest the moral malaise that threatens our culture, our families, and our children.

You and I have a golden opportunity to step in and stand up with an answer that can protect our communities and children from the anguish and grief of a society gone mad. We can provide an answer that takes us back to bedrock morals. But we must be careful to choose our issues wisely—particularly in the beginning.

A campaign to remove lurid magazines from the local convenience mart may not be the place to start, for example, particularly if an adult book store is selling child pornography just a few miles away. Both are promoting immorality, of course, but the latter is obviously the wiser place to start. Choose issues that are a clear violation of moral decency and you will be more likely, especially in your first encounter, to gain a hearing.

☐ 2. BUILD A COALITION

There is influence in numbers. Find other people who want to see your community regain its moral bearings and network with them. Talk to others in your church, school system, and community. Agree on the issues that are

244

intolerable—those issues that all agree upon must be ad-dressed. A coalition of men and women concerned about the moral and ethical well-being of a community can be a powerful force for making it right.

3. KNOW THE "WHYS" BEHIND THE WRONG

When you choose an issue and have a solid coalition behind you, be sure you are prepared to answer questions about why the issue is wrong—and what will make it right. The Bible instructs us to ". . . sanctify Christ as Lord in your hearts, always being ready to make a defense to everyone who asks you to give an account for the hope that is in you, yet with gentleness and reverence" (1 Pet. 3:15, NASB).

I would suggest two levels of preparation: be prepared to offer a moral and ethical defense for your position; and give inward attention to your spiritual convictions. Because we live in a pluralistic society, you may be more effective in rebuilding community values by promoting the values vig-orously, and presenting your faith gently. Appeal to basic decency and the violation of common sense, rather than appealing to biblical or church doctrine when making your case. People are far more responsive when they sense some-one has their children's best interest at heart, for example, than when they suspect someone is trying to "save lost souls." This doesn't mean people should not eventually understand that the principles for which you stand are based on the character of God and the Lordship of Christ; it means that we should obey the biblical instruction to "Let your speech always be gracious, seasoned with salt, so that you may know how you ought to answer every one" (Col. 4:6, RSV).

4. BE PREPARED FOR OPPOSITION

Of course, the moment we—or our children—support biblical values in public, we will be accused of intolerance. "That's the problem with you people," we'll be told. "It's either your way or no way. You have no right to force your morality on anyone else."

Tolerance has arisen as the sole virtue of western culture, and intolerance the sole vice. Tolerance is extolled as the new measure of morality. It has become synonymous with goodness and open-mindedness; intolerance has come to connote bigotry.

Chuck Colson describes the problem succinctly in his book, *The Body*:

> . . . the only stable virtue left in this relativistic world is un-bridled tolerance: the modern broadmindedness which purports that any and all values, if sincerely held, are equally valid (except a value that claims allegiance to absolute truth, of course). There are no absolutes except the absolute that there can be no absolutes.[2]

If a parent opposes public school curriculum that promotes homosexuality and homosexual unions, he is labeled "intolerant." If a Christian objects to pornography being paraded in public under the banner of "artistic expression," she is labeled "intolerant." If someone takes a stand against condom distribution in high schools, he is labeled "intolerant." Tolerance has been so cleverly promoted that when anyone advocates moral values in a community or school, that person is criticized for opposing personal rights.

That's the trouble with absolute truth: it arouses the disapproval of relativists, who interpret a belief in an absolute standard of truth as an assault on their faith and freedom. But standing for truth does not violate the personal rights or freedom of others. We must understand that personal rights are only valid when moral boundaries exist, because an appeal to "rights" is an appeal to an objective standard of justice, which can only exist in a moral society. Those who denounce moral values (even in the name of tolerance) threaten the very principles to which they appeal.

It is no virtue to tolerate behavior that threatens the morality or safety of our children. The Bible makes it clear that "To fear the LORD is to hate evil" (Prov. 8:13). We may upset those who "use [their] freedom to indulge the sinful nature" (Gal. 5:13), but Jesus warned us, "If the world hates you, keep in mind that it hated me first" (John 15:18). We must not seek confrontation or opposition, but we should not be surprised when it occurs.

☐ 5. COUNTER PRINCIPLES, NOT PEOPLE

It *is* people, of course, who advance wrong thinking and behavior. But to be effective in making it right in our communities, we must attack immoral principles, not people. A humble, non-combative spirit that stands firmly for principles will often win out over a belligerent fighter who fights fire with fire.

Just before the apostle Peter admonished Christians to always be "ready to make a defense," he commanded us to "be harmonious, sympathetic, brotherly, kindhearted, and humble in spirit; not returning evil for evil, or insult for insult, but giving a blessing instead . . ." (1 Pet. 3:8–9, NASB). And just following his endorsement of a ready defense, he advised, "keep a good conscience so that in the thing in which you are slandered, those who revile your good behavior in Christ may be put to shame" (1 Pet. 3:16, NASB).

Relativists may attack you and try to diffuse the message by deriding the messenger. But a Christlike attitude can put them to shame. Remember that ultimately it's not you they argue with; it is the truth. It is not you they reject; it is the Truth, Jesus Himself. That realization may help to remind us that the opponents of truth should not be the objects of our hate or scorn; we should instead be "sympathetic, brotherly, kindhearted, and humble in spirit" toward them, knowing that they "are perishing . . . because they [refuse] to love the truth and so be saved" (2 Thess. 2:10).

It is possible to "make it right" in our homes and in our churches. We can even begin making it right in our communities. "If the foundations be destroyed, what can the righteous do?" (Ps. 11:3, KJV). We can recover "the fear of God" in ourselves and in our families and churches, acknowledging Him as the Source of all good things; we can equip ourselves—and our youth—with the Test of Truth and Evidence of Truth; and we can take a godly stand for truth in our communities. Once we are equipped with the "*full* armor of God," which includes "the belt of truth," we are ready to make it right "so that when the day of evil comes, [we] may be able to stand [our] ground, and after [we] have done everything, to stand" (Eph. 6:13).

PART 4

THE
RESEARCH
ANALYSIS

Introduction to the
Research Analysis

THE FINAL FOUR CHAPTERS contain the results and analyses of responses from the 3,795 youth from thirteen denominations who participated in the 1994 Churched Youth Survey. The eight-page survey questionnaire each young person completed consisted of 193 questions; the survey has been divided into four categories for this analysis: Love and Sex; Marriage and Family; Faith and Religion; and Attitudes and Lifestyles. These four categories derived from the survey questionnaire encompass eleven dimensions of our young people's lives. They are:

- Attitudes about family and marriage
- Personal relationship with parents and family
- Sexual behavior and perspectives
- Lifestyle activities
- Self-view
- Perspectives related to "truth"
- Life choices and views
- Desirable life circumstances
- Religious practices
- Religious beliefs
- Spiritual commitment

251

In some cases the survey questions duplicated nationwide studies of the general youth and adult population conducted by The Barna Research Group, Ltd. of Glendale, California. Some questions also replicated the 1987 study among churched youth we commissioned during the "Why Wait?" campaign. This has allowed us to make interesting comparisons between the various studies.

The survey questionnaire was initially drafted by The Barna Research Group. Each denominational contact person provided input and modification to the survey questionnaire until all thirteen groups approved of the final questionnaire used. The survey questionnaire was then pre-tested by The Barna Research Group prior to its final distribution to each participating group.

The survey was completed anonymously by the 3,795 churched youth at their normal youth group meetings between November 1993 and March 1994. Each denomination was given the goal of surveying five hundred youth from their total church list using a "multistage stratified random probability sample." Each group was supplied with a survey manual, local leader's instruction guide, confidential survey questionnaires, envelopes, and other materials to assist proper administration of the survey.

The chart on the facing page lists the participating denominations and their proportionate survey number of the total tabulated.

Regarding the statistical weighting of the data, The Barna Research Group points out:

> Readers of these data should be aware that there is no statistical weighting of the data, which means that the results are weighted according to the responsiveness of the denomination's churches, rather than in response to each denomination's magnitude within the Protestant church world, or among the thirteen participating denominations.[1]

Though we believe the thirteen denominations reflect a good cross section of evangelical churches (and there was not a major statistical difference across participating denominations), we do not suggest that this study accurately reflects *all* churched youth in America. We do believe, however, that this study reflects the typical evangelical young person in America and the data within the participating denominations provides each group with an accurate reading of their youth.

The survey questionnaire used in this study, listing the percentage of youth who answered each of the 193 questions, is printed verbatim on succeeding pages. Following the questionnaire is an explanation of the seven statements regarding truth which respondents answered, and the profile of those who answered all seven questions from a pro-truth perspective compared to those who didn't. The last four chapters provides a full analysis of the data, including numerous tables which cross-tabulate the data. Many of these statistics and analyses have been quoted throughout this book; we will be repeating some of them, however, to provide you with a complete report of the data as they relate to each data table.

Denomination	Usable returns	% of all returns
Assemblies of God	319	9%
Church of God, Cleveland	232	6
Church of God, Gen. Conference	309	8
Church of the Nazarene	232	6
Foursquare Gospel	326	9
Free Methodist	175	5
Friends	236	6
Mennonite (Board of Cong.)	326	9
Mennonite (Gen. Conference of)	307	8
Pentecostal Holiness	500	13
Salvation Army	183	5
Southern Baptist Convention	176	5
Wesleyan	454	12
no identification	20	*
total: 13 denominations	3,795	100%

CONFIDENTIAL SURVEY QUESTIONNAIRE

The following Survey Questionnaire was administered anonymously and in confidence to 3,795 youth while attending their youth group meetings from thirteen evangelical denominations.

SECTION A: Background Characteristics

1. What is your gender?   48% =Male   52%=Female

2. What is your age?   11=1%   12=6%   13=17%   14=18%   15=20%
   16=16%   17=13%   18=7%   19=2%

3. What grade are you currently enrolled in at school?
   6th=3%   7th=13%   8th=16%   9th=21%   10th=19%   11th=14%
   12th=12%   College=2%

4. What is your grade average in school?   29%=A/A-   44%=B+/B/B-
   23%=C+/C/C-   4%=D+/D/D-

5. In what state is your home located?   East=18%   South=34%   Central=32%
   West=13%   Canada=1%

6. Which of the following best describes you?
   86%=White/Caucasian   4%=Hispanic/Latino   2%=Native American
   3%=Black/African-American   8%=Asian   4%=Other

7. My parents are:
   72%=Married   10%=Divorced/Remarried   3%=One has died
   13%=Divorced/Separated .3%=Both have died   2%=Other

8. I live with:
   73%=My natural father and mother   2%=My natural father or stepfather only
   .7%=Parents who are both stepparents   13%=Other
   11%=My natural mother or stepmother only

SECTION B: Family Relationships

1. Which <u>one</u> of the following descriptions comes closest to describing how you would define a family?
   32%=all of the people related to each other by birth, adoption, or marriage.
   59%=any person or group whom you love or care about deeply, or who love or care about you deeply.
   5%=any group of people who live together.
   4%=any group of people who share the same set of values and goals in life.

2. Please indicate whether or not you would consider each of the groups of people described below to be a family. Is this a family?

Situation	Yes	No	Not Sure
a. a man and woman who are not married but are living together and have no children	14%	72%	14%
b. a man and woman who are not married, are living together, and have had children together	40%	41%	19%
c. two homosexual men living together	8%	81%	11%
d. two homosexual women living together	9%	80%	11%
e. an unmarried mother and her children	74%	15%	11%
f. two divorced women who share housing but do not have a sexual relationship with each other	21%	58%	21%

3. How would you describe your relationship with your father? (Circle <u>one</u> answer.)

32%=we are very close   7%=we are not at all close
42%=we are fairly close   2%=my father is not alive — (Go to #6)
14%=we are not too close   3%=do not know my father — (Go to #6)

4. Indicate **how frequently** each of the following situations occur. How often do you . . .

Situation	frequently	occasionally	seldom	never
a. talk with your father about your personal concerns?	12%	34%	32%	22%
b. wonder whether or not your father loves you?	8%	14%	21%	57%
c. seek advice from your father?	26%	38%	21%	15%
d. feel proud of your father?	56%	28%	9%	7%
e. do something special with your father that involves just the two of you?	19%	39%	28%	14%
f. show your love for your father?	41%	36%	18%	5%
g. feel your father shows his love for you?	51%	29%	14%	6%

5. In a <u>typical week</u>, about how much time do you spend talking with your father about things that really matter to you? (Circle <u>one</u> answer.)

16%=no time   12%=between 31–60 minutes
14%=less than 5 minutes   10%=1 hour to less than 2 hours
20%=between 5–15 minutes   7%=2 hours to less than 4 hours
16%=between 16–30 minutes   5%=4 hours or more per week

6. How would you describe your relationship with your mother? (Circle <u>one</u> answer.)

52%=we are very close   3%=we are not at all close
36%=we are fairly close   1%=my mother is not alive — (Go to #9)
 8%=we are not too close   0%=do not know my mother — (Go to #9)

7. Indicate **how frequently** each of the following situations occur. How often do you . . .

Situation	frequently	occasionally	seldom	never
a. talk with your mother about your personal concerns?	39%	35%	18%	8%
b. wonder whether or not your mother loves you?	9%	13%	19%	59%
c. seek advice from your mother?	40%	34%	18%	8%
d. feel proud of your mother?	58%	31%	8%	3%
e. do something special with your mother that involves just the two of you?	30%	37%	25%	8%
f. show your love for your mother?	52%	34%	11%	3%
g. feel your mother shows her love for you?	68%	22%	7%	3%

8. In a <u>typical week</u>, about how much time do you spend talking with your mother about things that really matter to you? (Circle <u>one</u> answer.)

 6%=no time   15%=between 31–60 minutes
 9%=less than 5 minutes   13%=1 hour to less than 2 hours
16%=between 5–15 minutes   12%=2 hours to less than 4 hours
16%=between 16–30 minutes   13%=4 hours or more per week

9. Listed below are some situations that some teenagers face. Indicate **how often** this is true of you. "My parents . . ."

Situation	frequently	occasionally	seldom	never
a. do not trust me	12%	26%	38%	24%
b. yell at me	18%	34%	40%	8%
c. fight with each other	9%	20%	44%	27%
d. do not allow me to do things I want to do	15%	36%	40%	9%
e. are really interested in who I am	50%	30%	15%	5%
f. spend time with me	46%	38%	13%	3%
g. admit when they are wrong or mistaken	27%	36%	25%	12%
h. are too strict	16%	28%	37%	19%
i. set good examples for me	54%	32%	10%	4%
j. show that they really love each other	56%	23%	10%	11%
k. expect more of me than is fair	19%	28%	33%	20%

10. My home is a place . . . (Circle <u>one</u> answer to complete the sentence.)
   62%=where I feel secure and loved.
    9%=where each of us is <u>trying</u> to love each other.
   14%=where sometimes I feel loved, other times I don't.
    8%=where I usually feel uncomfortable and would rather be elsewhere.
    7%=where I feel comfortable, although we are not a close, loving family.

11. Please mark <u>one</u> answer for each statement below to indicate your reaction to the statement about marriage.

Statement	Agree	Disagree	Not Sure
a. If there are children involved in the marriage, the parents should not get divorced, even if they do not love each other anymore	21%	46%	33%
b. Overall, you feel that your family experience has been positive	72%	14%	14%
c. If the traditional family in America falls apart, American society will collapse	47%	28%	25%
d. These days it is very hard to have a successful marriage	43%	44%	13%
e. Anyone who gets married these days should expect that their marriage will end in divorce	6%	86%	8%
f. Marriage problems have been exaggerated; most married couples have fulfilling, healthy marriages	34%	32%	34%
g. I want a marriage like my parents	48%	36%	16%
h. God intended for marriage to last a lifetime	90%	4%	6%
i. I would like to be a virgin at marriage	73%	13%	14%
j. If I wasn't a virgin now and I could change the past, I would wait to have sex after marriage	76%	10%	14%

SECTION C: Relationship With Members of the Opposite Sex

1. Which of the following have you done with a member of the opposite sex?

Activity	----- have done -----		
	Yes	No	Not Sure
a. hold hands	89%	10%	1%
b. embracing and some kissing	73%	25%	2%
c. heavy "French" kissing	53%	45%	2%
d. fondling of breasts	34%	63%	3%
e. fondling of genitals	26%	71%	3%
f. sexual intercourse	16%	81%	3%

2. For two people who are not married but are both in love with each other and are willing, please indicate whether the actions described below are morally acceptable or not.

- - - - - - - morally acceptable - - - - - - -

Activity	Always	Sometimes	Never	Not Sure
a. hold hands	85%	14%	0%	0%
b. embracing and some kissing	68%	29%	2%	1%
c. heavy "French" kissing	33%	48%	10%	9%
d. fondling of breasts	10%	25%	49%	16%
e. fondling of genitals	9%	20%	55%	16%
f. sexual intercourse	7%	13%	68%	12%

3. If the opportunity presented itself <u>today</u>, how likely would you be to have sexual intercourse with another person if:

Situation	More Likely	Less Likely	No Difference
a. your friends strongly encouraged you to do so?	11%	31%	58%
b. you were in love with the person?	45%	19%	36%
c. you really intended to marry that person?	44%	19%	37%
d. you were positive that a pregnancy would not result?	26%	25%	49%
e. you knew that your parents would not find out?	25%	24%	51%
f. you felt that your parents would not mind?	22%	24%	54%

SECTION D: Daily Challenges

1. Think about your life during the past three months. Please indicate which, if any, of these activities you did during that period of time.

- - - did this? - - -

Activity	Yes	No
a. watched MTV at least once a week	45%	55%
b. watched an X-rated or pornographic movie	16%	84%
c. used some type of illegal, non-prescription drug	8%	92%
d. cheated on an exam or other evaluation	36%	64%
e. stole money or some other material possession	15%	85%
f. lied to a parent, teacher, or other older person	66%	34%
g. lied to one of your friends or peers	59%	41%
h. attempted suicide	5%	95%
i. read a pornographic magazine	12%	88%

Activity (cont.)	Yes	No
j. drank enough alcohol to be legally drunk	12%	88%
k. intentionally tried to physically hurt someone	20%	80%
l. intentionally tried to emotionally hurt someone	23%	77%
m. gambled or bet your money on something	20%	80%
n. smoked a cigarette or used another tobacco product	23%	77%

2. Overall, how satisfied are you with your life these days?

31%=Very satisfied   13%=Not too satisfied
53%=Somewhat satisfied   3%=Not at all satisfied

3. Which of the following words or phrases, if any, accurately describes you?

	accurate?			accurate?	
	Yes	No		Yes	No
a. too busy	54%	46%	n. have high hopes	87%	13%
b. stressed out	50%	50%	o. disappointed	35%	65%
c. optimistic	54%	46%	p. confused	55%	45%
d. content	59%	41%	q. always tired	46%	54%
e. lazy	41%	59%	r. religious	78%	22%
f. angry with life	26%	74%	s. lonely	36%	64%
g. skeptical	33%	67%	t. encouraged	74%	26%
h. upbeat	63%	37%	u. seeking answers	74%	26%
i. lacking purpose	20%	80%	v. resentful	25%	75%
j. unmotivated	21%	79%	w. reliable	86%	14%
k. physically attractive	61%	39%	x. an achiever	80%	20%
l. mistrust people	32%	68%	y. respected by others	86%	14%
m. high integrity	60%	40%	z. temperamental	47%	53%

Section E: Beliefs and Perspectives About Life

1. Please mark one answer next to each statement to indicate whether you agree or disagree with that statement.

Statement	- - - - - agree? - - - - -		
	Yes	No	Not Sure
a. freedom means being able to do anything you want to do, as long as it is legal	54%	35%	11%
b. there is no such thing as "absolute truth;" people may define "truth" in contradictory ways and still be correct	29%	43%	28%
c. the Bible does not provide today's people with practical standards for living	17%	67%	16%

	- - - - - agree? - - - - -		
Statement	Yes	No	Not Sure
d. everything in life is negotiable	23%	55%	22%
e. there's nothing wrong with breaking the law as long as it doesn't hurt anybody	12%	80%	8%
f. lying is sometimes necessary	38%	48%	14%
g. only the Bible provides a clear and indisputable description of moral truth	72%	12%	16%
h. nothing can be known for certain except the things that you experience in your life	39%	38%	23%
i. when it comes to matters of morals and ethics, truth means different things to different people; no one can be absolutely positive that they have the truth	48%	29%	23%
j. what is right for one person in a given situation might not be right for another person who encounters that same situation	70%	15%	15%
k. God may know the meaning of truth, but humans are not capable of grasping that knowledge	31%	44%	25%
l. every religion offers a different explanation of the meaning of life and truth	59%	18%	23%
m. the best philosophy for life is: do whatever feels or seems right, as long as it doesn't harm anyone else	22%	62%	16%
n. you know that something is morally or ethically right if it works	16%	54%	30%
o. God established the limits for humankind; acting in conflict with His laws has negative consequences for those people	57%	13%	30%
p. the Bible isn't very relevant for today's problems	15%	68%	17%
q. the moral standards of Americans these days are just as high as ever	20%	59%	21%
r. the only intelligent way to live is to make the best choice you can in every situation based on your feelings at the moment	33%	48%	19%

2. Read the list of life conditions described below. If each of these conditions were possible for you to achieve in your future, please indicate how much you desire that condition for your future: a lot, some, a little bit, or not at all.

	- - - - how desirable is this? - - - -			
Condition	A lot	Some	Little Bit	Not at all
a. good physical health	83%	14%	3%	0%

- - - - how desirable is this? - - - -

Condition	A lot	Some	Little Bit	Not at all
b. a high-paying job	55%	30%	8%	7%
c. being active in a church	64%	24%	10%	2%
d. influence other people's lives	64%	25%	8%	3%
e. having a close relationship with God	77%	15%	6%	2%
f. live close to family and relatives	48%	31%	16%	5%
g. achieve fame or public recognition	25%	28%	30%	17%
h. having a comfortable lifestyle	70%	23%	6%	1%
i. having close, personal friendships	81%	13%	4%	2%
j. having a fulfilled sex life within marriage	61%	21%	9%	9%
k. having a clear purpose for living	81%	14%	4%	1%
l. high personal integrity	69%	23%	6%	2%
m. to make a difference in the world	62%	24%	11%	3%
n. having a spouse and children	73%	15%	6%	6%
o. having one marriage partner for life	85%	7%	3%	5%

3. Please mark one answer next to each statement to indicate whether you agree or disagree with that statement.

- - - - - agree? - - - - -

Statement	Yes	No	Not Sure
a. the main purpose of life is enjoyment and personal fulfillment	29%	55%	16%
b. it's better to get even than to get mad	12%	79%	9%
c. in times of trouble or crisis, I feel all alone	40%	47%	13%
d. sometimes, I wonder if life is worth living	38%	53%	9%
e. one person cannot really make a difference in this world	22%	66%	12%
f. everyone needs a hero in their life	62%	23%	15%
g. I know one or more adults who I feel really have it together	75%	11%	12%
h. there is nobody whom I consider to be my hero or model for life	24%	65%	11%
i. life is too complex these days	49%	34%	17%
j. what I think doesn't matter	19%	68%	13%
k. the future will be better than today	34%	30%	36%

Section F: Religious Background

1. How often do you and others in your life attend services at a Christian church?

Person	every week	2–3 times a month	once a month	rarely	never	not applicable
a. myself	82%	12%	2%	4%	0%	0%
b. my father	56%	10%	2%	10%	15%	7%
c. my mother	70%	9%	3%	8%	9%	3%
d. brothers/sisters living at my home	62%	11%	2%	7%	6%	12%

2. How often do you do each of the activities listed below?

Activity	Daily	Weekly	Monthly	Rarely	Never
a. read part of the Bible	20%	28%	13%	30%	8%
b. pray to God	65%	19%	5%	9%	2%
c. attend a church youth group	11%	73%	8%	6%	2%
d. attend a Bible study group	7%	36%	7%	21%	29%
e. attend a Sunday school class	11%	67%	5%	8%	9%
f. lead a small group	6%	11%	6%	25%	52%

3. Overall, how important is the Christian faith in your life these days?

64%=very important   6%=not too important
29%=somewhat important   1%=not at all important

4. About how many youth attend your youth group meetings at a typical meeting?

1–9=17%   10–19=32%   20–29=23%   30–39=12%
40–49= 5%   50–59= 3%   over 60= 8%

5. Please mark one answer next to each statement to indicate whether you agree or disagree with that statement.

Statement	Yes	No	Not Sure
a. the Christian faith is relevant to the way I live today	69%	12%	19%
b. the Christian churches in my area are relevant to the way I live today	56%	19%	25%
c. the Bible is totally accurate in all of its teachings	70%	10%	20%
d. I, personally, have a responsibility to tell other people about my religious beliefs	68%	15%	17%
e. the devil, or Satan, is not a living being, but is a symbol of evil	31%	49%	20%

	- - - - - agree? - - - - -		
Statement	Yes	No	Not Sure
f. there is really a place of permanent suffering, which is known as hell	80%	8%	12%
g. if a person is generally good, or does enough good things for others during their life, they will earn a place in Heaven	23%	62%	16%
h. what I do for other people is more important than what I believe about Jesus Christ...	14%	74%	12%
i. there are a lot of hypocrites in my church	32%	29%	39%
j. all good people, whether or not they consider Jesus Christ to be their Savior, will live in Heaven after they die	13%	69%	18%
k. Jesus sometimes made mistakes	17%	67%	16%
l. it does not matter what religious faith you follow because all faiths teach similar lessons..........................	21%	54%	25%
m. no one can really prove which religion is absolutely true .	40%	34%	26%
n. a person can experience a relationship with God personally	84%	5%	11%
o. Muslims, Buddhists, Christians, Jews and all other people pray to the same God, even though they use different names for their god	21%	52%	27%
p. when it comes to religion, what you do in life is more important than what you believe	15%	62%	23%
q. when it comes to religion, what type of person you are is more important than what you accomplish..................	43%	27%	30%
r. there are some sins or crimes which are so serious that they cannot be forgiven by God	18%	68%	14%

6. Have you ever made a personal commitment to Jesus Christ that is still important in your life today?
   86%=Yes   14%=No

7. If so, at what age did you make that commitment?   at age 5=8%
   at age 10=10%   at age 12=12%   at age 15=6%   at age 18=1%

8. Which one of the following descriptions comes closest to describing your view of God? (Circle one answer.)
   2%=Everyone is god.
   85%=God is the all-powerful, all-knowing, perfect creator of the universe who rules the world today.
   4%=God refers to the total realization of personal, human potential.

1%=There are many gods, each with different power and authority.
2%=God represents a state of high consciousness that a person may reach.
4%=There is no such thing as God.
5%=I don't know what I believe about God.

9. Which of the following statements best describes what I believe will happen to me after I die?
6%=When you die you will go to Heaven because you have tried to obey the Ten Commandments.
3%=When you die you will go to Heaven because you are basically a good person.
75%=When you die you will go to Heaven because you have confessed your sins and have accepted Jesus Christ as your Savior.
3%=When you die you will go to Heaven because God loves all people and will not let them perish.
1%=When you die you will not go to Heaven.
12%=You do not know what will happen after you die.

10. When you graduate from high school or move away from home, how likely is it that you will attend a church on a regular basis?
63%=very likely   7%=not too likely
28%=somewhat likely   2%=not at all likely

■ HOW OUR YOUTH VIEW THE TRUTH ■

The responses of churched youth to seven statements regarding the existence of absolute truth indicate that relatively few of our young people believe in absolute truth. Fewer still refer to objective standards of truth and morality in making life decisions.

Table D-1.1 depicts the responses of 3,795 churched youth to the seven separate survey questions. Their answers to those questions reveal that our youth are not sold on the existence of absolute truth and objective standards of morality. Cumulatively, only 9 percent of the students interviewed provided a "pro-truth" reply to each of the seven statements. In other words, only one in eleven of our youth give evidence that they possess a consistent, cohesive belief in absolute truth. "This is an astoundingly low proportion," says the researcher, George Barna, "given that the sample is *churched* kids."

A significant number of our youth endorse the concept that some things are true for all people, for all times, and for all places, in some circumstances, but reject the idea when the question is phrased differently. This intimates that many of our kids are struggling with the concept of truth and grappling not only with how to understand it, but also with how it applies to them.

It is apparent from the survey that our youth have had little training or education regarding truth (whether it exists, for example, and how to discern it and apply it); consequently, they don't know what to think or do with the truth when they meet it.

Reactions to Statements About Absolute Truth			
Statement	Agree	Disagree	Not Sure
• Only the Bible provides a clear and indisputable description of moral truth.	72%	12%	16%
• What is right for one person in a given situation might not be right for another person who encounters that same situation.	71%	15%	15%
• When it comes to matters of morals and ethics, truth means different things to different people; no one can be absolutely positive they have the truth.	48%	29%	23%
• Nothing can be known for certain except the things that you experience in your life.	39%	38%	23%
• God may know the meaning of truth, but humans are not capable of grasping that knowledge.	31%	44%	25%
• There is no such thing as absolute truth; people may define truth in contradictory ways and still be correct.	29%	43%	28%
• Everything in life is negotiable.	23%	56%	22%
All statements: Took a pro-truth position	9%	91%	

Table D-1.1

Table D-1.1 makes it clear that many of our youth have no choice but to make conditional decisions—choosing what seems to be best in any given instance—without referring to the truth that God has revealed to us. "It appears," says Barna, "that expecting today's youth to live in awareness of and accordance with a group of moral absolutes is unrealistic at this time."

Such a circumstance presents us with a challenge: to equip our youth with a belief in biblical truth that can guide their decisions and behavior, leading them to choose right in a world that so often encourages wrong choices.

15

Survey Analysis on Love and Sex

OUR CHILDREN ARE GROWING UP in a sex-sated culture. Television, movies, music, magazines, books, and billboards—even the curriculum of many public schools—communicate messages about sex that are in stark contrast to biblical values. Teenagers today see and hear sexual messages everywhere, and they're paying attention. And it shows.

According to general research by George Barna, of The Barna Research Group, only 23 percent of the entire Baby Buster generation (churched and unchurched) claim to be virgins. More than three-quarters admit to having had sexual intercourse with another single person. Two out of ten single Busters say they have had sex with a married person. One in fourteen married Busters has had extramarital sex. Almost half (47 percent) of the babies born to Baby Buster females in 1992 were born to unmarried mothers.[1] And girls are having sex much earlier these days; the median age for a young woman's first act of premarital sex has fallen from nineteen in 1960 to seventeen in 1990.

■ SEXUAL ACTIVITY OF CHURCHED YOUTH ■

Those figures are disturbing enough; but the 1994 research among churched youth reveals that our kids—kids from Christian homes and good churches—are also crumbling under the constant pressures of a sex-crazed society.

By age eighteen, 27 percent of churched youth have experienced sexual intercourse, and 55 percent have engaged in fondling breasts; in other words, your son or daughter faces a one-in-four chance of engaging in sexual intercourse by the age of eighteen.

■ SEXUAL ACTIVITY COMPARED BY AGE GROUPS ■

Our kids are sold on sex, and they apparently become less—not more—resistant as they mature. From the youngest segment (eleven to twelve years old) to the next age category (thirteen to fourteen), the proportion of kids involved in heavy kissing doubled; the fondling of breasts increased fivefold; fondling of genitals increased by a factor of seven; and the incidence of intercourse (experienced by 1 percent of the youngest age group) increased eight times (to one in eleven).

Activity at each level of sexual involvement—fondling of breasts, fondling of genitals, sexual intercourse—doubled among fifteen- to-sixteen-year-olds (compared to those in the next youngest age group). By the age of sixteen, two in five (41 percent) have engaged in (or permitted) the fondling of breasts; nearly one in three (30 percent) have fondled genitals; about one in five (18 percent) have taken part in sexual intercourse (see Table B-2.2).

A majority are involved in heavy kissing and fondling of breasts by the time they reach the seventeen-to-eighteen-year-old age group. About two-thirds of the boys of that age have fondled breasts, an increase of 34 percent over the next youngest age group; nearly half of seventeen- and eighteen-year-old boys and girls have fondled the genitals of at least one other person, a 47 percent increase. And, due to a 50 percent rise in the incidence of

Sexual Activity With Persons of the Opposite Sex, by Age Group

ACTIVITY	ALL	11–12	13–14	15–16	17–18
Held hands	89%	74%	84%	92%	95%
Embracing & some kissing	73%	39%	65%	80%	86%
Heavy "French" kissing	53%	15%	38%	61%	74%
Fondling of breasts	34%	4%	20%	41%	55%
Fondling of genitals	26%	2%	14%	30%	44%
Sexual intercourse	15%	1%	8%	18%	27%

Table B-2.2

intercourse among seventeen- to-eighteen-year-olds (compared to the next youngest age group), over one in four (27 percent) admit to having gone "all the way."

■ SEXUAL ACTIVITY COMPARED TO 1987 ■

A ray of hope shines amid all the bad news, however. The research gives us reason to believe that there has been considerable improvement in teens' sexual involvement in the past several years. The 1994 figures, compared with the results obtained in the

Sexual Activity With Persons of the Opposite Sex, 1987 vs. 1994

ACTIVITY	1994	1987
Held hands	89%	91%
Embracing & some kissing	73%	81%
Heavy "French" kissing	53%	63%
Fondling of breasts	34%	42%
Fondling of genitals	26%	33%
Sexual intercourse	16%	24%

Table B-2.5

national "Why Wait?" survey done in 1987, suggests a nearly 10 percent decline in each area of sexual involvement among teens in the time between the two surveys.

This decline, which may reflect the influence of the "Why Wait?" campaign and similar programs, indicates that it is possible to equip our youth to resist the all-out assault of a godless culture. It is possible—if we clearly proclaim biblical standards to our kids and give them solid reasons to behave morally—to steel them against the traps and temptations of a sex-sated society. We must not only heed the research that portrays a generation in grave danger; we must also hear when it strikes a note of hope, and gives us reason to believe that we *can* do something.

■ WHAT DO THEY CONSIDER MORALLY ACCEPTABLE? ■

The study reveals that sexual activity is not at all uncommon among our kids. It also reveals that a surprising number see nothing wrong with premarital sexual involvement.

Over half of our kids (51 percent) could not state that fondling of breasts was morally unacceptable (see Table B-3.1). More than one-third (35 percent) consider the fondling of breasts to be morally acceptable. Nearly that many (29 percent) view the fondling

Activities Deemed Morally Acceptable Among Two People Who Are In Love, Are Willing, But Are Not Married

ACTIVITY	ALWAYS	SOMETIMES	NEVER	NOT SURE
Holding hands	85%	14%	1%	1%
Embracing & some kissing	68%	29%	2%	1%
Heavy "French" kissing	33%	48%	11%	9%
Fondling of breasts	10%	25%	49%	16%
Fondling of genitals	9%	20%	55%	16%
Sexual intercourse	7%	13%	68%	12%

Table B-3.1

of genitals as moral behavior. And one in five of our kids (20 percent) see sexual intercourse outside of marriage as moral. The study reveals that many of our kids think that heavy petting—even sexual intercourse—between two unmarried individuals is perfectly moral.

Moreover, for nearly every practice measured in the study, nearly all of the kids who define that behavior as "morally acceptable" have engaged in it. For example, 36 percent of our kids say that fondling of breasts between unmarried people is morally acceptable; 33 percent have engaged in that behavior (see Table B-3.2). Twenty-nine percent view the fondling of genitals as moral; 25 percent admit to having done so themselves. And 20 percent approve sexual intercourse outside marriage; 15 percent have participated in that activity. These figures clearly indicate the relationship between our kids' truth views and their behaviors. In each case, there is a close correlation between judging a behavior to be "OK" morally, and engaging in that behavior.

A frightening implication lies buried in those figures, like a snake slumbering in tall grass: the fact that the number of our kids who deem those activities to be morally acceptable is higher than the number who are involved in each activity suggests that there

Activities Deemed Morally Acceptable, And the Incidence of Such Behavior
(base: acceptable "always" or "sometimes")

Activity	Morally Acceptable	Engaged in This Activity
Holding hands	99%	88%
Embracing and some kissing	97%	72%
Heavy "French" kissing	80%	51%
Fondling of breasts	36%	33%
Fondling of genitals	30%	25%
Sexual intercourse	20%	15%

Table B-3.2

is probably more illegitimate sexual behavior yet to be unleashed among our youth. There are some kids who judge premarital sex to be moral who have not yet engaged in that behavior themselves; the study indicates that they are not restrained by any moral conviction. Therefore, it is apparent that we have yet to "max out" the proportion of kids who, based solely on moral judgments, feel perfectly justified in engaging in sexual intercourse.

■ MORAL VIEWS BY AGE GROUP ■

One of the interesting insights of the study reveals that our kids form their ideas about the right and wrong of sexual behavior well before they enter high school. Over a quarter (26 percent) of our eleven- and twelve-year-olds consider premarital fondling of breasts to be morally acceptable; one in five (21 percent) of that age group deem fondling of genitals among unmarried persons as moral, and nearly as many (19 percent) say that premarital sex is moral (see Table B-3.3).

While the numbers in each category above do change as our youth mature, they change incrementally, indicating that their sexual mores are largely in place before they even enter their teens.

Activities Deemed Morally Acceptable, By Respondent Age Group (base: acceptable "always" or "sometimes")				
ACTIVITY	**11–12**	**13–14**	**15–16**	**17–18**
Holding hands	97%	99%	99%	99%
Embracing & some kissing	92%	96%	98%	98%
Heavy "French" kissing	64%	79%	84%	83%
Fondling of breasts	26%	35%	39%	38%
Fondling of genitals	21%	29%	32%	30%
Sexual intercourse	19%	21%	22%	18%

Table B-3.3

This suggests that attempts to educate and influence our children's ideas about sexual morality *must not* be put off until they enter a high-school youth group; we must build a firm foundation of biblical sexuality well *before* our kids enter high school.

Furthermore, those numbers—already too high among eleven- and twelve-year-olds—do not decline as our kids mature. The percentage of our kids who judge these behaviors as immoral increases from the youngest age group we studied to the next (thirteen- to fourteen-year-olds), and peaks among fifteen- and sixteen-year-olds. At those ages, two in five (39 percent) believe fondling of breasts among unmarried people is morally acceptable; one in three (32 percent) say that fondling of genitals is OK; and more than one in five see nothing wrong with premarital sexual intercourse. Although a slight decrease in each category occurs among seventeen- and eighteen-year-olds (38 percent approve fondling of breasts, 30 percent condone fondling of genitals, and 18 percent endorse intercourse among unmarried partners), the study clearly indicates that our kids are becoming older, but no wiser, about matters of sexual morality.

■ MORAL VIEWS COMPARED TO 1987 ■

These results differ little from the attitudes of kids surveyed in 1987 for the national "Why Wait?" campaign. The percentage of kids who regard the fondling of breasts and genitals among unmarried persons as a moral activity declined by three points in the seven years between the two studies (see Table B-3.6, next page).

A slightly larger decline occurred among those who viewed premarital intercourse as "morally acceptable" (25 percent in 1987, 20 percent in 1994). This is not a significant increase in our kids' moral convictions. They may be engaging less in unacceptable behavior, but it's not due largely to their moral convictions against it. This is not encouraging for me as a father. I want my kids to be able to recognize what things are wrong, and I want that knowledge to embolden them to choose right.

Activities Deemed Morally Acceptable, 1994 vs. 1987

(base: acceptable "always" or "sometimes")

ACTIVITY	1994	1987
Holding hands	99%	98%
Embracing & some kissing	97%	96%
Heavy "French" kissing	81%	82%
Fondling of breasts	36%	39%
Fondling of genitals	29%	32%
Sexual intercourse	20%	25%

Table B-3.6

■ WHAT MAKES PREMARITAL SEX ACCEPTABLE TO THEM? ■

In spite of the fact that one in five of our kids (20 percent) said they think sexual intercourse between unmarried persons is morally acceptable, more than twice that number (46 percent) said that they would be more likely to have sex with someone if they "were in love with the person." In other words, nearly half of our kids would tend to agree with Brittney's attitude that love—not marriage—makes it right.

To many of our kids, that is also true of an intention to marry. Forty-four percent say that they would be more likely to have sex with a person they "really intended to marry." Thus, nearly half of our kids stop short of endorsing the marriage commitment alone as the proper context of sex, but consider the intention to marry (a determination that may pale or disappear tomorrow, or next week, or next month) a suitable incentive for sexual involvement—another indication of our kids' willingness to compromise sexually in advance of marriage.

Similarly, one in four of our kids (26 percent) say that they would be more likely to have sex if they were positive a pregnancy would not result. An identical number responded that they would be more likely to "go all the way" if they could know that their parents would not find out, and one in five (22 percent) said

	CONDITIONS MAKE INTERCOURSE:		
Conditions	More Likely	Less Likely	Doesn't Matter
You were in love with the person	46%	19%	36%
Really intended to marry them	44%	19%	37%
Positive a pregnancy would not result	26%	25%	49%
Knew your parents would not find out	26%	24%	51%
Felt your parents would not mind	22%	25%	54%
Friends strongly encouraged you to do so	11%	31%	58%

Conditions Under Which Churched Youth Would Have Sexual Intercourse Today

Table B-3.7

they would be more likely to have sex if they felt that their parents "would not mind." Perhaps the sole encouragement we can glean from the data is that only one in nine (11 percent) said that being "strongly encouraged" by friends to have sex would make them more likely to do so (see Table B-3.7).

Such responses reveal that our kids' morals are not based on fundamental, fixed principles, but on fluid concepts of right and wrong. As a result, our children's decisions about the morality and advisability of sexual involvement are subject chiefly to their youthful emotions or intentions. There has not been a significant change in how our youth responded to this set of questions from 1987 (see Table B-3.8, next page).

These statistics point out the fact that our youth are floundering and flailing; they are being tempted and tossed because they do not have a sound moral and spiritual standard to anchor them when they are faced with difficult choices. As we will see, that single factor—the possession of a strong truth view—will make a world of difference in what they think and do.

■ WHAT DIFFERENCE DOES TRUTH MAKE? ■

The research strongly indicates that a deep conviction about the existence of truth and objective moral standards will anchor

Conditions Under Which Churched Youth Would Have Sexual Intercourse
1994 versus 1987
(base: said conditions would make such intercourse more likely)

Conditions	1994	1987
You were in love with the person	46%	NA
Really intended to marry them	44%	39%
Positive a pregnancy would not result	26%	29%
Knew your parents would not find out	26%	28%
Felt your parents would not mind	22%	22%
Friends strongly encouraged you to do so	11%	16%

Table B-3.8

our youth, even when they are pushed and pulled by a culture in crisis. Without such a conviction, our kids won't know which way is up or which choice is right; they'll be buffeted by the culture and, more likely than not, they'll succumb to its pressures. This is not just something I believe; the cold, hard facts of the study bear it out.

The study reveals that youth are much more likely to accept sexual petting and intercourse before marriage as moral if they lack a strong pro-truth view. Youth who *do not* affirm the existence of absolute truth are twice as likely to classify fondling of breasts (between unmarried persons) as moral. Young people who are not equipped with a consistent view of truth and morality are three times as likely to regard fondling of genitals (between unmarried persons) as morally acceptable. And kids who lack a "truth lens" are four times as likely to approve premarital sexual intercourse as a "moral" choice.

The data also indicate that nearly all of the kids who define a behavior as "morally acceptable" have engaged in it. Consequently, it is likely that those kids who define premarital petting or intercourse as "moral" have succumbed (or will soon) to the temptation to engage in that behavior. Therefore, while a strong foundation of biblical views about truth and morality is no guarantee that your kids will not become sexually involved before marriage, the *lack* of a strong foundation may nearly guarantee that they will!

■ THE DIFFERENCE FAITH MAKES ■

Among the students participating in the survey, 65 percent were classified as "born again" (that is, they said they had made a personal commitment to Jesus Christ that is still important in their lives today, *and* affirmed that when they die they will go to heaven because they have confessed their sins and have accepted Jesus Christ as their Savior).

Not surprisingly, the study revealed that a young person's faith commitment plays a role in determining his or her views about sexual morality. Compared to born-again students, non-Christians (35 percent of the total) were twice as likely to regard the fondling of breasts and the fondling of genitals among unmarried partners as moral. And for every three non-Christian youth who stated that premarital sex is "morally acceptable," only one born-again youth took the same stand. And what born again students believe is morally acceptable by and large allows them to engage in that activity (see Tables B-3.5 and B-2.3, next page).

■ TRUTH MORE INFLUENTIAL THAN FAITH ■

Perhaps the most shocking revelation of the study, however, is the indication that our kids' attitudes and behaviors are influenced more by their truth views than by whether or not they are born again. The two groups are not mutually exclusive, but born-again kids are 50 percent more likely than those who accept absolute truth to say that fondling of breasts or genitals is morally acceptable between unmarried persons. And born-again youth are two times as likely to consider premarital sex a moral activity. In other words, your child's morality will be positively affected by a born-again experience, but even more so by the development of strong

The Moral Acceptability of Sexual Activity with Persons of the Opposite Sex, by Faith Commitment
(base: acceptable "always" or "sometimes")

Activity	All	Born Again Christians	Non-Christians
Holding hands	99%	99%	98%
Embracing and some kissing	97%	97%	97%
Heavy "French" kissing	81%	79%	85%
Fondling of breasts	36%	27%	52%
Fondling of genitals	29%	20%	45%
Sexual intercourse	20%	11%	37%

Table B-3.5

convictions regarding morality (and, of course, still more if the those two factors are combined). This applies not only to the area of sexual involvement; it is true across the board, in every area of behavior and belief.

The implications of this discovery may take some thinking through, but perhaps it will help us understand why so many

Sexual Activity with Persons Of the Opposite Sex, by Truth Views

Activity	Believe in Absolute Truth?	
	Yes	No
Held hands	86%	89%
Embracing and some kissing	71%	74%
Heavy "French" kissing	51%	53%
Fondling of breasts	35%	34%
Fondling of genitals	25%	26%
Sexual intercourse	13%	16%

Table B-2.3

Christian kids, who seem to love the Lord, are falling into harm-ful, sinful behaviors—they have the desire to please God, but because they believe truth is subjectively determined, they more readily accept the counterfeit as a means of fulfilling their desires.

■ THE IMPORTANCE OF CONVICTIONS ON TRUTH ■

The study revealed yet another startling fact. If your kids do not accept the existence of objective moral standards, they will be twice as likely to consider having illicit sexual relations in certain circumstances. For example, kids who do not accept truth to be absolute are twice as likely to consider having sex "if they were in love with the person." In fact, in almost every circumstance suggested by the study ("if you really intended to marry," "if you were positive a pregnancy would not result," "if you knew your parents would not find out," and "if your friends strongly encour-aged you to do so"), youth who did not possess a pro-truth view were two times as likely to say that the cited condition would make them "more likely" to have sex (the exception: kids who denied the existence of absolute truth were 64 percent more likely, if they "felt [their] parents would not mind," to consider engaging in sexual intercourse). See Table B–3.9, next page.

Moreover, the data again indicates that, while a born-again experience does have an impact on how our kids plan to make future sexual decisions, it is in every case *half* as influential as that person's convictions about truth.

In other words, the likelihood of young people being persuaded to engage in premarital sex based on emotional or practical cir-cumstances (not moral considerations) increases significantly if they are not equipped with solid, foundational views about truth and morality (see Table B–3.4).

This study shows that the most important thing we can do for our children—the investment that will do the most good—is to introduce them to the person of Truth and instill within them a conviction that His truth is right for all people, for all times, for all places. The research indicates that doing that will double, triple, even quadruple their chances of making moral choices in an immoral world.

Conditions Under Which Churched Youth Would Have Sexual Intercourse Today, by Their Views on Truth
(base: said conditions would make such intercourse more likely)

Conditions	Is there absolute truth?	
	Yes	No
You were in love with the person	25%	48%
Really intended to marry them	24%	47%
Positive a pregnancy would not result	14%	27%
Knew your parents would not find out	13%	27%
Felt your parents would not mind	14%	23%
Friends strongly encouraged you to do so	6%	12%

Table B-3.9

Morally Acceptable Sexual Activity with Persons of the Opposite Sex, in Relation to the Respondent's Truth Views
(base: said these activities are morally acceptable among unmarried, in love, consenting individuals)

Conditions	Believe in absolute truth?	
	Yes	No
Holding hands	99%	99%
Embracing and some kissing	96%	97%
Heavy "French" kissing	73%	82%
Fondling of breasts	18%	37%
Fondling of genitals	11%	31%
Sexual intercourse	5%	21%

Table B-3.4

16

Survey Analysis on Marriage and Family

ACCORDING TO WILLIAM J. BENNETT'S "Index of Leading Cultural Indicators," the divorce rate has climbed from 9.2 (per 1,000 married women) in 1960 to 20.9 in 1991, a 120 percent jump. Within that same period, the percentage of children who live with single mothers has rocketed from 8 percent to 22 percent (an increase of 175 percent), while births to unwed mothers have increased from 5.3 percent (of total births) in 1960 to 28 percent in 1990 (a leap of 400 percent).[1]

We must face it; our kids are growing up in a day and age that glorifies sex and motherhood outside of marriage, and often demeans the institution of marriage as restrictive and outdated. Reasonably healthy depictions of two-parent families on prime time television are rare and are outnumbered substantially by single-parent households or multiple-parent households.

Don't get me wrong. I'm not saying that television is the culprit; but at the very least, it reflects what people in our society think and feel. And the message of our culture very often seems to be that a happy marriage and a two-parent family is unrealistic, unnecessary, and boring.

If we expect our children to develop strong biblical values about marriage and the family, we must prepare them to do battle with the values of contemporary society. And the battle begins in our own families. What do our children say about their homes and families? Do they feel loved? How much time are they spending with Mom and Dad, as opposed to MTV? And how are their own family experiences shaping their views of marriage and family?

■ FAMILY PORTRAIT ■

Technology these days is so advanced that we're shocked by very little. Telephone calls from planes, interactive virtual-reality games, entire libraries on CD-ROM discs—every new development is greeted with aplomb. But I remember the first time I saw a Polaroid camera. It struck me as an amazing piece of technology. I considered it miraculous to be able to point the lens at a subject, snap the shutter, extract the photo from the camera, tick off sixty seconds, and then separate the print from the protective paper to reveal the final photo.

Many years later, Polaroid came out with yet another advancement, a camera they called the "One Step." This photographic wonder spat out a stiff print instantly, which developed from a blank square of smelly chemicals into a color photo before my very eyes! The photographer could watch the picture emerge without leaving the scene.

Our survey of 3,795 youth allows us to do much the same thing; by careful study and analysis, we can watch our own family portrait emerge before our very eyes.

The first portrait of marriage and family in the church that emerges reveals that nearly three in four (73 percent) of our kids live with both their mother and father; about one in four (23 percent) are the children of divorced parents. Thirteen percent of our kids live in single-parent homes, and 1 percent live with both a stepfather and stepmother.

■ WHAT IS THEIR RELATIONSHIP TO DAD? ■

Three-fourths of our kids (74 percent) say that they are fairly or very close to their father. However, the study suggests that father-child relationships become more distant, not closer, as teens mature. For instance, junior-high-school students are much more likely than senior-high students to feel "very close" to their father.

Our kids seem to have positive feelings toward their fathers. A majority (56 percent) state that they frequently feel proud of their fathers. Half claim that their fathers frequently show love for them. One in five (19 percent) say they frequently do something special with Dad that involves just the two of them. Less than one in eleven (8 percent) say they frequently wonder if their fathers love them (see Table A-2.2).

A further warning appears in the midst of that news, however. In spite of the thriving relationships that many churched kids seem to enjoy with their fathers, the study clearly communicates the fact that fathers are not among the primary counselors churched youth confide in or turn to for advice. One out of

Frequency of Conditions Related to One's Father

Conditions	Frequently	Occasionally	Seldom	Never
• Feel proud of your father	56%	38%	9%	7%
• Feel your father shows his love for you	51%	29%	14%	7%
• Show your love for your father	41%	36%	18%	5%
• Seek advice from your father	26%	38%	21%	15%
• Do something special with your father that involves just the two of you	19%	39%	28%	15%
• Talk with your father about your personal concerns	12%	34%	32%	22%
• Wonder whether or not your father loves you	8%	14%	21%	58%

Table A-2.2

every four (26 percent) say they frequently seek advice from their fathers, and about one in nine (12 percent) frequently discuss personal concerns with Dad. The implication is that, while most of our kids enjoy positive father-child relationships, they do not often hear Dad's perspective on intimate or sensitive matters.

There appears to be little difference between how boys and girls describe their relationships with their fathers. While boys are slightly more likely to say they feel very close to Dad, the gap was minute (35 percent for males, 29 percent among females). Sons were only slightly more likely than daughters to frequently seek advice from their father (28 percent to 23 percent). Females were less likely than males to say they frequently did something special with just their father (15 percent for females, 22 percent among males). The largest difference in how boys and girls relate to their fathers occurs in how frequently they demonstrate their love for Dad: half of the girls (47 percent) say they express love to their dads frequently, compared to just one-third of the boys (34 percent) who make the same claim.

■ TIME SPENT WITH DAD ■

Though our kids seem to enjoy positive relationships with their dads, they seem to spend precious little time with them. The median amount of time spent with a father in a typical week was seventeen minutes. Though one in four of our kids say they spent an hour or more each week in meaningful conversations with their fathers, one of every seven kids claim to spend no time in such interaction with Dad.

There was virtually no difference between the amount of time sons spent in conversation with fathers and the amount of time daughters spent with dads in a typical week. This area was, however, the single instance in which the responses in the 1994 study differed significantly from the results of the 1987 "Why Wait" survey among churched youth; in most cases, the state of father-child relationships today is unchanged from the way things appeared seven years ago. But the median amount of time spent with fathers rose, from twelve minutes per week among the youth participating in the "Why Wait?" survey, to seventeen minutes a week for the youth in the 1994 survey. While there is still ample room for improvement, the increase suggests that fathers may be giving more attention to their relationships with their children today than they have in the past—a welcome development, indeed. See Tables A-2.1; A-2.3; and A-2.4.

Closeness to One's Father

Closeness with Father	1994	1987
Very close	32%	30%
Fairly close	42%	43%
Not too close	14%	17%
Not at all close	7%	6%
Not alive/don't know father	5%	4%

Table A-2.1

Frequency of Conditions Related to One's Father, 1987 vs. 1994
(base: occurs "frequently")

Conditions	1994	1987
• Feel proud of your father	56%	59%
• Feel your father shows his love for you	51%	47%
• Show your love for your father	41%	33%
• Seek advice from your father	26%	27%
• Do something special with your father that involves just the two of you	19%	16%
• Talk with your father about your personal concerns	12%	11%
• Wonder whether or not your father loves you	8%	7%

Table A-2.3

Time Spent with Father in a Typical Week

Amount of Time Spent	1994	1987
No time	16%	15%
Less than 5 minutes	14%	17%
Between 5 and 15 minutes	20%	23%
Between 16 and 30 minutes	16%	17%
Between 31 and 60 minutes	13%	14%
1 Hour or more	23%	14%
Media (minutes)	17%	12%

Table A-2.4

■ WHAT IS THEIR RELATIONSHIP TO MOM? ■

Greg Howard and Craig MacIntosh, authors of the newspaper comic strip, "Sally Forth," depicted the reality of many families with a series of panels that showed a mother setting the breakfast table as she talked to her daughter.

"Tonight," the mother said, "we're going to have a dinner where we all sit down together. We'll spend a nice leisurely hour talking about the kinds of things families should talk about."

"An hour?" the daughter responded.

"Sure. There are so many things we can discuss that the time will fly by."

"An hour?" the daughter repeated.

"It'll be fun," Mom continued. "We'll turn off the TV and . . ."

The daughter turned to her father. "Shouldn't you at least tell me what I'm being punished for?"

It's funny, of course. But it's also sad. Many families today—our families—spend little time in meaningful conversation and interaction between parents and children.

While many fathers are apparently giving more attention to their relationships with their children, mothers still fare significantly better in building good relationships and initiating meaningful conversation with their sons and daughters.

Our kids indicate that they are more likely to feel close to their mother than to their fathers. A majority (52 percent) say they feel very close to their mother, substantially more than the one in three (32 percent) who feel very close to their fathers. Altogether, nine in ten (88 percent) characterize their relationships with Mom positively ("very close" or "fairly close"), compared to three in four (74 percent) who regard their relationships with Dad as positive.

The pattern continues, as two-thirds of our youth (68 percent) say that their mothers frequently show love to them (compared to 51 percent who make the same claim about Dad). Six out of ten (59 percent) say they frequently feel proud of Mom, and half (52 percent) frequently show their affection for their moms. Three in ten (30 percent) claim to frequently "do something special with your mother that involves just the two of you." Only one in eleven (9 percent) say they frequently wonder if their mothers really love them (see Table A–3.2).

The picture that emerges from the study is a portrait of kids who feel loved, and have generally positive impressions of their

Frequency of Conditions Related to One's Mother

Conditions	Frequently	Occasionally	Seldom	Never
• Feel proud of your mother	59%	31%	8%	3%
• Feel your mother shows her love for you	68%	22%	7%	3%
• Show your love for your mother	52%	34%	12%	3%
• Seek advice from your mother	40%	34%	18%	8%
• Do something special with your mother that involves just the two of you	30%	37%	25%	8%
• Talk with your mother about your personal concerns	39%	35%	18%	8%
• Wonder whether or not your mother loves you	9%	13%	19%	59%

Table A-3.2

parents, especially of Mom: mothers are more likely than fathers to frequently show their love for a child, to receive demonstrations of love in return, and to engage in special one-on-one activities with a child.

■ THEY SPEND TWICE AS MUCH TIME WITH MOM ■

Our youth also turn to their mothers more often than their fathers to ask advice or discuss personal concerns. Two out of every five (40 percent) of our children say they frequently seek advice from Mom. Not surprisingly, daughters more often take their problems or questions to their mothers. Girls are 50 percent more likely than boys to ask their mothers for advice (47 percent to 31 percent) and twice as likely as boys (51 percent to 27 percent) to talk with their mothers about personal concerns.

Our kids—both male and female—spend about twice as much time in meaningful conversation and interaction with Mom than they do with Dad. Our youth claim that Mom spends about thirty-seven minutes a week "talking [with them] about things that really matter." This figure has climbed 40 percent in

Frequency of Conditions Related to One's Parents
(base: occurs "frequently")

Conditions	Mother	Father
• Shows love for you	67%	51%
• Feel proud of her/him	57%	56%
• Show your love for her/him	50%	41%
• Seek advice from her/him	38%	26%
• Talk about your personal concerns	38%	12%
• Do something special that involves just the two of you	28%	19%
• Wonder whether or not she/he loves you	9%	8%

Table A-3.3

the seven years since the "Why Wait?" survey, indicating that mothers, too, are devoting more time and attention to influencing their children. See Tables A-3.3; A-3.1; and A-3.5.

At the same time, however, spending roughly one-half hour a week in meaningful dialogue with our kids is certainly insufficient to address all their struggles or answer all their questions. While it is encouraging to see the combined amount of time parents typically spend with their children increase from thirty-nine minutes a week in 1987 to fifty-four minutes a week in 1994, we must recognize the need to redouble our efforts to understand and influence what our children think and believe.

Closeness to One's Mother		
Closeness with Mother	**1994**	**1987**
Very close	52%	48%
Fairly close	36%	39%
Not too close	8%	9%
Not at all close	3%	2%
Not alive/don't know mother	1%	1%

Table A-3.1

Time Spent with Mother in a Typical Week		
Amount of Time Spent	**1994**	**1987**
No time	6%	5%
Less than 5 minutes	9%	10%
Between 5 and 15 minutes	16%	20%
Between 16 and 30 minutes	16%	29%
Between 31 and 60 minutes	15%	17%
1 Hour or more	38%	28%
Median (minutes)	37%	27%

Table A-3.5

■ WHAT ARE THEIR ATTITUDES ABOUT HOME? ■

"Be it ever so humble, there's no place like home." That old adage is accurate for most of the churched youth we surveyed. Three out of every five of our kids (62 percent) state that they feel their home is a place where they feel secure and loved. One in seven identify their homes as "a place where sometimes I feel loved, but other times I don't." One in eleven (9 percent) characterize their homes primarily as a place where "each of us is trying to love each other." Eight percent say they usually feel uncomfortable at home and "would rather be elsewhere." Seven percent say home is a place "where I feel comfortable, although we are not a close, loving family." This has not changed significantly since 1987. See Table A-4.1.

Descriptions of "Home"		
Description	**1994**	**1987**
• A place where I feel secure and loved	62%	52%
• A place where sometimes I feel loved, but other times I don't	14%	18%
• A place where each of us is trying to love each other	9%	11%
• A place where I usually feel uncomfortable and would rather be elsewhere	8%	10%
• A place where I feel comfortable, although we are not a close, loving family	7%	9%

Table A-4.1

The impression that most of our kids enjoy a largely positive home life is also reflected in how they view their parents. Nearly six out of ten (56 percent) say that their parents frequently show that they really love each other; four out of five (79 percent) say their parents do so at least occasionally. This response suggests that most of our kids have the benefit of parents who model loving marriages, a tremendously encouraging finding of the study (see Table A-4.2).

How Often Parents Exhibit Specified Behaviors

My Parents... Description of the behavior	Frequently	Occasionally	Seldom	Never
• Show that they really love each other	56%	23%	11%	11%
• Set good examples for me	54%	32%	10%	4%
• Are really interested in who I am	51%	30%	15%	5%
• Spend time with me	46%	37%	13%	3%
• Admit when they are wrong or mistaken	27%	36%	25%	12%
• Expect more of me than is fair	19%	28%	33%	20%
• Yell at me	18%	34%	40%	9%
• Are too strict	16%	27%	37%	19%
• Do not allow me to do the things I want to do	15%	36%	39%	9%
• Do not trust me	12%	26%	38%	24%
• Fight with each other	10%	20%	44%	27%

Table A-4.2

By and large, then, we see that when we talk about the kids participating in this survey, we're talking about *our* kids—children from good Christian homes, children of good conscientious parents, children whose mothers and fathers provide a generally positive model of marriage and family life.

Keep that in mind, because we will discover that, despite the fact that three in four (73 percent) say that their family experiences have been positive, our kids entertain some disturbing ideas and concepts about marriage and the family.

■ WHAT ARE THEIR VIEWS ON MARRIAGE? ■

For years now, many voices in the popular culture have proclaimed the demise of traditional concepts of marriage and family.

291

New terms, like "open marriages," "domestic unions," "palimony," and "blended families" have been coined as a response to societal changes.

But recent research[2] indicates that most adults in America (not just Christian adults, but the entire adult population) believe that marriage is an important and solid institution; that divorce is a cancer on society and a person's own life; that the benefits of a happy marriage are to be desired. Most adults also believe that the traditional family is critical to the health of the nation.

Our survey of churched youth reveals that they espouse many traditional views regarding marriage and family. Nine out of ten (90 percent) affirm that God's intention was for marriage to last a lifetime. Three in four (73 percent) agree with the statement, "I would like to be a virgin at marriage"—an interesting response, considering the fact that 15 percent have already engaged in sexual intercourse; consequently, it seems that more than one in nine (12 percent) of our kids who are still virgins don't necessarily plan to remain so until marriage. Among those who have had sexual relations, three in five admit that if they could change their pasts, they would wait until after marriage to become sexually involved.

Although they overwhelmingly attest that their parents love them and each other, our youth are wrestling with a disturbing degree of confusion, fear, and anxiety about marriage. Less than half of our kids (48 percent) say that they want marriages like those of their parents. More than one-third say that they definitely do *not* wish to duplicate their parents' relationships. One-sixth of our kids claim that they don't know if they want marriages like Mom and Dad's, suggesting that they may not like what they see in their parents' marriages, but don't know if they can hope for anything better.

Our kids aren't convinced of the societal importance of marriage and family. Less than half (47 percent) agreed that "if the traditional family in America falls apart, American society will collapse," a notion to which 70 percent of the adult population (churched and otherwise) subscribe. Three in ten of our kids (28 percent) agreed with this statement, and one in four (25 percent) were not sure what to think.

Our youth are even more convinced than their elders that "these days it is very hard to have a successful marriage." Forty-three percent of our kids agree with that statement; 44 percent disagree (only 32 percent of the adult population agrees with the statement).

One in three (34 percent) of our youth agree that "marriage problems have been exaggerated; most married couples have fulfilling, healthy marriages." A comparable proportion (32 percent) disagree with the statement, with the remaining third (34 percent) answering, "Don't Know." See Table B-1.1, next page.

■ THEIR VIEWS ON DIVORCE ■

Another disturbing revelation of the survey is the fact that our kids favor divorce—by a two-to-one margin—for parents who do not love each other. Nearly half (46 percent) of our kids disagree with the statement, "if there are children involved in the marriage, the parents should not get divorced, even if they do not love each other anymore." One-fifth (21 percent) favor staying together for the kids' sake.

Put simply, our kids—the products of loving marriages and intact families—are not convinced that marriage is an important and solid institution, nor that divorce is an improper response to marital strife.

One message that comes through loud and clear in all these statistics is the message that our youth are wrestling to make sense of all the pressures, opportunities, and philosophies they encounter in life. As in other areas, the root of this struggle is related to the fact that most of them do not have a strong, cohesive moral standard to serve as a guide for what they think and what they do.

Attitudes and Perspectives
Regarding Marriage and Family

Perspective	Agree	Disagree	Don't Know
• God intended marriage to last a lifetime.	90%	4%	6%
• I would like to be a virgin at marriage.	73%	13%	14%
• Overall, you feel that your family experience has been positive.	73%	14%	14%
• If I wasn't a virgin now and I could change the past, I would wait to have sex until after marriage.*	62%	25%	13%
• I want a marriage like that of my parents.	48%	36%	16%
• If the traditional family in America falls apart, American society will collapse.	47%	28%	25%
• These days it is very hard to have a successful marriage.	43%	44%	13%
• Marriage problems have been exaggerated; most married couples have fulfilling, healthy marriages.	34%	32%	34%
• If there are children involved in the marriage, the parents should not get divorced, even if they do not love each other anymore.	21%	46%	33%
• Anyone who gets married these days should expect that their marriage will end in divorce.	6%	86%	8%

[*percentages are for respondents who admit to having had sexual intercourse already]

Table B-1.1

■ HOW DO THEY DEFINE THE FAMILY? ■

Recent studies by The Barna Research Group among American adults indicate a major shift in the ways people define "family." People once defined a family as a group of individuals related to each other by marriage, birth, or adoption. That is no longer true; these days, a majority of adults define a family as "all of those people whom I deeply care about, and all of those people who deeply care about me."

That definition means that one's family tomorrow may not encompass the same group that constitutes the family today. Family members may be added or subtracted according to feelings; I may care for a different set of people tomorrow, or next month, or next year. Family is no longer based upon legal or biblical foundations; it is based upon feeling. In other words, a "nineties kind of family" has assumed a very fluid and temporary meaning.

Our survey indicates that the majority of churched youth have adopted this viewpoint. A large majority of our youth—three out of every five (60 percent)—buy into the idea of this "nouveau family," defining family as "those who deeply care about you, or whom you deeply care about." Only one in three (32 percent) possesses a traditional perspective of what constitutes a family ("people related to each other by birth, adoption, or marriage"). Five percent of our kids say a family is "people living together," and 4 percent consider "people sharing the same goals and values" to be a family. To put it another way, two-thirds of our kids, when given a choice of four definitions of "family," select a definition that reflects a "no risk, no commitment" kind of arrangement (see Table A-1.1).

However, it is apparent from the study that, while most of our kids embrace the nouveau family definition, many of them are not fully aware of the implications of their view; they are still

Defining "Family"

Definition	All	Male	Female	11–14	15–18
• Those who deeply care about you, or you deeply care about	60%	56%	62%	61%	59%
• People related to each other by birth, adoption, or marriage	32%	34%	30%	30%	33%
• People living together	5%	5%	4%	5%	4%
• People sharing same goals and values	4%	5%	4%	4%	4%

Table A-1.1

working through how their idea of "family" applies to real life. For instance, although two-thirds of our kids have a fluid definition of family, they aren't yet willing to apply that definition to specific cases.

For example, three-fourths of our kids (74 percent) define "an unmarried mother and her children" as a family, but only two in five (40 percent) apply the same appellation to "a man and a woman who are not married but are living together and have had children together." These answers highlight the confusion that exists among our kids, confusion that is exacerbated by the adult world all around them.

One in five of our kids (21 percent) labels "two divorced women who share housing but do not have a sexual relationship with each other" as a family. One in seven (14 percent) says that "a man and a woman who are not married but are living together and have no children" constitutes a family.

One in eleven (9 percent) of our youth characterize two homosexual women living together as a family, and a comparable number (8 percent) say that two homosexual men living together is a family as well.

Keep in mind that each of these "families" fits within the construct of "those who deeply care about [each other]," to which three in five (60 percent) of our kids subscribe. Most of our kids possess a concept of the family that would define cohabiting couples and homosexual unions as a legitimate family; the study indicates that they do not fully realize the implications of their view, but it is there, nonetheless, to shape their reasoning—and their behavior—in the future (see Table A-1.2).

We may take heart from this. The fact that our kids have not yet realized or explored all the ramifications of the nouveau family indicates that they may not have totally rejected biblical concepts of the family; as in other areas, they may simply lack the ability to distinguish the real from the counterfeit. They may yet be open to sound biblical teaching and careful, loving guidance. Furthermore, our kids' views about family are not as disturbing as the views of the adult population at large. According to The Barna

Is This a Family?

Description of Family Unit	Percent who say it is a family:	
	Youth	Adults
• An unmarried mother and her children	74%	81%
• A man and a woman who are not married but are living together and have had children together	40%	77%
• Two divorced women who share housing but do not have a sexual relationship with each other	21%	21%
• A man and a woman who are not married but are living together and have no children	14%	NA
• Two homosexual women living together	9%	21%
• Two homosexual men living together	8%	20%

Table A-1.2

Research Group, one in five *adults* (20 percent) says that two homosexuals living together constitutes a family; one in five adults (21 percent) endorses the living arrangement of two divorced women sharing housing as a "family," and three in four adults (77 percent) define cohabiting couples as a family.

On the other hand, there is cause for concern, not only because our own kids don't know what to make of the family, but because they are surrounded by a culture that approves "alternative families." Our children's teachers, professors, coaches, employers, and neighbors perceive a family as practically any type of domestic partnership. Our kids' views about the family will be constantly questioned and challenged by the dominant culture, and those of our children whose concepts of family do not rest on solid biblical principles will be easily led into tragic error.

■ WHAT DIFFERENCE DOES TRUTH MAKE? ■

Strong convictions in matters of truth have a definite effect on our youth's views of marriage and family. Our study of churched youth suggests that convictions about truth provides a network of roots for our children's concepts of marriage and family. For example, those youth who have formed a strong pro-truth view are more likely to say that God intended marriage to last a life-time, and to characterize their family experience as positive.

Kids with strong convictions that there is an absolute right and wrong are more apt to value chastity before marriage; they are 23 percent more likely to say, "I would like to be a virgin at marriage," and 30 percent more likely to say, "If I wasn't a virgin now and I could change the past, I would wait to have sex until after marriage."

Youth who are thoroughly convinced of the existence of ab-solute moral standards will probably have a more optimistic view of marriage than their peers who deny the existence of absolutes. They'll be 40 percent less likely to think that it is "very hard to have a successful marriage" these days, and two-and-a-half times (150 percent) less likely to say that "anyone who gets married these days should expect that their marriage will end in divorce."

Youth who believe in objective truth are 65 percent more likely to say that "if there are children involved, the parents should not get divorced, even if they do not love each other anymore." In other words, kids who lack a pro-truth view are 65 percent more likely to accept divorce as an option, even when children are involved.

According to the study, your children are also more likely to view the alternative family as legitimate if they lack a strong con-viction about the existence of absolute truth and objective moral standards. For example, young people who hold a pro-truth view are 75 percent more likely to consider the traditional family as a vital part of a healthy society.

Youth who *lack* a pro-truth view are much more accepting of cohabitation (unmarried couples living together); they are 46 percent more likely to say that "a man and a woman who are not married but are living together and have had children together" qualifies as a family, and two-and-a-half times (150 percent) more likely to say that an unmarried couple with no children make up a family.

The gap between the attitudes of youth who accept objective standards of truth and those who do not is most striking when they are asked to classify homosexual unions. Young people who lack a consistent pro-truth view are four-and-a-half times (350 percent) more likely to say that two homosexuals—male or female—living together are a legitimate family! (see Table A-1.3)

How Perceptions of Absolute Truth Impact Views of Family		
	Percent who say it is a family: believe in absolute truth?	
Description of Family Unit	Yes	No
• An unmarried mother and her children	76%	74%
• A man and a woman who are not married but are living together and have had children together	28%	41%
• Two divorced women who share housing but do not have a sexual relationship with each other	19%	21%
• A man and a woman who are not married but are living together and have no children	6%	15%
• Two homosexual women living together	2%	9%
• Two homosexual men living together	2%	9%

Table A-1.3

The study consistently reveals a gap between the views of youth who embrace the existence of truth and those who reject it. That means that youth who are not equipped to evaluate moral matters in an objective way are liable to see marriage as an unnecessary (and, usually, negative) institution. If their morals are not based on fundamental, fixed principals, they will tend to view divorce as an appropriate solution to marital difficulties. If they do not have a sound spiritual and moral standard, they will be more likely to regard "alternative" arrangements (such as cohabitation or homosexual unions) as acceptable "family" settings.

Neither do youth hold these ideas and opinions in a vacuum; what they think about marriage and family will determine their behavior in these areas. The young person who does not value marriage highly will approach a relationship from an entirely different perspective than someone who possesses a biblical perspective of marriage. A young adult who sees divorce as an option will be more likely to end the relationship during a difficult period. A teen who does not object to "alternative families" will be more likely to consider cohabiting with a boyfriend or girlfriend.

The study intimates that equipping youth for the challenges of preparing for and building a lifelong marriage and healthy family requires strong convictions that truth is right for all people, for all times, for all places.

17

Survey Analysis on Faith and Religion

THE GENERATION that is now approaching or embarking upon adulthood, called the Baby Busters (those born from 1965–1983) exhibits an interesting combination of religious practice and belief. In many respects, "Busters," while somewhat suspicious of organized religion, appear more interested in spiritual matters than their parents were. General research published by The Barna Research Group indicates that a majority of the current generation are involved in some type of religious activity. One-third of all Busters (the general population, not just those participating in our survey) claim to have attended religious worship services within the past week; over half say they have done so within the past month. One-third of all Busters say they have read from the Bible within the past seven days, and the same proportion indicate that they have shared their faith within the last week.

George Barna, in his informative book, *Baby Busters: The Disillusioned Generation,* reveals that nearly four in ten of today's youth say they watch religious television programming in a typical month (again, these responses represent the entire population, not just churched kids), and three in ten listen to Christian radio. One in four say they read Christian books or magazines with some regularity.

While those results may be surprising—even encouraging—the 3,795 churched youth participating in our 1994 survey are—in some respects, at least—in an entirely different class from the rest of their generation.

Four out of five of these youth (82 percent) say that they attend worship services every week. That degree of religious participation is about twice the national average among the rest of their generation, indicating that the study deals with youth who exhibit an extraordinary involvement in church, far above that of the rest of their generation (see Table E-1.1).

Their record of church attendance becomes more impressive in light of the fact that our youth are more likely than either of their parents to attend church in a given week. In fact, one-fourth of our kids (25 percent) say that their fathers rarely or never attend worship services, and one-sixth (16 percent) make the same statement about Mom.

As we might expect, our youth say that their mothers are more likely than their fathers to attend church regularly. However, almost

Church Service Attendance

Person Evaluated	Every Week	2-3 times Each Month	Once a Month	Rarely	Never	N/A
• Respondent	82%	12%	2%	3%	1%	1%
• Father	56%	10%	2%	10%	15%	7%
• Mother	70%	9%	2%	8%	9%	3%
• Brothers/Sisters living at home	62%	11%	3%	7%	6%	12%

Table E-1.1

Influence of Family Church Attendance on Own Attendance

Family Member	Weekly	1-3 times per month	Infrequent	N/A
• *Among kids who attend church weekly:*				
Father	65%	9%	21%	6%
Mother	80%	6%	12%	2%
Brothers/Sisters	73%	7%	8%	12%
• *Among kids who attend church monthly or less often:*				
Father	9%	13%	72%	7%
Mother	17%	17%	64%	2%
Brothers/Sisters	12%	16%	59%	13%

Table E-1.2

six out of ten come from households where Dad attends church weekly, and seven in ten say that Mom does so. See Table E-1.2.

The study clearly and indisputably shows the importance of Mom and Dad's church attendance on their children. Teens and pre-teens who attend church weekly are seven times more likely to have fathers who attend church weekly than those youth who attend only monthly or less frequently; similarly, youth who attend church every week are nearly five times more likely to have mothers who attend weekly. In other words, the study supports the widely held belief that children whose parents do not attend church will be very unlikely to develop a pattern of faithful church attendance themselves.

■ WHAT IS THEIR CHURCH INVOLVEMENT? ■

Our youth are also exceptional among their generation in their involvement in other forms of religious expression. For example, one-fifth of our youth (21 percent) say they read the

Bible daily; nearly half do so at least once a week (49 percent). That exceeds the national average among their generation by almost 50 percent.

Almost two-thirds (65 percent) say they pray daily; the "flip side" of that statistic, however, is that one in four (24 percent) of born-again youth lack a daily prayer habit, while (interestingly) four in ten non-Christian youth *do* pray daily.

More than four out of five (85 percent) of our youth state that they attend their church youth group every week, and a slightly smaller proportion (78 percent) attend Sunday school on a weekly basis (more than three times the national average among their generation). Four in ten (43 percent) attend a Bible study group (other than a Sunday school class) every week, more than double the national average among the entire "Buster" population (see Table E-1.3).

Most of our young people profess that they plan to continue attending church on a regular basis when they "graduate from high school or move away from home:" almost two-thirds (63 percent) say they are very likely to do so, one-quarter (28 percent) say they are "somewhat likely," and one-eleventh (9 percent) say that they are not too likely or not at all likely. Those intentions must be qualified, however, with the realization that (as George Barna states), "the behavioral testing we have conducted over the past decade [suggests] that stated intentions are, at best,

Religious Activity

Activity	Daily	Weekly	Monthly	Rarely	Never
Read part of the Bible	21%	28%	12%	30%	9%
Pray to God	65%	19%	6%	9%	2%
Attend church youth group	12%	73%	7%	21%	29%
Attend a Bible study group	7%	36%	7%	21%	29%
Attend Sunday School	11%	67%	5%	8%	8%

Table E-1.3

a moderately accurate predictor of behavior." In other words, in spite of the fact that 63 percent of our children *say* they intend to make church attendance a way of life, it is unlikely, based on the research currently available, that more than 40 percent will do so. That degree of commitment would coincide with other trends and, Barna says, "remains consistent with our contention that this disillusioned generation may remain spiritually inclined, but not necessarily Christian."

■ WHAT DO THEY BELIEVE ABOUT FAITH AND RELIGION? ■

A substantial proportion of our youth (86 percent) say that they have made personal commitments to Jesus Christ that is still important in their lives today, and the median age at which the commitments were made was ten years old. This may not necessarily mean that all 86 percent are truly "born again." For example, while 86 percent say they had made a personal commitment to Christ, just 75 percent say they will go to heaven when they die because they have confessed their sins and accepted Christ; others responded that they will go to heaven because they try to obey the Ten Commandments, that they will not go to heaven, and that they "don't know" what will happen when they die.

In other words, the survey data indicate that about three-quarters of the teens who attend Christian youth groups and claim to have made a personal commitment to Christ are, in fact, trusting Christ alone for their salvation (rather than seeking to earn their place in heaven).

Many of our youth, however, seem to be confused about biblical truth and Christian doctrine. They seem genuinely perplexed when they're asked to express an opinion on such subjects as God, the Bible, the devil, heaven, hell, and salvation. In the majority of cases, one in five of our kids had to admit that they could not express an opinion.

Not all the signs are discouraging, however. Four out of five of our youth (84 percent) did assert that "a person can experience a relationship with God personally," and seven in ten (70 percent) said "the Christian faith is relevant to the way I live today." This appears to be an encouraging response; however, it also intimates that not all of our youth who attest to a "born-again experience" are convinced that their faith is relevant to the way they live their lives, indicating that some are failing to make the connection between belief and behavior, between faith and conduct.

Unlike their generational peers outside the church, our youth overwhelmingly reflect a biblical understanding of God. More than four out of five (85 percent) identify God as the "all-powerful, all-knowing, perfect Creator of the universe who still rules the world today." Only 4 percent characterized God as the "total realization of personal, human potential." Other responses included definitions of God as "a state of higher consciousness that a person may reach" (2 percent), "everyone is God," (2 percent), "there are many gods, each with different power and authority" (1 percent), and 6 percent who say they do not know what they believe about God.

More than two-thirds of our youth (71 percent) consider the Bible to be totally accurate in all its teachings; about the same proportion (67 percent) disagree with the statement, "Jesus sometimes made mistakes."

Two-thirds (68 percent) agree with the statement that "I, personally, have a responsibility to tell other people about my religious beliefs," but just over half (56 percent) say that "the Christian churches in my area are relevant to the way I live today."

Four out of five (80 percent) believe that there is "a place of permanent suffering, which is known as hell," but less than half (49 percent) could affirm a belief in a literal devil; the rest tended toward the opinion that Satan is "a symbol of evil."

Our young people seem to suffer the greatest confusion when they attempt to relate biblical belief to other religions and lifestyles. For example, an alarming number of our children do not believe that their faith can be objectively shown to be true; four in ten (40 percent) endorse the statement, "no one can prove which religion is absolutely true."

One in five of our youth (21 percent) believe that "Muslims, Buddhists, Christians, Jews, and all other people pray to the same god, even though they use different names for their god." An identical number (21 percent) aver that "it does not matter what religious faith you follow because all faiths teach similar lessons." Not only that, but one in five teens (22 percent) agree with the statement, "if a person is generally good, or does enough good things for others during their life, they will earn a place in heaven," and the one in eight (13 percent) who conclude that "all good people, whether or not they consider Jesus Christ to be their Savior, will live in heaven after they die."

These responses indicate that, in the mind of one out of every five of our young people—youth who are predominantly from good, church-going families and highly involved in church activity—Christianity is nothing special; it is no more true, no more correct in its teachings, no more central to salvation than any other religion (see Table E-3.1, next page).

Still, our young people fare better than American adults in matters of faith and doctrine (note that the adult sample in Table E-3.2 compares churched *and* non-churched adults to churched youth). We may take heart from the fact that our youth score significantly better in every category except in their estimation of the relevance of the Christian faith and in their concept of Satan (see Table E-3.2, p. 313.).

■ WHAT DIFFERENCE DOES TRUTH MAKE? ■

The study shows that the youth who have formulated cohesive views about truth are immensely better equipped in spiritual matters. For example, our youth are more likely to be committed to church attendance if they are equipped with a conviction that objective standards of truth and morality exist. More than nine out of ten (94 percent) of those who possess a positive truth view attend church weekly, compared to just four out of five (80 percent) of those who reject the concept of absolute truth. Moreover,

What Church Kids Believe

Statement	Agree	Disagree	Not Sure
• A person can experience a relationship with God personally.	84%	5%	11%
• There really is a place of permanent suffering, which is known as Hell.	80%	9%	12%
• The Bible is totally accurate in all of its teachings.	71%	10%	20%
• The Christian faith is relevant to the way I live today.	70%	12%	19%
• I personally, have a responsibility to tell other people about my religious beliefs.	68%	15%	18%
• The Christian churches in my area are relevant to the way I live today.	56%	19%	25%
• When it comes to religion, what type of person you are is more important than what you accomplish.	43%	27%	31%
• No one can really prove which religion is absolutely true.	40%	34%	25%
• There are a lot of hypocrites in my church.	32%	29%	39%
• The devil, or Satan, is not a living being, but is a symbol of evil.	31%	49%	20%
• If a person is generally good, or does enough good things for others during their life, they will earn a place in Heaven.	22%	62%	16%
• Muslims, Buddhists, Christians, Jews and all other people pray to the same god, even though they use different names for their god.	21%	52%	27%
• It does not matter what religious faith you follow because all faiths teach similar lessons.	21%	54%	25%
• There are some sins or crimes which are so serious that they cannot be forgiven by God.	18%	68%	15%
• Jesus sometimes made mistakes.	17%	67%	16%
• When it comes to religion, what you do in life is more important than what you believe.	15%	62%	23%
• What I do for other people is more important than what I believe about Jesus Christ.	14%	74%	12%
• All good people, whether or not they consider Jesus Christ to be their Savior, will live in Heaven after they die.	13%	69%	18%

Table E-3.1

A Comparison of the Faith Views of Church Kids and American Adults

Statement	Kids	Adults
• The Christian faith is relevant to the way I live today.	70%	81%
• The Bible is totally accurate in all of its teachings.	71%	59%
• I, personally, have a responsibility to tell other people about my religious beliefs.	68%	45%
• The Christian churches in my area are relevant to the way I live today.	56%	66%
• The devil, or Satan, is not a living being, but is a symbol of evil.	31%	32%
• If a person is generally good, or does enough good things for others during their life, they will earn a place in Heaven.	22%	61%
• Muslims, Buddhists, Christians, Jews and all other people pray to the same god, even though they use different names for their god.	21%	64%
• It does not matter what religious faith you follow because all faiths teach similar lessons.	21%	62%
• Jesus sometimes made mistakes.	17%	36%
• There are some sins or crimes which are so serious that they cannot be forgiven by God.	18%	32%
• All good people, whether or not they consider Jesus Christ to be their Savior, will live in Heaven after they die.	13%	40%

[Adult base: drawn from five different OmniPoll surveys, all using a nationwide sample of 1,000 or more adults.]

Table E-3.2

if your child accepts objective standards of truth, he or she will be more likely to attend Sunday school, church youth group, and a Bible study group on a weekly basis.

The research suggests a relationship between spiritual disciplines and truth convictions. Young people are 32 percent more likely to develop a daily habit of prayer if they see truth as absolute and

A Profile of Those Who Believe in Truth, Compared to Those Who Reject Truth

Characteristic	Believe in Objective Standard of Truth?	
	Yes	No
• Life Satisfaction: Very	14%	86%
Less Than Very	8%	92%
• Purpose Of Life Is Enjoyment: Agree	3%	97%
Disagree	15%	85%
• Attend Church: Weekly	11%	89%
2-3 Times/Month	4%	96%
Monthly or Less	3%	97%
• Read Bible: Every Week	16%	84%
Less Than Weekly	4%	96%
• Bible Is Totally Accurate Teaching: Agree	13%	87%
Disagree	2%	98%

Table D-1.2

eternal: 83 percent of youth with a pro-truth view pray every day, compared to 63 percent of those who lack a pro-truth view. Similarly, youth who accept the existence of moral absolutes are more than twice as likely (125 percent) to read their Bibles daily (see Table D-1.2).

The study shows that what youth believe about truth also influences whether or not they make lasting personal commitments to Jesus Christ. Nearly every young person who affirms a belief in absolute truth (98 percent) testifies to having made a personal commitment to Christ, compared to eight in ten (84 percent) of those who lack such a conviction. Similarly, youth who have formed a pro-truth view are 48 percent more likely to say that they will go to heaven when they die because they have confessed their sins and accepted Jesus Christ as their Savior.

Those youth who accept truth are also the most likely to understand and embrace biblical Christianity. For example, nearly all youth (97 percent) with a pro-truth view describe God in biblical terms ("all powerful, all-knowing Creator"), while four in five (83 percent) who lack a conviction of absolute truth reflect the same understanding of God.

If your youth possess solid convictions about truth, they will be 38 percent more likely to regard the Bible as "totally accurate in all of its teachings," and half as likely to say that "Jesus made some mistakes."

A solid view of truth will make your children 30 percent more likely to recognize a connection between their faith and their behavior, saying that "the Christian faith is relevant to the way I live my life today," and 34 percent more likely to consider witnessing to non-Christians a priority.

If your children are equipped with a pro-truth world view, they will be nearly 20 percent more likely to posit a belief in a literal hell and, amazingly, more than two times as likely (136 percent) to believe in a real devil.

The effects of strong truth convictions are most apparent in what our young people think about the relative truth and distinctiveness of Christianity. Teens who *lack* a strong pro-truth position are 83 percent more likely to say "it doesn't matter what religious faith you follow because all faiths teach similar lessons." Those who do not believe in absolute truth are more than two times more likely (115 percent) to say that "no one can prove which religion is absolutely true," and nearly three times more likely (188 percent) to state that "Muslims, Buddhists, Christians, Jews, and all other people pray to the same god, even though they use different names for their god."

A glaring disparity occurs between those youth who espouse truth and those who reject it in their understanding of salvation and the way to heaven. Youth who do not accept objective standards of truth are more than two times more likely to think that "all good people, whether or not they consider Jesus Christ to be their Savior, will live in heaven after they die," and nearly three-and-a-half times more likely to say that "if a person is generally

What Church Kids Believe
(% who agree with statement)

Statement	Truth Acceptor?		Age:	
	Yes	No	11–12	17–18
• A person can experience a relationship with God personally.	95%	83%	74%	89%
• There really is a place of permanent suffering, which is known as Hell.	94%	79%	78%	84%
• The Bible is totally accurate in all of its teachings.	94%	68%	69%	74%
• The Christian faith is relevant to the way I live today.	88%	68%	64%	76%
• I, personally, have a responsibility to tell other people about my religious beliefs.	91%	65%	64%	72%
• The Christian churches in my area are relevant to the way I live today.	73%	54%	50%	61%
• When it comes to religion, what type of person you are is more important than what you accomplish.	49%	42%	33%	48%
• No one can really prove which religion is absolutely true.	20%	43%	36%	37%
• There are a lot of hypocrites in my church.	30%	32%	21%	40%
• The devil, or Satan, is not a living being, but is a symbol of evil.	14%	33%	45%	21%
• If a person is generally good, or does enough good things for others during their life, they will earn a place in Heaven.	7%	24%	28%	17%
• Muslims, Buddhists, Christians, Jews and all other people pray to the same god, even though they use different names for their god.	8%	23%	21%	17%
• It does not matter what religious faith you follow because all faiths teach similar lessons.	12%	22%	27%	18%
• There are some sins or crimes which are so serious that they cannot be forgiven by God.	20%	17%	19%	17%
• Jesus sometimes made mistakes.	9%	18%	19%	12%
• When it comes to religion, what you do in life is more important than what you believe.	11%	16%	13%	14%
• What I do for other people is more important than what I believe about Jesus Christ.	8%	15%	15%	12%
• All good people, whether or not they consider Jesus Christ to be their Savior, will live in Heaven after they die.	6%	14%	18%	9%

Table E-3.3

good, or does enough good things for others during their life, they will earn a place in heaven" (see Table E-3.3).

If we take a moment to review all that we've learned about our children's spiritual experience and belief, one fact emerges: the study suggests that, if you wish your children to remain active in church throughout their teen years, if you desire for them the assurance of salvation in Jesus Christ, if you want them to espouse biblical Christian belief, then teaching them that God determines what is right for all people, for all times, and for all places, may be the single most influential gift you can give them.

18

Survey Analysis on Attitudes and Lifestyles

SPIKE LEE'S 1989 FILM, *Do the Right Thing,* was the story of a white pizza parlor owner in a black neighborhood who sparks a riot. However, the film, which created a firestorm of controversy because it seemed to endorse violence, leaves the viewer to wonder whether anyone has done the right thing . . . or even what "the right thing" is.

Unfortunately, many of our own youth face the same dilemma; the statistics indicate that churched kids seem willing—even determined—to do the right thing, but they're uncertain as to what "the right thing" is. In some cases, it appears that our kids' desires to do (and think) the right thing are hampered by ignorance and confusion.

In religious matters, for instance, churched kids display more confusion about religious realities than they do in other areas of their lives. An average of 22 percent responded uncertainly to statements relating specifically to religious perspectives (see Table D-2.1, next page). Although about three out of every five

315

What Churched Kids Think About Life and Its Choices

Statement	Agree	Disagree	Not Sure
• Every religion offers a different explanation of the meaning of life and truth.	59%	18%	23%
• God established the limits for humankind; acting in conflict with his laws has negative consequences.	57%	13%	30%
• Freedom means being able to do anything you want to do, as long as it's legal.	54%	35%	12%
• Lying is sometimes necessary.	38%	48%	15%
• The only intelligent way to live is to make the best choice you can in every situation, based on your feelings at the moment.	33%	48%	19%
• The best philosophy for life is: do whatever feels or seems right, as long as it doesn't harm anyone else.	22%	62%	16%
• The moral standards of Americans these days are just as high as ever.	20%	59%	21%
• The Bible does not provide today's people with practical standards for living.	18%	66%	16%
• You know that something is morally or ethically right if it works.	16%	54%	30%
• The Bible isn't very relevant for today's people.	15%	68%	17%
• There's nothing wrong with breaking the law as long as it doesn't hurt anybody.	12%	80%	8%

Table D-2.1

churched kids echoed the traditional Christian view on these statements, the high proportion of "not sure" responses suggests that even those who took a stand (one way or the other) may not be thoroughly convinced of their stated position, and probably could not convincingly defend their position.

Our youth also display misunderstanding and confusion in moral areas too. Note that two out of five say that lying is sometimes necessary. One in six believe that the measure of whether an action is right or wrong is whether "it works." One in eight say that breaking the law is acceptable as long as it does not harm others. Taken altogether, about half of our kids display confusion when answering questions pertaining to ethics and morality.

Nearly half say they would base their choices in moral matters on feelings and emotions (rather than objective, constant, and universal standards). For instance, one in three (33 percent) say they would make choices, in any given situation, based on their feelings at that moment. One in five (22 percent) say they would act according to "whatever feels . . . right," as long as no one got hurt in the process. One in seven (18 percent) would not turn to the Bible for guidance in moral decisions; they say the Bible does not provide people with practical standards for living. Another 16 percent were not sure whether the Bible provided such practical standards.

■ WHAT ARE THEIR VIEWS ABOUT LIFE AND CHOICES? ■

The research revealed that the age of a young person seems to have a limited impact on his or her views about life, and his or her approach to decision-making. The age of individuals seemed to affect their answers less than half of the time. For example, roughly 60 percent of youth say that "every religion offers a different explanation of the meaning of life and truth," regardless of whether they are in the youngest age group among those surveyed (eleven to twelve) or the oldest (seventeen to eighteen).

In areas where age was an apparently significant in the response, the oldest youth tended to give answers that reflected biblical beliefs and behaviors. In light of other indications within the research, this probably reflects the fact that most seventeen-to-eighteen-year-olds who remain active in the church are those who possess strong commitments and convictions; those who

317

lack such commitments and convictions tend to become inactive before age seventeen (see Table D-2.1a).

In other words, whether our children are twelve or eighteen figures little in determining what basis—subjective or objective, emotional or rational—they use for making moral and ethical decisions.

Life Views and Choices by Age Group
(indicates percentage of "agree" answers)

Statement	11-12	13-14	15-16	17-18
• Every religion offers a different explanation of the meaning of life and truth.	60%	60%	59%	61%
• God established the limits for humankind; acting in conflict with his laws has negative consequences.	52%	52%	59%	67%
• Freedom means being able to do anything you want to do, as long as it's legal.	58%	58%	52%	50%
• Lying is sometimes necessary.	32%	39%	40%	37%
• The only intelligent way to live is to make the best choice you can in every situation, based on your feelings at the moment.	46%	38%	32%	25%
• The best philosophy for life is: do whatever feels or seems right, as long as it doesn't harm anyone else.	19%	25%	21%	19%
• The moral standards of Americans these days are just as high as ever.	26%	24%	19%	14%
• The Bible does not provide today's people with practical standards for living.	21%	20%	18%	12%
• You know that something is morally or ethically right if it works.	17%	17%	17%	14%
• The Bible isn't very relevant for today's people.	18%	17%	16%	11%
• There's nothing wrong with breaking the law as long as it doesn't hurt anybody.	11%	13%	14%	10%

Table D-2.1a

■ WHAT DIFFERENCE DOES TRUTH MAKE? ■

Our young people's acceptance or rejection of absolute truth greatly affects how they view life and decisions—a more distinctive effect, in fact, than whether they testified to a personal commitment to Christ.

Being born again does influence the views and behavior of our youth in how they view choices and how they make decisions; the difference between the answers of Christian and non-Christian youth to ten of the eleven statements was statistically significant; the same was true when comparing the answers of youth who affirm consistent standards of absolute truth to those who reject absolute truth. However, those youth who accept absolute truth were more likely than born-again youth to give a biblical response to the questions (see Table D-2.2, next page).

If our youth do not believe in absolute truth, they will be over two times more likely to believe that "lying is sometimes necessary," and over two times more likely to say that the Bible is not relevant and does not provide practical standards for living for today's people.

Youth who do not affirm objective standards of truth and morality are two-and-a-half times more likely to say that "there's nothing wrong with breaking the law as long as it doesn't hurt anybody," and almost three times more apt to judge something to be morally or ethically right "if it works."

Most importantly, perhaps, our young people's views about absolute truth affect whether they base their moral decisions on feelings and guesswork, or on objective standards of right and wrong. Our study reveals that youth who lack strong convictions of biblical truth are three times more likely to say that "the only intelligent way to live is to make the best choice you can in every situation, based on your feelings at the moment," and six times more likely to believe that the best philosophy for life is to "do whatever feels or seems right, as long as it doesn't harm anyone else."

319

Life Views and Choices
by Faith Commitment and Truth View
(indicates percentage of "agree" answers)

Statement	Born again?		Accept truth?	
	Yes	No	Yes	No
• Every religion offers a different explanation of the meaning of life and truth.	60%	58%	56%	60%
• God established the limits for humankind; acting in conflict with his laws has negative consequences.	62%	48%	79%	55%
• Freedom means being able to do anything you want to do, as long as it's legal.	48%	64%	31%	56%
• Lying is sometimes necessary.	34%	46%	17%	40%
• The only intelligent way to live is to make the best choice you can in every situation, based on your feelings at the moment.	28%	44%	12%	36%
• The best philosophy for life is: do whatever feels or seems right, as long as it doesn't harm anyone else.	15%	35%	4%	24%
• The moral standards of Americans these days are just as high as ever.	17%	25%	7%	21%
• The Bible does not provide today's people with practical standards for living.	13%	25%	8%	19%
• You know that something is morally or ethically right if it works.	12%	23%	6%	17%
• The Bible isn't very relevant for today's people.	10%	24%	7%	16%
• There's nothing wrong with breaking the law as long as it doesn't hurt anybody.	8%	21%	5%	13%

Table D-2.2

The research reveals that, when it comes to making moral choices, properly evaluating faith systems, or taking a biblical stand on moral and ethical issues, the ages of our youth—and even their faith commitment—are less influential than whether they possess strong, cohesive views about absolute truth.

■ WHAT IS THEIR PHILOSOPHY OF LIFE? ■

The news and entertainment media have widely reported and often repeated the claim that today's youth, popularly called "Generation X" in the media, has no heroes. Other research has asserted that most of today's kids do not have individuals in their lives whom they feel they can look to as role models. However, our study reveals that churched kids fly in the face of those claims and findings.

Almost two-thirds of our youth do claim to have a hero or role model, although more of our kids say they know adults who "really have it together" than claim to have role models or heroes, indicating that even people whose lives appear to be fulfilling and enviable may not be perceived as worthy role models by many of our young people (see Table D-2.3).

Role Models and Philosophies of Life

Statement	Agree	Disagree	Not Sure
• You know of one or more adults whom you feel really have it together.	75%	13%	12%
• Everyone needs a hero in his or her life.	62%	23%	15%
• Life is too complex these days.	49%	34%	17%
• In times of trouble or crisis, I feel all alone.	41%	47%	13%
• Sometimes I wonder if life is worth living.	38%	53%	9%
• The future will be better than today.	34%	31%	36%
• The main purpose of life is enjoyment and personal fulfillment.	29%	55%	16%
• There is nobody whom you consider to be your hero or model for life.	24%	65%	11%
• One person cannot really make a difference in the world today.	23%	66%	12%
• What I think doesn't matter.	19%	68%	13%
• It's better to get even than to get mad.	12%	79%	9%

Table D-2.3

In spite of their personal hope for a better tomorrow, our kids are not convinced that things will be better in the days ahead. Their responses were almost evenly divided; one-third believe things will be better, roughly one-third do not believe things will improve, and over one-third confess that they aren't sure what to expect. This uncertainty may be related to the feelings of stress and anxiety that many of our youth express.

This disparity between hopes and expectations is intriguing in light of the fact that most of our youth say they believe that their thoughts matter and that they, personally, can make a real difference in the world. In fact, the kids who say they can change the world outnumber those who reject that idea by a three-to-one margin, and those who believe that what they think matters outnumbered those who disagreed by a four-to-one margin.

Such mixed signals may be better understood if we recognize that our youth—many of whom express hope for the future—feel overwhelmed and trampled by life. Half (49 percent) of them say that life has become too complex. Four in ten (41 percent) feel isolated and alone during times of personal crisis or hardship. Four in ten (38 percent) admit that they sometimes question whether life is worth living.

Once again, the responses of Christian youth are more encouraging than those given by non-Christian youth. The most positive attitudes, however, are again expressed by young people who consistently affirm the existence of absolute truth. Youth who believe in absolute truth, for example, are much less likely to wonder if life is worth living or to say that life is too complex these days. They are less than half as likely to say that they feel alone in times of trouble or crisis. And youth who possess a pro-truth view are half as likely to believe that "what I think doesn't matter," and that "one person cannot really make a difference in the world today."

In other words, the research indicates that a belief in absolute truth is related to the cultivation of a positive, hopeful outlook in our young people.

Role Models and Philosophies of Life by Faith Commitment and Truth View
(indicates percentage of "agree" answers)

Statement	Born again?		Accept truth?	
	Yes	No	Yes	No
• You know of one or more adults whom you feel really have it together.	80%	66%	82%	75%
• Everyone needs a hero in his or her life.	64%	57%	68%	61%
• Life is too complex these days.	48%	50%	36%	50%
• In times of trouble or crisis, I feel all alone.	37%	47%	20%	43%
• Sometimes I wonder if life is worth living.	34%	46%	23%	40%
• The future will be better than today.	33%	36%	32%	34%
• The main purpose of life is enjoyment and personal fulfillment.	21%	44%	10%	31%
• There is nobody whom you consider to be your hero or model for life.	21%	30%	17%	25%
• One person cannot really make a difference in the world today.	20%	28%	12%	24%
• What I think doesn't matter.	15%	26%	11%	20%
• It's better to get even than to get mad.	7%	21%	5%	13%

Table D-2.3a

■ WHAT DO THEY WANT OUT OF LIFE? ■

What are young people today looking for in life? What do they expect—or hope—to get out of life? What circumstances or achievements do they consider to be the most desirable?

More than four out of five of our youth identify having one marriage partner for life, having good physical health, having close personal friendships, and having a clear purpose for living as very desirable goals or aspirations for their lives (see Table D-3.1, next page).

Approximately three in four identified having close relationships with God, having a spouse and children, having a comfortable

How Desirable Are Specified Life Circumstances?
Born again?
Accept truth?

Circumstance	very	some	a little	not at all
• One marriage partner for life	85%	7%	3%	5%
• Good physical health	83%	14%	3%	1%
• Close personal friendships	82%	13%	4%	2%
• Clear purpose for living	81%	14%	4%	2%
• Close relationship with God	77%	15%	6%	2%
• Having a spouse and children	73%	15%	6%	6%
• Having a comfortable lifestyle	70%	23%	6%	1%
• Having high personal integrity	69%	23%	6%	2%
• Influencing other people's lives	64%	25%	8%	3%
• Being active in a church	64%	24%	9%	2%
• Make a difference in the world	62%	24%	11%	3%
• Having a fulfilling sex life within marriage	61%	21%	9%	9%
• Having a high-paying job	55%	30%	8%	7%
• Living close to family and relatives	48%	31%	16%	5%
• Achieving fame and public recognition	25%	28%	30	17%

Table D-3.1

lifestyle, and having high personal integrity as highly desirable. The fact that more than three-fourths of our kids (77 percent) considered having a close relationship with God as highly desirable is not surprising (considering the respondents were all involved in church life to some degree), but it is nonetheless heartening to hear that sustaining or improving their relationships with God constitutes a dominant hope for many of our youth.

Less important to our youth are such goals or aspirations as influencing other people's lives, being active in a church, having a fulfilling sex life, making a difference in the world, and having a high-paying job. Though these were not among the ideals most often cited, they were still indicated as "very desirable" by the majority of our youth.

The least appealing objectives among our young people are living close to family and relatives, which is highly valued by 48 percent, and achieving fame or public recognition, highly valued by 25 percent.

In contrast to other areas, our young people's faith commitment and their views of absolute truth seem to produce strikingly similar results in determining what life circumstances they favor. For example, born-again youth are 68 percent more likely to value "being active in a church" than non-Christian youth—a practically identical margin to that which separates the opinion of youth who espouse absolute truth from those who reject it.

A similar correspondence occurs in the answers to other questions. A young person's faith commitment and truth view seem to strongly (and similarly) affect whether they consider one marriage partner for life, high personal integrity, and a close relationship with God to be "very desirable" aims.

It is interesting, and perhaps informative, to note that today's youth display the greatest difference from adults (both churched and unchurched) in three areas. They tend to be more concerned with close personal relationships than adults; they value a comfortable lifestyle, high-paying job, and fame or recognition more highly than adults; and they are considerably less concerned about living close to other family members. Some of these perspectives are somewhat characteristic of every generation that approaches adulthood. It may also be an indication of the shifting emphases occurring within our society, away from "family" and toward "friends" (or "significant others" as they have come to be called), away from spiritual and toward more materialistic goals. Such trends are, happily, less pronounced among churched youth, but they may be worthy of our attention nonetheless.

The over-all impact of our kids' views about life and the future, however, should encourage us, because the possibility of instilling our youth with strong, biblical values is a goal that is well within our reach.

■ THE CONCLUSION ■

"The conclusion," Solomon said, "when all has been heard, is: fear God and keep His commandments, because this applies to every person" (Ecc. 12:13, NASB).

One cannot get more profound and concise than that. Our challenge is to know God for who He is and fear Him accordingly; to resist the cultural shift that has rejected God as the determiner of truth, and acknowledge that He and He alone defines right and wrong; to model before our families, our churches, and our communities a life of dependence upon God; and to diligently teach our children to fear God and keep His commandments, because His truth is right and beneficial for all people, for all times, for all places.

Additional Resources

To obtain a free catalog of Josh McDowell resources that includes the latest "Right from Wrong" campaign products, write:

Josh McDowell Ministry
P.O. Box 1000 C
Dallas, TX 75221

Resources for Adults

Books

- *How to Be a Hero to Your Kids*, by Josh McDowell and Dick Day—Word, Inc.

- *"Why Wait?"—What You Need to Know about the Teen Sexuality Crisis*, by Josh McDowell and Dick Day—Thomas Nelson Publishers

- *How to Help Your Child Say No to Sexual Pressure*, by Josh McDowell—Word, Inc.

- *What I Wish My Parents Knew about My Sexuality*, by Josh McDowell—Thomas Nelson Publishers

- *The Myths of Sex Education*, by Josh McDowell—Thomas Nelson Publishers

- *The Secret of Loving*, by Josh McDowell—Thomas Nelson Publishers

- *Building Your Self-Image*, by Josh McDowell—Thomas Nelson Publishers

- *Sex, Guilt, and Forgiveness*, by Josh McDowell—Tyndale House Publishers

- *How to Love Your Teenager*, by Ross Campbell—New American Library

- *Preparing for Adolescence*, by Dr. James Dobson—Bantam Books

- *Forty Ways to Teach Your Child Values*, by Paul Lewis—Tyndale House Publishers

- *The Five Cries of Youth*, by Merton Strommen—Harper and Row

- *Evidence That Demands a Verdict, volumes 1 and 2*, by Josh McDowell—Thomas Nelson Publishers

- *Answers to Tough Questions*, by Josh McDowell and Don Stewart—Thomas Nelson Publishers
- *A Ready Defense*, by Josh McDowell—Thomas Nelson Publishers
- *More Than a Carpenter*, by Josh McDowell—Tyndale House Publishers

Videos

- "Let's Talk About Love and Sex," by Josh McDowell—Word, Inc.
- "The Myths of Sex Education," by Josh McDowell—Word, Inc.

Resources for Youth

- *The Teenage Q&A Book*, by Josh McDowell and Bill Jones—Word, Inc.
- *The Love Killer*, by Josh McDowell and Bob Hostetler—Word, Inc.
- *Givers, Takers and Other Kinds of Lovers*, by Josh McDowell—Tyndale House Publishers
- *Under Siege*, by Josh McDowell and Chuck Klein—Word, Inc.
- *Thirteen Things You Gotta Know to be a Christian* (Devotional), by Josh McDowell and Bob Hostetler—Word, Inc.
- *Thirteen Things You Gotta Know to Keep Your Love Life Alive and Well* (Devotional), by Josh McDowell and Bob Hostetler—Word, Inc.
- *It Can Happen to You* (a book on date rape), by Josh McDowell—Word, Inc.
- *Don't Check Your Brains at the Door*, by Josh McDowell and Bob Hostetler—Word, Inc.

Videos

- "God Is No Cosmic Killjoy," by Josh McDowell—Word, Inc.
- "Why Waiting is Worth the Wait," by Josh McDowell—Word, Inc.
- "How to Handle the Pressure Lines," by Josh McDowell—Word, Inc.
- "A Clean Heart for a New Start," by Josh McDowell—Word, Inc.
- "Who Do You Listen To?," by Josh McDowell—Word, Inc.
- "It Can Happen to You," by Josh McDowell—Word, Inc.

Resources for the Church

- "Right from Wrong" Video Series for Adults (March 1995 release), by Josh McDowell—Word, Inc.

- "How to Be a Hero to Your Kids" Video Series, by Josh McDowell—Word, Inc.

- "Evidence for Faith" Video Series, by Josh McDowell—Word, Inc.

- "The Body" Video Series, by Chuck Colson—Word, Inc.

- "Preparing for Adolescence" Audio Package, by Dr. James Dobson—Word, Inc.

Video Curriculum for Youth

- Revised "No—The Positive Answer," by Josh McDowell—Word, Inc.

- "Teenage Q&A Series," by Josh McDowell—Word, Inc.

- "See You at the Party," by Josh McDowell—Word, Inc.

- "Won by One," by Josh McDowell and Dann Spader—Word, Inc.

- "Don't Check Your Brains at the Door," by Josh McDowell—Word, Inc.

- "Life on the Edge," by Dr. James Dobson—Word, Inc.

NOTE: The video series for junior-high and high-school youth and the children's video series were untitled at the release date of this book. They are planned to be available in mid-1995. Ask your local Christian bookstore for the "Right from Wrong" campaign series for youth and children.

Ministries That Can Help

Focus on the Family
P.O. Box 35500
Colorado Springs, CO 80935
Ph: 800-232-6459
(Resources for entire family)

Family Life
P.O. Box 23840
Little Rock, AR 72221
Ph: 800-333-1433
(Resources for marriage and family)

Sonlife Ministries
1119 Wheaton Oak Ct.
Wheaton, IL 60187
Ph: 800-770-GROW
(Youth worker training)

Student Venture
Campus Crusade for Christ
100 Support Lane
Orlando, FL 32809
(High-school ministry)

Notes

CHAPTER 1

1   Michelle Ingrassia with Peter Annin, Nina Archer Biddle, and Susan Miller, "Life Means Nothing," *Newsweek* 19 July, 1993, 16–17.

2   Bill Hewitt, Lyndon Stambler, Julie Klein, and Doris Bacon, "The Body Counters," *People,* 12 April, 1993, 35–37.

3   Roland Nethaway, "Missing Core Values," Cox News Service appearing in the *Hamilton* (OH) *Journal-News,* 3 November, 1993.

4   Compiled from figures published by the Childrens Defense Fund and the book, *13th Generation,* by Neil Howe and Bill Strauss.

5   Christina Hoff Sommers, associate professor of philosophy, Clark University (Worcester, Massachusetts), as quoted in *Christianity Today,* 13 December, 1993, 33.

CHAPTER 2

1   Statistics compiled by the Childrens Defense Fund.

2   William J. Bennett, *The De-Valuing of America,* (New York: Summit Books, 1992), 56.

3   Allan Bloom, *The Closing of the American Mind,* (New York: Simon and Schuster, 1987), 25.

CHAPTER 3

1   Stanley Newbigin, *The Gospel in a Pluralist Society.*

2   David F. Wells, *No Place for Truth* (Grand Rapids, MI: William B. Eerdmans Publishing Company, 1993), 259–260.

3   Chris Wright, "All Our Gods Have Failed," *Themelios,* (April 1993), as quoted in *Christianity Today,* 22 November, 1993, 37.

4   Francis Schaeffer, *How Should We Then Live?* (Old Tappan, NJ: Fleming H. Revell Co., 1976), 145.

5   Ibid., 182.

6   These figures represent the median of all respondents.

7   Os Guiness, *The American Hour* (New York: The Free Press, 1993), 82–83.

8   Ibid., 84.

9   James A. Michener, "After the War: Victories at Home," *Newsweek,* 11 January, 1993, 27.

10 H. Stephen Glenn and Jane Nelsen, *Raising Self-Reliant Children in a Self-Indulgent World* (Rocklin, CA: Prima Publishing & Communications, 1989), 26–27.

11 Larry Pierce, "Baby Busters: A Lost Generation Finds Its Place in God's Plan," *National & International Religion Report,* Vol. 7, No. 21, 4 October, 1993, 1.

12 Francis Schaeffer, *How Should We Then Live?,* (Old Tappan, NJ: Fleming H. Revell Co., 1976), 145.

CHAPTER 4

1 Judges 2:7,10–12a, NIV.

2 I am indebted to Os Guiness for these five pairs of contrasts which (with others) appear in his book, *The American Hour,* 30.

CHAPTER 5

1 Figures cited in *Baby Busters: The Disillusioned Generation* (Chicago, IL: Northfield Publishing, 1994), 122–123.

2 Such as that reported by George Barna in *The Future of the American Family* and Andrew Greeley in *Faithful Attraction.*

CHAPTER 6

1 Collected Papers, V, 211.

2 C.S. Lewis, *Mere Christianity* (New York: Macmillan Publishing Co., 1943).

3 Stephen L. Carter, *The Culture of Disbelief.*

4 Exodus 20:13; Exodus 20:17; Leviticus 19:14.

CHAPTER 7

1 Bill Hybels, *Laws That Liberate* (Wheaton, IL: Victor Books, 1985), 10.

2 Os Guiness, *The American Hour,* 379.

3 S.I. McMillen, M.D., *None of These Diseases* (Westwood, NJ: Spire Books, 1968), from the Preface.

CHAPTER 8

1 Peter Bocchino, "How Does Green Taste?," *Just Thinking,* Winter 1994, 5.

2 Josh McDowell and Dick Day, *How to Be a Hero to Your Kids* (Dallas, TX: Word Publishing, 1991).

CHAPTER 10

1 *USA Weekend,* March 25–27,1994, based on a national poll of 252 teenagers conducted February 18–22 by ICR Research.

2 Josh McDowell, *Teens Speak Out: What I Wish My Parents Knew About My Sexuality* (San Bernardino, CA: Here's Life Publishers, 1987), 177–178.

3 Anne Catherine Speckhard, "Psycho-Social Aspects of Stress Following Abortion," (doctoral dissertation, University of Minnesota, 1985), n.p.

4 Barbara Dafoe Whitehead, "Dan Quayle Was Right," *The Atlantic Monthly,* April 1993, 48.

5 "Young Love: How to Talk to Your Kids About You-Know-What," Minnesota Institute of Public Health, Anoka, MN, n.d., 5.

6 Stacy Rinehart and Paula Rinehart, *Choices* (Colorado Springs, CO: Navpress, 1982), 94.

7 Robert J. Levin, "The *Redbook* Report on Premarital and Extramarital Sex: The End of the Double Standard?," *Redbook,* October 1975, 40.

CHAPTER 11

1 Barbara Dafoe Whitehead, "Dan Quayle Was Right," *The Atlantic Monthly,* April 1993, 47.

CHAPTER 12

1 Anonymous letter published in "Family Feedback," *Focus on the Family,* May 1994, 23.

2 Barbara Dafoe Whitehead, "Dan Quayle Was Right," *The Atlantic Monthly,* April 1993, 65.

3 Judith Wallerstein and Sandra Blakesee, *Second Chances: Men, Women, and Children a Decade After Divorce* (New York: Ticknor & Fields, 1990).

4 As quoted by Barbara Dafoe Whitehead, "Dan Quayle Was Right," *The Atlantic Monthly,* April 1993, 82.

CHAPTER 13

1 As quoted by S. I. McMillen in *None of These Diseases* (Westwood, NJ: Fleming H. Revell, 1968), 77.

2 William Shakespeare, *The Merchant of Venice,* Act IV, Scene 1, line 187.

3 William Shakespeare, *The Merchant of Venice,* Act IV, Scene 1, lines 194–196.

4 William Shakespeare, *The Merchant of Venice,* Act IV, Scene 1, line 186.

CHAPTER 14

1 Francis A. Schaeffer, *The Great Evangelical Disaster* (Wheaton, IL: Crossway Books, 1984), 150.

2 Charles Colson, *The Body* (Dallas, TX: Word Publishing, 1992), 171.

INTRODUCTION TO THE RESEARCH ANALYSIS

1 George Barna, 1994 Churched Youth Research Analysis, 1994.

CHAPTER 15

1 Figures cited in *Baby Busters: The Disillusioned Generation* by George Barna, (Chicago, IL: Northfield Publishing, 1994),122–123.

CHAPTER 16

1 As cited in "The Virtue Man," by Michael Cromartie, *Christianity Today,* 13 September 1993, 32.

2 Such as that reported by George Barna in *The Future of the American Family* and Andrew Greeley in *Faithful Attraction.*

Passing on the Truth to Our Next Generation

The "Right From Wrong" message, available in numerous formats, provides a blueprint for countering the culture and rebuilding the crumbling foundations of our families.

Read It and Embrace a New Way of Thinking

The Right From Wrong Book to Adults

Right From Wrong - What You Need to Know to Help Youth Make Right Choices
by Josh McDowell & Bob Hostetler

Our youth no longer live in a culture that teaches an objective standard of right and wrong. Truth has become a matter of taste. Morality has been replaced by individual preference. And today's youth have been affected. Fifty-seven percent (57%) of our churched youth cannot state that an objective standard of right and wrong even exists!

As the centerpiece of the "Right From Wrong" Campaign, this life-changing book provides you with a biblical, yet practical, blueprint for passing on core Christian values to the next generation.

Right From Wrong, Tradepaper Book
ISBN 0-8499-3604-7

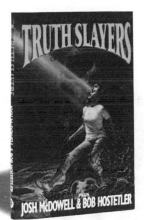

The Truth Slayers, Tradepaper Book
ISBN 0-8499-3662-4

The Truth Slayers Book to Youth

The Truth Slayers - A Battle of Right From Wrong
by Josh McDowell & Bob Hostetler

This book—directed to youth—is written in the popular NovelPlus format and combines the fascinating story of Brittney Marsh, Philip Milford and Jason Withers and the consequences of their wrong choices with Josh McDowell's insights for young adults in sections called "The Inside Story."

The Truth Slayers conveys the critical "Right From Wrong" message that challenges you to rely on God's word as the absolute standard of truth in making right choices.

Hear It and Adopt a New Way of Teaching

Right From Wrong Audio for Adults
by Josh McDowell

What is truth? In three powerful and persuasive talks based on the book *Right From Wrong*, Josh McDowell provides you, your family, and the church with a sound, thorough, biblical, and workable method to clearly understand and defend the truth. Josh explains how to identify absolutes and shows you how to teach youth to determine what is absolutely right from wrong.

Right From Wrong, Audio–104 min.
ISBN 0-8499-6195-5

See It and Commit to a New Way of Living

Video Series to Adults

Truth Matters for You and Tomorrow's Generation
Five-part Video Series featuring Josh McDowell

Josh McDowell is at his best in this hard-hitting series that goes beyond surface answers and quick fixes to tackle the real crisis of truth. You will discover the reason for this crisis, and more importantly, how to get you and your family back on track. This series is directed to the entire adult community and is excellent for building momentum in your church to address the loss of values within the family.

This series includes five video sessions, a comprehensive Leader's Guide including samplers from the five "Right From Wrong" Workbooks, the *Right From Wrong* book, the *Truth Slayers* book, and a 12-minute promotional video tape to motivate adults to go through the series.

Truth Matters, Adult Video Series
ISBN 0-8499-8587-0

Video Series to Youth

Setting Youth Free to Make Right Choices
Five-part Video Series featuring Josh McDowell

Through captivating video illustrations, dynamic teaching sessions, and creative group interaction, this series presents students with convincing evidence that right moral choices must be based on a standard outside of themselves. This powerful course equips your students with the understanding of what is right from what is wrong.

The series includes five video sessions, Leader's Guide with reproducible handout including samplers from the five "Right From Wrong" Workbooks, and the *Truth Slayers* book.

Setting Youth Free to Make
Right Choices, Youth Video Series
ISBN 0-8499-8585-4

Practice It and Make Living the Truth a Habit

Workbook for Adults

Truth Matters for You and Tomorrow's Generation
Workbook by Josh McDowell with Leader's Guide

The "Truth Matters" Workbook includes 35 daily activities that help you to instill within your children and youth such biblical values as honesty, love, and sexual purity. By taking just 25 - 30 minutes each day, you will discover a fresh and effective way to teach your family how to make right choices—even in tough situations.

The "Truth Matters" Workbook is designed to be used in eight adult group sessions that encourage interaction and support building. The five daily activities between each group meeting will help you and your family make right choices a habit.

Truth Matters, Member's Workbook ISBN 0-8054-9834-6
Truth Matters, Leader's Guide ISBN 0-8054-9833-8

Workbook for College Students

Out of the Moral Maze
by Josh McDowell with Leader's Instructions

Students entering college face a culture that has lost its belief in absolutes. In today's society, truth is a matter of taste; morality of individual preference. "Out of the Moral Maze" will provide any truth-seeking collegiate with a sound moral guidance system based on God and His Word as the determining factor for making right moral choices.

Out of the Moral Maze, Member's Workbook with Leader's Instructions
ISBN 0-8054-9832-X

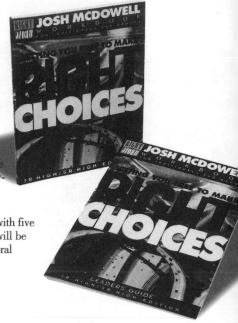

Workbook for Junior High and High School Students

Setting You Free to Make Right Choices
by Josh McDowell with Leader's Guide

With a Bible-based emphasis, this Workbook creatively and systematically teaches your students how to determine right from wrong in their everyday lives–specifically applying the decision-making process to moral questions about lying, cheating, getting even, and premarital sex.

Through eight youth group meetings followed each week with five daily exercises of 20-25 minutes per day, your teenagers will be challenged to develop a life-long habit of making right moral choices.

Setting You Free to Make Right Choices, Member's Workbook
ISBN 0-8054-9828-1
Setting You Free to Make Right Choices, Leader's Guide
ISBN 0-8054-9829-X

Workbook for Children

Truth Works - Making Right Choices
by Josh McDowell with Leader's Guide

To pass on the truth and reclaim a generation, we must teach God's truth when our children's minds and hearts are young and pliable. Creatively developed, "Truth Works" is two workbooks, one directed to younger children grades 1 - 3 and one to older children grades 4 - 6.

In eight fun-filled group sessions, your children will discover why such truths as honesty, justice, love, purity, self-control, mercy, and respect work to their best interests and how four simple steps will help them to make right moral choices an everyday habit.

Truth Works, Younger Children's Workbook ISBN 0-8054-9831-1
Truth Works, Older Children's Workbook ISBN 0-8054-9830-3
Truth Works, Leader's Guide ISBN 0-8054-9827-3